A TERM AT THE FED

A TERM AT THE FED

An Insider's View

LAURENCE H. MEYER

HarperBusiness
An Imprint of HarperCollins*Publishers*

HarperCollins books may be purchased for educational, business, or sales promotional use. For information, please write: Special Markets Department, HarperCollins Publishers Inc., 10 East 53rd Street, New York, NY 10022.

FIRST EDITION

Designed by Joy O'Meara

Library of Congress Cataloging-in-Publication Data
Meyer, Laurence H.
A term at the Fed : an insider's view / Laurence H. Meyer.—1st ed.
p. cm.
Includes index.
ISBN 0-06-054270-5
1. Board of Governors of the Federal Reserve System (U.S.) 2. Federal Reserve banks. 3. Monetary policy—United States. 4. United States. Federal Open Market Committee. I. Title.
HG2563.M48 2004
332.1'1'0973—dc22 2004047317

04 05 06 07 08 DIX/RRD 10 9 8 7 6 5 4 3 2

To Flo, for her love, support, and encouragement

CONTENTS

ACKNOWLEDGMENTS

Writing this book turned out to be much more challenging than I anticipated. Fortunately I had a lot of help along the way.

Daniel Greenberg, my agent and a partner in the Levine Greenberg Literary Agency, stayed focused on the project until the very end and indeed helped put it back on track at a critical point. Don Gastwirth, a close friend and also a literary agent, helped me focus on the broader vision for the book and also provided much appreciated encouragement along the way. Erik Calonius provided superb editorial assistance, guiding me from the substance of the first manuscript to a more readable, better-organized, and hopefully more engaging book.

I am particularly grateful to Mike Prell, who read and made detailed comments on both the first and second drafts. I am also grateful to a number of former and current colleagues and friends who reviewed drafts along the way. This group included Alan Blinder, Bill Dudley, Rick Mishkin, Joel Prakken, Chris Varvares, and Janet Yellen. Ed Ettin, Ellen Meade, Pat Parkinson, Jeremy Siegel, Ted Truman, and David Wessel made helpful suggestions on one or more chapters. Karen Alexander provided valuable editorial assistance on the first draft, and Pat Fewer helped with the final manuscript.

My assistant at the Center for Strategic and International Studies, Adam Bowman, provided excellent research assistance and took charge of the fact checking for the book with a passion that made it seem as if it were his reputation on the line.

I have some personal intellectual debts that I also want to acknowledge. I owe much of my success as an economist to Franco Modigliani, my mentor at MIT, who continued to provide advice and encouragement throughout the remainder of his illustrious career. Hy Minsky, my colleague at Washington University in St. Louis where I taught for twenty-seven years, helped to broaden my intellectual vision. I was also fortunate to have done my graduate work in economics at MIT, surrounded by dedicated teachers and stimulating classmates, to have spent my academic career at Washington University, where I had the opportunity to grow as an economist, and to have landed at the Center for Strategic and International Studies when I left the Board.

I was especially fortunate to have met Joel Prakken and Chris Varvares at Washington University. They were both graduate students of mine there and later were my partners at Laurence H. Meyer & Associates, a consulting firm specializing in forecasting and policy analysis, renamed Macroeconomic Advisers when I went to the Board. Our success as economic forecasters put me in position to be nominated to the Board, and what we learned together about macroeconomic modeling and forecasting prepared me well for my new responsibilities.

I am also grateful to all the staff I worked with at the Board, my colleagues on the Board and the FOMC, and especially Alan Greenspan for making my term at the Fed such an enjoyable, uplifting, and intellectually stimulating experience.

Finally, I want to thank my family for putting up with me while I was writing the book. They provided me with emotional support and encouragement and showed remarkable patience. My daughter, Stephanie, provided valuable editorial help during the early stages of the project. My wife, Flo, read the entire final manuscript and demonstrated that she had a better memory for detail than I did, making a series of corrections about my recollection of experiences during my term at the Fed. My son focused on managing my business (as well as the rest of my life) so I could focus on the book. Ken and my daughter-in-law, Kathy, also provided advice about managing the project from start to end. Most important, Ken and Kathy produced Abigail Rose, and my visits with Ken, Kathy, and Abby down the stretch kept me on an emotional high as I finished the book.

PREFACE

The Federal Reserve of the United States is often called the most powerful institution in America. Arguably it is, at least in the economic sphere: The monetary policy decisions made by the Fed can lift markets overnight, bring people out of unemployment, keep growth on track, and hold inflation in check.

Yet the workings of the Fed are obscure. Its key decisions are made by nineteen people—whose names are known to only a minute percentage of our population—meeting regularly behind closed doors. The financial markets of the world wait expectantly for the policy decisions that come out of this meeting room—basically whether to raise interest rates, lower them, or keep them steady—and then react, sometimes violently.

I was a governor of the Federal Reserve between June 1996 and January 2002. These were extraordinary times: There was the booming economy of the late 1990s, the "irrational exuberance" of the sky-rocketing stock market, the creation of the highly worshipped New Economy—and then, like the downward run of a roller coaster, the bursting of the stock bubble, September 11, and the lingering post-bubble hangover. I not only watched these events come and go, I had a seat at the table where the decisions were made. I listened to the economic reports and forecasts, participated in the vigorous discussions, and voted on the choices before us.

Writing a book about all of this came to my mind during my last weeks as a governor. I had spent most of my career as a professor—

twenty-seven years teaching economics at Washington University in St. Louis—and as you know, teachers are storytellers at heart. Now I had a great story to tell. It was one, I hoped, that would help demystify the Fed and the conduct of monetary policy. I felt compelled to get it down on paper.

In writing this book, I had no journal or diaries to refer to, nor did I have access to confidential material. I relied mostly on my memory of the events and discussions, aided by the transcripts of the meetings which are made available after a five-year delay, and the minutes for the more recent period.

EARLY IN MY TERM at the Federal Reserve, I was at a luncheon. It was one of the weekly gatherings for senior Fed staff and senior Treasury staff, hosted by a Fed governor. It was my turn to host. At one point during the event, a very senior member of the Treasury staff asked me if I knew what "FOMC" stood for. This was a strange question coming from so knowledgeable a person. I replied that I thought I did, but, just to be sure, what did he think it stood for? He replied, "Fruit of the Month Club." I knew he wasn't serious, but this remark encouraged me to write a paper, "Come with Me to the FOMC." It describes what the FOMC is all about and became the most widely read paper I wrote while at the Fed.[1]

So that you won't make the same gaffe, I'll tell you what FOMC stands for: the Federal Open Market Committee. That's the group that sits at the oval table making decisions about monetary policy. It's the group that I was a part of for five and a half years as a governor of the Federal Reserve. The FOMC, in large part, is what this book is all about. So what is the FOMC and what does it do? Glad you asked.

In 1913, the Congress created the Federal Reserve. The Fed was to be America's central bank. As the central bank, it would manage the growth of the money supply and credit, supporting the nation's economic health and steering it away from financial crises. But by the 1930s, the Congress became concerned that there was a lack of coordination between the Federal Reserve Board in Washington, D.C., and the far-flung regional Federal Reserve Banks. As a result, in 1935, Congress created the FOMC.

The voting members of the FOMC consist of the seven Federal Reserve Board governors and five of the presidents of the twelve Federal Reserve Banks (although all twelve Reserve Bank presidents attend and otherwise fully participate in FOMC meetings). The President nominates the governors (who are also subject to confirmation by the Senate), while the directors of the Reserve Banks (who are mostly businesspeople and bankers in the respective districts) choose the Reserve Bank presidents (subject to the veto of the Board).

This structure is designed to protect the independence of the FOMC by balancing the politically appointed governors and the Reserve Bank presidents selected outside the political process. It also ensures a geographical balance on the Committee (since the Reserve Bank presidents represent twelve districts that span the entire nation).[2] The structure also gives a special weight to the Board, whose members constitute a majority of the voting members.

The FOMC steers the economy by setting the federal funds rate. The federal funds rate is the rate on loans from one bank to another. It eventually determines the interest rates charged to businesses and households and, hence, affects a broad range of financial conditions. When interest rates are high, businesses and households will borrow and spend less. When they're low, they'll borrow and spend more. The FOMC tries to keep the country at full employment and price stability, the objectives that Congress has set for monetary policy. It does this by raising, lowering, and sometimes just maintaining the federal funds rate. It sounds easy, but as you will see in the following chapters, it is not.

SO I PLAN TO DISCUSS the economy in this book and how the FOMC tries to manage it. But let me tell you what this book is not. If you were hoping for a book that would be filled with nasty stories about either the Fed or my colleagues there, you bought the wrong book. Sorry. I had a great time at the Fed. I loved every day. I had a wonderful relationship with the staff, my fellow governors, the Reserve Bank presidents—and Chairman Alan Greenspan. Yes, I did have my differences with the Chairman, and I will explain these in the book. But the point is that we were all learning together as the world's economies whipsawed about, and this is the story that I will try to tell.

Nor is this book a political revelatory piece. Other books have done a decent job of digging through the political landscape, particularly in describing the Chairman's relationships in Washington. But I have to tell you that, as a mere governor, I was not exposed to the political end of things very often, other than during the process of being nominated by the President and confirmed by the Senate and during my many congressional testimonies. That political side—dealing with the administration and the Congress—was the Chairman's bailiwick. For the rest of us, the FOMC was actually a safe harbor, a place consciously constructed to keep us away from the political winds. So you won't see much of politics in this book.

For many, understandably, "monetary" policy is viewed as being about the Fed's control of the "money" supply. Yet you will not hear very much about the money supply in this book. Let me explain why.

For literally centuries it has been understood that, in the long run, the rate of inflation will mirror the rate of growth in the money supply.[3] But the FOMC (and other central banks around the world) have historically set monetary policy in terms of a target for some short-term interest rate (the federal funds rate, in the case of the Fed), rather than in terms of a target for money growth.[4] Once a central bank sets a target for a certain short-term interest rate, the money supply will be determined by how much money households and firms want to hold at that interest rate. In the end, there will still be a relationship between the money supply and the price level and between money growth and inflation, but the central bank does not directly make its decisions in terms of the money supply. So we can (and I do) tell the story about monetary policy without referring to what happens to the money supply.

In the 1970s, when inflation rose to an unacceptably high level, Congress required the FOMC to start identifying ranges for the growth of various measures of the money supply (and of credit), believing this would encourage a more disciplined monetary policy. By the time I arrived at the Fed, however, the discussions about the ranges for the money supply were about the only times the words *money supply* were uttered at FOMC meetings.[5] The discussion about the ranges was generally mechanical and disinterested, with the main objective being to avoid making any changes to them that would suggest that the Committee was paying more attention to the monetary aggregates than they had recently.

Toward the end of my term, the Committee asked that it be released from the requirement to set ranges for the monetary aggregates, and the Congress obliged. I have therefore said as much about the money supply as is necessary to understand the Committee's approach to the conduct of monetary policy.[6]

BECAUSE I'VE FOCUSED this book on the Fed's monetary policy, I've also given short shrift to the regulatory and other non-monetary policy responsibilities of the governors. There are many, including consumer protection, bank supervision and regulation, the efficient operation of the payments system, as well as the oversight of the internal operations of the Board (and of the operations of the regional Federal Reserve Banks). Some simply involve the day-to-day running of the institution. The Board has 1,700 employees, and the governors, like the board of directors of a private sector corporation, oversee everything from salaries to capital expenditures. Because these responsibilities are so wide-ranging, a governor has to be a generalist. This is a challenge for most governors, who get there generally because they are distinguished specialists.

I arrived, for instance, with a lot of experience about economic forecasting and monetary policy. That left me to pick up much of the rest on the run—with a lot of help from the staff specialists in each field, of course. My wife, by the way, clearly appreciated my standing as a specialist. She sometimes refers to me as an idiot savant—lovingly, to be sure—meaning that I am a near genius on matters of economics, but a near idiot on virtually everything else. You can always count on your wife to see your better qualities. After all, I wouldn't really call myself a near genius on economic matters.

Of course, the Fed also uses members' specialties to its best advantage. There are, for example, five Board committees—each typically comprised of three governors—covering the various areas of Board responsibilities, from bank supervision and regulation to consumer and community affairs, the internal operations of the Board, and oversight of the operations of the Reserve Banks. The various committee chairs, in particular, are offered to whoever has had some expertise and experience in the area, or at least exhibits some inclination to learn the subject. The role one plays on the Board, in fact, is greatly shaped by the committees you are placed on.[7] I was oversight governor for bank supervision and regulation, a position I held for most of my term on the Board.

Greenspan plays a disproportionate role in shaping monetary policy and often takes control on regulatory issues when the outcome could affect the Fed's reputation or importance in banking supervision and regulation. But he's also a great delegator, leaving the other governors with the key decisions about other regulatory issues, internal management of the Board, and oversight of the Reserve Banks.

In truth, most governors spend more time on these other responsibilities than they do on monetary policy. They are important assignments, to be sure. But frankly, they are not nearly so exciting a tale as the Fed and monetary policy—which is the story of how we stand at the helm, with our hands on the big wheel, and navigate through the storm.

—w—

EXPLAINING HOW the economy works and how monetary policy is made is my strong suite. I have my PhD in economics and, as I said, taught economics for many years. I also founded an economic forecasting firm (with two partners) that has distinguished itself frequently through its forecasting accuracy and economic insights. I've also served as an outside economic adviser to the economics teams of three U.S. presidents, as well as the Federal Reserve Board itself. And, of course, I can talk about monetary policy from the perspective of an insider, a member of the inner sanctum of monetary policymakers.

In this book, I am going to have to lay a few basic economic concepts on you. This is like having to understand a few things about horse racing before you go to the track.

One is the NAIRU. This is a concept that I'm attached to and that has attached itself to me. NAIRU stands for Non-Accelerating Inflation Rate of Unemployment. It is the minimum sustainable unemployment rate—the lowest unemployment rate that can be sustained without lifting inflation. The NAIRU is central to the FOMC's decisions, since it sets the limits to where the unemployment rate should be pushed.

The problem is that no one really knows precisely (or perhaps even not so precisely) what level of the unemployment rate represents the NAIRU. Many of us have an opinion. But as you will see in the following chapters, those opinions became the point of heated debate around the FOMC table. Chairman Greenspan, in fact, has said he doesn't even know if the NAIRU exists at all. That sometimes put the Chairman and me on opposite sides of the debate.

I also spend a lot of time in this book helping you to understand the strategy of monetary policy: that is, how monetary policy responds to economic developments. In the abstract models of academic theorists, monetary policymakers act systematically on the basis of a set of simple principles that guide their decisions.

I will refer on occasion to a specific set of principles—summarized by the Taylor rule—that identifies how monetary policy should be set in order to promote full employment and price stability.[8] Specifically, the Taylor rule identifies how aggressively monetary policymakers should adjust the federal funds rate in response to movements in output and inflation.

But while such a simple set of principles is useful in explaining the strategy of monetary policy, monetary policymakers in practice have to be flexible enough to respond to unusual shocks and unexpected developments. It is, as a result, impossible to write down a simple set of principles that could cover every contingency. So this book is both about the principles that provide a point of departure for the strategy of monetary policy and the judgment that monetary policymakers inevitably have to exercise in the conduct of monetary policy in practice.

—∾—

THIS BOOK IS NOT just about the past (as interesting as I believe the period I served on the FOMC was). It is also about the present and the future. Remarkably, economic events in this country, as of this writing, are nearly replicating the experience of the latter half of the

1990s. For the future to repeat the past is not that unusual. After all, forecasting is about extrapolating from past experiences and observations. What is striking today, however, is that we appear to be repeating not one of the more normal periods in our economic history, but one of the most unique and remarkable.

There is a bit of a déjà vu going on here: We are seeing, for example, another unexpected acceleration in the productivity of workers. We have another bull market on our hands. And the policy issues facing the Fed are also remarkably similar to those faced in the second half of the 1990s: Will the Fed tighten soon in response to robust growth and a further decline in the unemployment rate, or will the low and perhaps still declining rate of inflation keep the Fed on the sidelines for some time? We also are watching how the FOMC will respond to what may be another period of soaring equity prices.

While we never precisely repeat the past, we certainly can learn from it. I have, and I hope my insights will help you better understand both monetary policy and the Fed.

A TERM AT THE FED

INTRODUCTION

SEPTEMBER 9, 2001

On the morning of September 9, 2001, I arrived in China, representing the Federal Reserve Board on a U.S. delegation led by Secretary of the Treasury Paul O'Neill. This was to be my last official trip to China, and I had asked my wife to accompany me, so that I could share my enthusiasm for this great nation with her.

After a brief side trip, in which Secretary O'Neill and I met with Chinese president Jiang Zemin, we arrived at the St. Regis Hotel in Beijing, set on a tranquil, tree-lined street in the city's embassy district. The following day, we had a full schedule of discussions with our Chinese counterparts.

Minister of Finance Xiang Huaicheng gave the first presentation, followed by Paul O'Neill. Then, Undersecretary of the Treasury John Taylor and I led a discussion on the issues at hand. The Chinese were most interested in broadening the capital markets in their country, resolving weaknesses in their banking system, and reforming their state enterprises. They wanted to know how we supervised our banks, how the securities market in the United States complemented our banking system, and how we regulated and supervised activities in the capital markets.

What struck me was how earnestly this Communist nation wanted to adopt the features of the capitalist system. The Chinese were incredibly pragmatic. They asked us for our recommendations. What would we do in their circumstances? They were very open and frank.

When the meetings concluded, Secretary O'Neill headed for Japan. My wife and I remained in Beijing, where I had talks the following day with a few Chinese academics and economists at local think tanks. Following that, my wife and I planned to see some of the local sights. I was especially excited about visiting the Great Wall. I had been in China four times and had not yet seen it, so I was committed on this trip to doing so.

The meeting ended with a brief reception at the ambassador's house, just around the corner from the hotel. Then my wife and I walked back to the St. Regis. We were looking forward to a quiet evening's dinner together. It was just before 9:00 p.m. in Beijing and 9:00 a.m., September 11, in New York.

As is our usual custom when abroad, we turned on CNN to see what was going on in the United States and the rest of the world. When I first glanced at the television screen, I saw smoke coming out of the North Tower of the World Trade Center. The broadcasters' voices were not yet thick with emotion, but still analytical. They were puzzling over the circumstances. It might have been a small plane, and its guidance system might have failed. I called my wife over.

Then we witnessed a horrifying sight, in real time, as the second plane hit the South Tower. The commentators did not immediately put it all together, but it soon became clear that these two events were really one. This was a premeditated act; these were not small planes, mistakenly crashing into buildings, but large passenger jets used as weapons, striking at the symbols of American capitalism.

My first thoughts were not about my role as a monetary policymaker, but about the lives lost, the families overcome by grief. Pretty soon it dawned on me, though, that the Fed would have an enormous task ahead.

Although the towers had not yet collapsed, my immediate concern was that the World Trade Center housed many financial operations. Others were nearby: The Federal Reserve Bank of New York and several of the nation's big clearing banks were within a few blocks.

What would happen to the payment system if those buildings were damaged or destroyed?

Obviously, there were plans to make and policy options to consider. But I was in Beijing, and it became clear that my first challenge was to get home.

—ꟺ—

I CALLED THE BOARD in Washington and spoke to Roger Ferguson, the Vice Chairman. Ironically, he was the only Federal Reserve governor in Washington; all the others were traveling domestically or overseas. The Chairman was in Basel. He caught a military flight back home, and since there were only slings in the back of the cargo plane to sit on, he returned to Washington in the copilot's seat.

Ferguson said they were putting together a team, setting up a command center. They needed to find out how much damage had been done and what steps to take. He said he realized that it would be difficult for me to get out of China for a few days, at least, and suggested that I might be more valuable on the ground, for the time being, where I could participate in FOMC conference calls on the phone.

The American embassy provided me with a cell phone, so the embassy could alert me to any Board briefings. But don't speak too freely, they warned me; it was not a secured line.

In the middle of the next night, the embassy staff took me down to the building's safe room, a cramped enclosure with bare metal walls that resembled a bank vault. They struggled for a few minutes to get the door open, and then we went inside. On a table, surrounded by some chairs, was a phone with a secured line. I settled in and waited for what would be the first meeting of FOMC members since 9/11.

Alan Greenspan was back at the Fed, but it was the senior staff who led off the hour-long conversation. The discussion centered not on what we should do in terms of monetary policy, but on what damage had been sustained by the financial infrastructure. Were the financial markets sound? What was the degree of threat to the functioning of the payments system? How extensive was the damage to the banks—and to the communications systems that helped the banking system clear payments? At the Fed, what was our role? How should we coordinate with other agencies? Despite the magnitude of the questions facing us, the meeting was calm, almost matter-of-fact.

When I got off the line, I sensed that Greenspan would schedule an FOMC meeting very soon, perhaps the following Monday, just ahead of the reopening of the stock market. For me, the question was whether I'd be able to get back to Washington in time for the meeting. This was Wednesday. I had only a few days to make it back.

It took until Saturday for my wife and me to get a commercial flight from Beijing to Tokyo. From Tokyo we were driven to a U.S. air force base, Yokota, home of the 374th Airlift Wing. We were joined at the base by members of Paul O'Neill's Treasury delegation and a few other government agency staff who had also been stranded in Tokyo.

The next morning we boarded a C-5, one of the largest transport planes in the world. After a long flight, we landed at McClellan Air Force Base, outside of Sacramento. The next morning, another C-5 was waiting for us. This time we were on our way to Andrews Air Force Base, outside of Washington, D.C. As we landed, I could see one of the Board's cars waiting for me. It was Sunday evening. I would have one night's rest before the FOMC meeting—and the opening of the stock market on September 17, at 9:30 a.m.

AT 8:00 a.m. we all gathered in the boardroom. The mood was somber. There were the five Fed governors (two positions were vacant), including, of course, Alan Greenspan, and several senior staff members. The Fed's bank presidents were connected by phone.

While I was still in Beijing, we had tried to determine how much damage had been done to the payments system. Now we turned our attention to the options for monetary policy. Following September 11, consumer confidence had been shaken. Businesses had become more cautious. We were facing the danger of a serious and prolonged economic downturn.

Everywhere across America, people were pulling together to get the country back on track. At the Fed, as the monetary policymaker, we had one basic tool, the federal funds rate—and we were prepared to use it. At the meeting we decided to cut the funds rate by 50 basis points (a ½-percentage-point cut), to calm the nerves of the financial markets. We wanted to assure the nation that we would do everything in our power to blunt the shock of the attack.

—ʍ—

WE HOPED for a quick turnaround. But nothing could have prepared us for how rapidly the recovery came: The economy began to stabilize in October, shaking off the brief recession that had begun before September 11. The fourth quarter of 2001 showed nearly a 3% rate of growth. The first quarter of 2002 advanced at a surprisingly strong 5% rate.[1] Ironically, this was even better than what I had expected *before* the terrorist attack.

By the time my term expired in January 2002, then, it appeared that the economy had shrugged off the terrorist attacks and was in the midst of a surprisingly strong recovery. On my last day at the Fed, I felt as though we had made it through the storm.

—ʍ—

IT'S BEEN MORE than two years since I left the Fed. I drive by its white marble facade frequently, the same solemn entrance that millions of tourists see every year. As a former governor, I go back and visit occasionally with the current governors, the staff, and, of course, the Chairman himself.

But sometimes, as I drive by, I can't help but reflect on the five and a half years I had there. Anyone who has ever served on the Fed, of course, has had his or her share of excitement. But between 1996 and 2001, I had witnessed truly extraordinary times. There was the great booming economy of the second half of the 1990s, driven by an unexpected acceleration in productivity; an equity bubble; the financial turbulence that raced through Asia; the Russian default and the collapse of the ruble; the implosion of Long-Term Capital Management (LTCM); the nail-biting over Y2K; and, finally, the bursting of the equity bubble, the economic slowdown, the recession, and the postbubble hangover.

In my first four years at the Fed, the U.S. economy was good—so good, in fact, that people were calling it the "New Economy," an economy fundamentally different from what we had experienced in at least twenty-five years. It was an economy that seemed to succeed by breaking the old rules. We were very happy at the Fed to take some credit for this. But behind the scenes, we were frantically trying to understand why.

When I arrived at the Board, for instance, I thought I understood how the macroeconomy worked—what determines growth and inflation and how monetary policy should be conducted to contribute to good economic performance. After all, I had been a professor of economics for twenty-seven years. I had written a textbook on macroeconomic models. Moreover, I had run an economic forecasting firm with my two partners for more than a dozen years. I had come to the Fed with economic models that my partners and I had spent many years developing and refining. I had a well-articulated view (or "paradigm") of how the economy worked. I expected those models and that paradigm to be my strength as a monetary policymaker. So it was a real shock to see economic performance thumbing its nose at my carefully developed and, I thought, well-tested models.

It was Alan Greenspan who figured it out before the rest of us. By the time I joined the Board in mid-1996 (and probably before that), he was saying that the new economy was being fueled by the new computer and communications technologies, which were pumping up productivity. It would take us several years after his first pronouncement to confirm that statement in the data and to fully appreciate all the ramifications of this mostly intuitive insight.

The Chairman was right about something else, too. The exceptional performance was being fueled by "irrational exuberance," the phrase he coined during a speech in December 1996. Everyone expected equity prices to rise during this period, given the exceptional performance and the apparent higher sustainable rate of economic growth. But no one expected them to rise 20% a year for more than four consecutive years—or for the technology-dominated NASDAQ to rise at a 40% annual rate, topping out at 100% for the year ending in March 2000.

The New Economy, in fact, kept the U.S. economy afloat through some very stormy weather. In the second year of my term, the Asian markets began to wobble and fall. First it was Thailand, then came Malaysia, Indonesia, the Philippines, and Hong Kong. At the Fed, we kept monitoring the overseas turmoil but found that Asia's woes weren't even putting a dent in the U.S. juggernaut. Even when South Korea's currency and stocks collapsed, the U.S. economy didn't flinch.

In 1998, we watched the Russian default and the collapse of the ruble and, following that, the collapse of LTCM, a large hedge fund that owed billions of dollars to the biggest U.S. banks. This collapse seemed capable of capsizing the U.S. financial system. But it didn't, thanks to a rescue by its private creditors, facilitated by the New York Federal Reserve Bank. Even the Y2K scare fizzled out in 2000 without marring the new economy. We were on a roll.

Throughout all this, of course, we at the Fed were trying to adjust monetary policy to keep the economy strong without burning it up. At the beginning of my term, we kept interest rates relatively stable, first because we saw no signs of increasing inflation and later because we feared the Asian crisis might slow the U.S. economy (it ultimately didn't). Still later, we eased rates in response to the escalation in global financial turbulence that followed the Russian default and devaluation and the implosion of LTCM.

As I entered the second to last year of my term, it seemed that we had steered Fed policy pretty well. The media felt that way, it seemed, from their year-end congratulatory columns. And we weren't unimpressed ourselves.

A VERY WISE ECONOMIST, Herb Stein, once quipped that if something isn't sustainable, it won't continue. And it didn't. The bubble burst in early 2000. Ultimately, the overall stock market would decline by almost 50%, technology stocks by nearly 80%, and Internet stocks by around 90%.

Now we were being blamed as mightily as we had been praised earlier. Of course, the bursting of the equity bubble didn't mean an immediate sinking of the economic ship. But in the second half of

2000, the economy slowed sharply and then slipped into recession in 2001. It took another two years for the stock market to hit bottom.

By the time of my trip to China, in fact, the United States was still staggering from the bursting of the equity bubble. The FOMC had cut the funds rate from 6½% at the end of 2000 to 3¾% by the time of this trip. But I told the Chinese delegation that we were seeing some encouraging signs. I thought the U.S. economy would begin to expand again by early 2002. This would coincide with the end of my term as governor. It would be nice to leave with the economy on the mend.

Of course, this was not to be. The economy continued to disappoint in the coming year, not so much because of September 11, but simply because the economy continued to suffer from its postbubble hangover. As it turned out, then, the challenges that I had faced in the latter part of my term continued after I left the Fed, falling onto the shoulders of those remaining at the FOMC.

I ALWAYS JUDGE my success at each point in my career not only by what I have contributed, but also by what I have learned. By that measure, my term at the Fed was a success. This was a learning experience, after all, not in the isolation of a library or a classroom, but on the front lines, making policy in real time. I learned something about myself in the process and a lot about the Federal Reserve.

The first lesson was that monetary policymaking is more challenging than I had ever anticipated. When I came to the Board, I thought that steering the economy was a matter of adjusting policy to take the economy from where it was to where you wanted it to be. I expected to apply the knowledge that I had accumulated as a teacher, a scholar, and a forecaster to the task at hand.

But I soon discovered that the Fed doesn't know precisely where the economy is (because of lagging and often revised economic data) or precisely where it wants the economy to go. It's easy to say that you want to achieve "full employment," but what does that really mean? Theoretically, full employment is the lowest unemployment rate that can be sustained without boosting inflation. That may be good enough for a classroom, but in real life one needs a number for that ideal rate of unemployment.

When I arrived at the Board, I thought I had a pretty good idea of what that number was. But the surprising economic developments during my term—especially the failure of inflation to rise despite declines in the unemployment rate to a level that, in the past, would have triggered higher inflation—soon made me realize that we didn't really know what that number was at the present moment or what it might be tomorrow. These developments and uncertainties challenged everything I had learned as an academic economist and forecaster.

A second lesson was about the importance of relationships inside the Fed. When I joined the Board, I thought that my expertise in macroeconomics and monetary policy alone would enable me to be an effective governor. The fact is that it's also relationships—with the staff, your peers, and the Chairman—that influence your effectiveness as a governor. That's why this book is as much about relationships as it is about economics.

A third lesson was that what the Fed says is often equally important to what it does, and often more so. The FOMC moves markets. That's why FOMC members have to be so careful about what they say (and why the Chairman would prefer they say as little as possible). I also learned that I could create damaging volatility in the markets through my public speeches far more easily than I could influence the markets in the direction that served the interests of the Fed—and the economy.

A fourth lesson was that independent central banks are one of the really great inventions and that the political insulation associated with "independence" makes the job of a central banker both easier and more enjoyable. When I was a student of economics, and then a young economist, I dreamed of becoming chairman of the President's Council of Economic Advisers (CEA) someday. That position would give me the opportunity to perform public service, as well as put me at the center of the exciting political process. But my experience at the Fed changed my mind. While I still regret that I was never a presidential adviser in my younger days, I'm pleased that the President chose me for the Fed rather than as his adviser.

The reason is that the Fed's independence ensures that governors are very well insulated from the short-term political pressures of the electoral cycle. In fact, I never witnessed wholesale partisan positioning and bickering inside the Fed, and I never once was pressured by anyone outside the Fed to toe the party line on any issue. My rather limited partisan efforts before joining the Board may have enhanced my chances of being nominated, but I will tell you that I left any partisanship at the Fed's doorstep when I walked in. It was a good thing, too: I needed all my energy for the policy issues ahead.

Those are some of the lessons I learned during my term at the Fed. In the following chapters of this book, I will attempt to explain how it all happened during those five and a half years, and why.

1

GETTING THERE

By the time I had completed my first economics class in college, I knew I wanted to be an economist. One attraction was that a career as an economist appeared to offer such a variety of opportunities and challenges: teaching, research, consulting, and serving in government. In addition, one didn't have to make a single choice within this set: One could pursue several options simultaneously or sequentially. By age fifty, I had already been a teacher, researcher, and consultant. Never for a day have I regretted my career choice.

But I had two unfulfilled dreams. The first was to play second base for the Dodgers. The second was to be chairman of the President's CEA, a position of stature and some influence and an ideal spot for an academic economist seeking an opportunity for public service. For some inexplicable reason, though, the Federal Reserve never made it into my dreams. And that's despite the fact that, in retrospect, it was truly the ideal spot for me.

In any case, in September 1995 I was sitting peacefully at a conference in Washington, D.C., organized by my consulting firm, when my adventure began. My partner handed me a note saying that Laura Tyson, chairman of President Clinton's National Economic Council, would like me to call her. My consulting firm had worked with the Clinton administration's economics team, as we had with the Bush and Reagan administrations' teams previously, so such a call, though unusual, didn't suggest anything out of the ordinary.

When I slipped out and returned the call, our conversation seemed innocuous enough. There were some openings on the Federal Reserve Board, and Laura asked me for some suggestions about possible nominees. She also asked if I would like to be considered for the position, but I viewed the latter question as more of a courtesy than a serious inquiry. I quickly provided a list of several potential candidates and gave no further thought to the possibility of being nominated.

But this call was indeed the beginning of the process that would result in my nomination and confirmation. Once I was nominated to the Board, incidentally, I was frequently asked, How does someone get to be on the Federal Reserve Board? The technical answer is, You have to be nominated by the President and confirmed by the Senate.

But to me, the question usually sounded more like How did someone like *you* get to be on the Board? The answer, generically, is really quite simple. It depends on some combination of whom you know, what you have accomplished, what your party affiliation is, and what you have contributed in support of your party. The relative importance of these considerations differs depending on the President and on his economics and political teams.

In my case, I knew most of the economics team that would make the decision; I had been a professor of economics at Washington University in St. Louis for twenty-seven years; I was an award-winning economic forecaster; and I was a valued consultant to several administrations, including the current one, as well as to the Board of Governors itself. In addition, I was widely recognized as a Democrat and modestly outspoken in support of Democratic positions on economic policy. My consulting firm had even earned a gold star by doing a much appreciated piece of policy analysis for the Clinton presidential campaign. So I had the credentials.

The next important event toward my nomination was a call from Joseph Stiglitz, chairman of the President's CEA. Joe told me that I would be on the administration's short list for the Fed position, provided I would commit to accepting the nomination if it was offered. Even though Laura Tyson had hinted at this possibility in the earlier call, Joe's call came as a total shock. I was immediately excited about the prospect of serving on the Board—and thrilled to have been asked.

But while it may seem hard to believe, I nevertheless didn't exactly jump at the opportunity. My first thought was about the prospects of my consulting firm and my two partners. They had taken all the risks in starting the firm. At the time, I was a tenured professor at Washington University. If the firm failed, I still had a nice position there. As a result of this asymmetry in risk taking, I felt I had an obligation to them. I told Joe I would think about it and talk to my partners.

CHRIS VARVARES AND JOEL PRAKKEN had been graduate students of mine at Washington University. Joel had gone on first to the Federal Reserve Bank of New York and then to IBM, where he had helped refine IBM's macroeconomic model. I had lusted after a large-scale model with which to do policy analysis and forecasting ever since my graduate school days at MIT, in fact, where I worked as a research assistant with Franco Modigliani (later a recipient of the Nobel Prize in economics), who was developing a large-scale model of the U.S. economy.

Chris, meanwhile, had taken a leave from the graduate program to serve on the staff of the CEA. Working at the CEA is a great opportunity to broaden and deepen one's knowledge of economics, and Chris benefited enormously from this experience. He was also a computer guru. This was perfect. One partner would bring the model, the other would know how to get it running and make it available to clients. And both wanted to start a firm with me.

By the way, I have a confession to make. The firm was started under the influence of, not alcohol, but drugs. I had a herniated disk and was ordered by my doctor to stay in bed and take Tylenol with codeine. The medication not only controlled the pain, it also made my mind incredibly clear. I wanted to work sixteen hours a day. So I snuck into my office and worked standing up at a tall filing cabinet. I began to dream of starting a forecasting firm with Chris and Joel. Not long after, Joel called and said, "Guess what? I'm quitting my job at IBM and coming to St. Louis to start a forecasting firm . . .

with you." So began my career as an economic forecaster, the success of which ultimately put me in the position to be nominated to the Board.

FIFTEEN YEARS LATER, when I sat down with Chris and Joel to discuss Joe Stiglitz's offer, they were both incredulous. This is a chance of a lifetime, they told me. You're an idiot for not immediately making a commitment to serve if nominated. We will take care of ourselves and the firm. Call Joe back and go for it! You might think that they were happy to be rid of me and have the firm for themselves, but trust me, we were like family (and still are). Fortunately, Joe called back. I indicated that I would indeed be delighted to be on the short list and would accept the position if nominated and confirmed. Joe ended our conversation by telling me that he didn't want to pressure me on any issues on behalf of the Clinton administration, but he did want me to know that the administration was strongly in favor of CRA.

I suspect we've all had moments when our response to a particular situation could change our lives and careers. This seemed like one of those moments to me. I could have said: Joe, I have heard of the NBA, the PTA, and CPAs, but CRA—I don't have a clue. But then, I figured, I would still be a professor of economics at Washington University and an economic forecaster. Not a bad life, to be sure, but I was already seeing myself on the Board of Governors.

Or I could have said: Joe, I am with you 100%—and figure out later what I had committed myself to. But that was definitely not my style. So I gave Joe the silent treatment. After a brief pause, Joe said good-bye, and I patted myself on the back for apparently dodging that bullet successfully. But a few seconds later I heard the telltale ring of the fax machine; coming across was a sixty-five-page history of CRA, courtesy of Joe.

This incident is full of lessons. First, political appointees are, naturally, subject to lobbying from the administration that appoints them. Administrations understandably nominate candidates whose views on policy and whose values are perceived to be consistent with their own. This is as it should be, although the pursuit of commitments from appointees can be taken to excess, particularly in the case of appointments to an "independent" central bank. But the main lesson here is that your political views and values do, of course, matter for political appointments.

The second lesson is about Joe Stiglitz. He handled my ignorance of CRA in a very gentle and indeed constructive way, confirming what I had already learned about him. Joe Stiglitz is a really smart guy. My silent treatment didn't fool him for a second. Joe, by the way, subsequently won the Nobel Prize in economics, to no one's surprise. He is one of the most brilliant economists of his (and my) generation. He always treated me kindly and as an intellectual equal, which I don't pretend to be.

I guess you are still wondering what CRA stands for and perhaps whether I ever figured it out. CRA stands for the Community Reinvestment Act. It was passed by Congress in 1977 to remind banks that they are obligated to meet the needs of their communities, with a special emphasis on meeting the needs of people in low- and moderate-income neighborhoods. Democrats love CRA because it demonstrates how the government can provide better opportunities for lower-income families. Republicans hate CRA because it represents interference by government in the operation of businesses (in this case, banks). By the way, not much more than a year later, I was named head of the Board's oversight committee on consumer and community affairs. I became the member of the Board to testify before Congress on issues related to CRA. I went around the country supporting the superb work that community groups and banks were doing in providing affordable housing for low- and moderate-income groups. In other words, I was CRA all the way. I guess I'm a fast learner.

THE NEXT STEP was the interview in Washington, D.C., with Clinton administration staffers. Since I knew virtually all the folks involved, this was a pleasant experience. Well, there was one little point of tension. The political staffer closest to the Fed appointments was Gene Sperling. Gene and I had a falling-out with each other in the early days of the Clinton administration. For that reason, I had significantly discounted my chances of any political appointment by the administration.

This problem arose just before the Clinton administration's first budget was to be voted on by Congress. The administration had been arguing that a tax increase was needed to stimulate the economy. Although a tax increase would diminish the federal budget deficit and lower bond rates, it was still unlikely to stimulate the economy in the short term. I felt the administration had dramatically overstated its case. I was quoted in a wire service story to the effect that the spin doctors must have been up all night thinking up that rationale.

Gene was the lead spin doctor on economic issues in the Clinton administration, and a very skilled spinner at that. He not only was personally offended by my quote, but believed I had undercut the prospects for passage of the core element of the President's economic program. He was always loyal to a fault and was a take-no-prisoners type of soldier. He called me shortly after the story crossed the wires and cursed at me nonstop for minutes. I tried to calm him down, but he insisted that the administration was holding me personally responsible if the budget failed in Congress the next day. I asked him if I could put him on hold, so that I could call my mother and tell her that the fate of the nation was being held in the balance because of something I said. I am sure my mother would have been very proud.

At any rate, there was Gene with his arms crossed in a menacing pose in front of Laura Tyson's door. Once I was inside, Laura took me aside and told me that she recalled there was some incident between the two of us but that I shouldn't worry about it because Gene didn't have a vote on my nomination. That relieved me. Incidentally, Gene went on to become chairman of the National Economic Council and one of the leading members of the economics team in the administration and seemed to get over the event more quickly than I did. When I left the Board, in fact, he wrote a very generous column about my accomplishments as a member of the Board. We have had a few laughs together about this incident in the years that followed.

AS THIS PROCESS was unfolding, and because of a serious concern about the direction of monetary policy, the administration was especially focused on the Fed appointments. Economic growth had slowed in 1995, following a period of sharp increases in the federal funds rate. These increases had begun in February 1994 and had extended through January 1995. At the same time, there was an ongoing debate about how fast the economy could grow and whether current monetary policy was an obstacle to faster growth.

The President seemed partial to the view that the obsession of the Fed (and specifically of its Chairman, Alan Greenspan) with inflation was resulting in a tighter monetary policy than was appropriate and slower growth than would otherwise have been possible. In order to make monetary policy more accommodative and growth oriented, Clinton wanted to appoint governors to the Board who shared his convictions and would challenge the Chairman.

Clinton had found the man to carry out this task: Felix Rohatyn, a well-known investment banker and a committed and active Democrat. Rohatyn had been more than outspoken for the party: He had been an energetic and effective fund-raiser. He had the stature to be appointed to the Board, and, equally or perhaps more important, he agreed with the President about Fed policy. Or perhaps it was the President who agreed with Rohatyn. There was, however, one problem—Congress. Rohatyn's nomination would have to be confirmed by the Republican-controlled Senate.

It's interesting to ponder what considerations are relevant to Senate confirmations. Certainly, competence is an issue. A candidate's policy views are also fair game, although it is understood that each adminstration will appoint people who share its perspective and values. Of course, appointments to the Fed are different from appointments to positions inside the administration itself. The administration's appointees serve at the President's discretion, can be removed at any time, and have a term of appointment that does not span administrations.

Governors of the Federal Reserve, on the other hand, serve for terms of fourteen years (if they serve full terms) and therefore may (and generally do) have terms that span administrations. Therefore, it is not unreasonable that somewhat greater scrutiny should be given to appointments to such independent agencies. In any case, Rohatyn was considered simply too political (or at least too philosophically objectionable) for the Republicans to stomach, and they made it clear that he could not be confirmed.

So the administration was in search of an alternative. Whereas the

Rohatyn nomination had been the President's idea, and then carried forward by the political side of the Clinton administration, the President's economics team now reasserted control of the nomination process, putting together a list of candidates with strong backgrounds in economics. I was a name that rose to the top of the list. When my name was leaked—a process that allows an administration to get some quick feedback about possible reactions to a nomination—the speculation was that I was chosen to fulfill the same task that Rohatyn would have cheerfully taken up, to challenge Alan Greenspan and move policy in a more accommodative and growth-oriented direction.

That speculation made me nervous. I didn't agree with Rohatyn at all on this issue. I believed that the economy was on a relatively low growth path, limited by the rate of increase in productivity, over which the Fed had little control. I wondered if this position would ultimately do me in. Still, I hoped for the best. The irony of my appointment was that, once appointed, I was perceived as occasionally challenging the Chairman, as the administration had hoped. But, as I will explain later, the Chairman and I actually traded places on the issues. Greenspan, apparently unbeknownst to the administration, had already become a convert to the view that the economy could grow faster. I, however, became the member of the FOMC most committed to the proposition that there was no evidence the economy could grow faster—and that monetary policy had no ability to contribute to that end. So much for political strategy.

I WILL ALWAYS REMEMBER the next call from Laura Tyson. She informed me that the Clinton economics team had chosen me as their preferred candidate, but that I would have to speak with the President and get his blessing. She asked if I would like to talk to him on the phone or come to Washington for a brief visit. That seemed like a no-brainer. At least I should get a face-to-face meeting with the President out of this experience. We agreed that I would come to Washington within a day or two, meet with the President, and return to St. Louis. The administration would then contact me shortly thereafter and let me know its decision. It seemed as though I had the nomination—if I didn't screw it up in my discussion with the President.

There was just one lingering issue—the conflict between what the President thought he could count on me to deliver as a member of the Board and my own strongly held views. I decided to try to head off a showdown at my meeting with the President. I asked Laura if the President was aware of my views about the sustainable rate of growth and monetary policy's limited role in influencing it. She wasn't sure. I told her that I didn't want to embarrass her and the other members of the economics team who had backed me, but that I would defend my position vigorously if the issue arose at the meeting. I asked Laura to take the initiative and explain this to the President in advance.

When I arrived for my meeting, I was informed that the President wasn't feeling well and that I should return the next morning. In the meantime, to occupy my time, I was shepherded around to meet several of the leading members of the administration—Robert Rubin, Secretary of the Treasury; Jerry Hawke, Undersecretary of the Treasury for Domestic Finance; and Mack McLarty, a close political adviser to the President. Everyone was friendly, and all seemed to assume that my nomination was a *fait accompli*. They presumed that I was here for a ceremonial visit with the President. That relaxed me a little, but only a little.

I CERTAINLY WILL NEVER forget my meeting with the President. He chose to visit with me in a room in the living quarters of the White House. When I arrived at the door to the White House, two marines greeted me and saluted. That sent a chill down my back. I was then taken to the Map Room to wait for the President. I figured that if I didn't faint or throw up on the President, the nomination was mine. I gave myself a 70% probability of meeting those conditions.

When the President walked into the room, I got a lump in my throat and worried I might not be able to speak. You may be thinking that that could have worked to my advantage, but I didn't see it that way at all.

My first impression was that the President was larger in person than I expected. His self-confidence and personal magnetism were immediately evident. We shook hands, and he asked me to have a seat on the couch. He slowly took off his suit jacket, folded it carefully, and laid it on a chair. He then proceeded for the next ten minutes to tell me about the history of the room and why it was a favorite of his and Hillary's. This was undoubtedly a device that he found useful in calming visitors and making them feel at home. It worked. I felt more comfortable. I even thought I might be able to speak, if invited to.

I wasn't. He sat on a chair next to the couch and launched into a discussion of his own political and economic priorities. The topic of monetary policy never came up. He never asked me a single question. Indeed, if I hadn't worked hard to find an opportunity to ask a question or make a comment, I think the entire visit might have concluded without a word from me. He never asked me to challenge the Chairman or to work to tilt monetary policy in a particular direction. I was relieved.

After the meeting, I returned to Laura Tyson's office to say goodbye and thank her for her role in getting me to this point, on the verge of a nomination to the Board. She suggested that I not rush away too fast but rather sit in the First Lady's office for a while (she was away on a trip) and see what the day would bring. A meeting was set up for me with the White House counsel, in which we discussed the disclosure forms that I would have to fill out if I was nominated. This included disclosing whether I had paid Social Security for cleaning help. Oops, I thought. So close, but so . . . Not to worry, I was told. This was no longer an obstacle, but I should, upon returning to St. Louis, immediately pay any back taxes that might be due and put this issue behind me. It never came up again.

Throughout the several hours of waiting, I was on the phone to my family. The staff took wonderful care of me, bringing me two full lunches so I would have plenty of choices. I recall a conversation with my son, Ken, in the midafternoon. "I've been surfing the Web," Ken told me. "It looks like the press conference is set for 4:00 p.m. Did you know that Alice Rivlin is the other nominee and she will be the Vice Chair?" Wow, I said, you're way ahead of me. Ken responded: "Dad, I don't like to give you advice, but when they come to let you know that you are being nominated today, act surprised."

Soon thereafter, a White House staffer dropped by to inform me that this was my last chance to reconsider: Did I really want this job? A few minutes later, they were back to let me know that there would be a press conference at 4:00 p.m. and that Alice Rivlin was the other nominee and that she would be the Vice Chair. I acted truly surprised. They bought it.

—~—

AFTER HELPING DRAFT the President's remarks about me, I was led outside the Oval Office to a meeting with Alan Greenspan, Alice Rivlin, and the cast from the West Wing—the real cast from the West Wing—including Vice President Gore, George Stephanopoulos, and Robert Rubin, along with the President. I was surprised that the President played the straight man and the Vice President was the comic in the group.

As we were chatting, someone asked what would happen to my consulting firm. A good question, I responded. I hadn't had too much time to think about it. Alan Greenspan volunteered that the rules might be less onerous today than when he had been appointed. Rather than sell my interest in the firm, I might just have to put it into some kind of blind trust. The White House counsel suggested that he could probably settle this issue quickly with a call to the ethics officer at the Federal Reserve Board. He went off in search of an answer.

A few minutes later, the President was taking me by the arm and leading me toward the Oval Office, where the press conference announcing my nomination was awaiting. I saw the White House counsel rushing down the hall, waving his hands. Stop, Mr. President, he blurted. He told me that the situation with my firm was worse than he'd expected. You will have to sell your interest and totally disassociate yourself from the firm. Do you still want to go ahead? I figured I had about fifteen seconds to make up my mind. I could see the headlines: PROSPECTIVE FED NOMINEE JILTS PRESIDENT AT THE DOOR OF THE OVAL OFFICE. So I said, "Let's go," and I hoped I would be able to sell my interest in the firm.

I was on a stage with the Chairman, Alice Rivlin, the President, and other members of the administration. I get very nervous in such situations. My knees were shaking. I know my wife and daughter, back in St. Louis, were watching and thinking, I just hope he doesn't faint. In any case, I survived being nominated.

—~—

NEXT CAME the vetting process, one of the more painful rites of passage for nominees. The cast of characters in this drama include the White House lawyers, accountants, and the FBI. They search through your past, everything you wrote, said, or were alleged to have said, and what you ate and, more important, smoked and drank. This is a time for regret about past actions, youthful or not-so-youthful indiscretions, and potentially embarrassing revelations about your character and judgment.

Fortunately, I am a pretty boring guy. It would have been hard to make much of a titillating movie about my life story. Still, when the friendly (truly) FBI officer asked if I had ever smoked marijuana, it was another of those situations I told you about earlier, when your future may hinge on a single response. My parents had told me never to lie, and I went into the interview convinced I had nothing to hide. So I confessed that I had had a couple of puffs on one or two occasions, at parties, when a joint was being passed around. (Hmm, how did I even know it was called a joint?)

Anyway, the minute I revealed this wild act of disregard for the law, I regretted it (both the puffs and the revelation). This was a one- (or two-) time event of no significance. But the headline flashed in front of me: PRESIDENT REVOKES NOMINATION OF POT-SMOKING PROFESSOR. Then I looked at that headline and noticed just a little incongruity. Not to worry. Thanks, Bill.

I was almost home, I thought. Then a few days after returning to St. Louis, I got an unexpected call from the White House Counsel's Office. A young lawyer informed me that the office had just done a LexisNexis search of everything I had written. She had some serious problems. I was dumbfounded. *Moi?* She then informed me that on April 2 the President had made a comment in support of a particular policy initiative, and just a few days later I had said that program was a bad idea. I had contradicted the President. And this pattern had been repeated on several other occasions.

I found this inquisition more than a bit irritating, but I immediately figured that I had the edge. I had already been nominated in front of thousands, if not millions, of viewers, and the President was not likely to revoke my nomination at this point because I had occasionally taken a different position on his policy proposals. So I decided to have a little fun. I told her there was a simple explanation: The President was wrong. That's what I do for a living.

Then I tried to soothe her by noting that the Republicans must have had some nasty things to say about me. That's the second problem, she replied. The Republicans seem actually to like you. Not to worry, I comforted her. So does the President. You might have been watching when he nominated me. If you have problems with my nomination, I think you should take it up with the President. I never heard from her again.

NOW I THOUGHT I was really home free. But I guess I had forgotten my civics lessons from high school, the part about the powers of Congress—and the Senate in particular. That lesson about advise and consent. But I figured I could make it through the congressional gauntlet. I had been nominated, after all, in part because I was viewed as easily confirmable. I wrote my opening statement and prepared for my confirmation hearings.

Someone in the administration called and asked if I would like him to run a mock confirmation hearing to prepare me for the real deal. At first, I wondered whether this would be a veiled attempt to lobby me on some particular issue. But the fact is the economics team had my best interests in mind and put me through an extraordinarily effective mock hearing. They were frankly better prepared than I was. The first question was about the stock market. I parried and obfuscated, and clearly was struggling, when one of my interrogators finally intervened with exceptional advice: Never, ever answer that question. Wow, I thought. You mean I don't have to answer every question that's asked? I am a bit naive sometimes.

At the mock hearing, I learned that there are three ingredients to a confirmation hearing. First, substance—the message you want to convey. Second, strategy—what issues you want to avoid being forced to take positions on. Third, style—how to deflect the questions you don't want to answer and, more generally, how to show appropriate respect for the people who have you by the . . . Well, you get the point.

The confirmation hearing in March 1996 began with Alice and me making our opening remarks. The Chairman was being renominated, so he, too, was supposed to be at this party. But he had informed the Senate committee that he would be late—something about an FOMC meeting.

Next came questions from the committee members. Someone asked me if I, as a highly regarded forecaster, would like to make a prediction about the stock market. I was ready. The reason I am regarded as such a good forecaster, I replied, is that I never make forecasts of the stock market. Everyone laughed. I had pulled off a skillful deflection, combining superb strategy and wonderful style. I think I saw someone hold up a sign: 9.7. I was on a roll.

Then, after just a few questions, the Chairman arrived. The committee nearly genuflected. They heaped praise on the Chairman and weighed every word he uttered. In the process, they seemed to forget about Alice and me. I almost wanted to stand up and shout: What about us? We were nominated, too. Ask us some questions! Perish the thought. Finally, the committee was exhausted—or at least famished—and they concluded the hearing. They quickly voted unanimously to send all three nominations to the floor for a vote.

SO CLOSE, but I was about to get another civics lesson. Alan Blinder, an academic colleague and former member of the Board, had called me immediately after the press conference to congratulate me—and educate me. He asked me if I understood the concept of a senatorial hold. I tried to envision the political equivalent of the hold in football, with a member of the Senate grabbing my suit jacket and preventing me from getting to the Senate hearing room where I was about to be confirmed. As it turns out, a hold allows a single Senator to hold up a nomination, sometimes indefinitely, without the public knowing who has put the kibosh on the confirmation or for what reason. Alan warned me to be wary of a hold on my nomination.

It was not my nomination, however, that had someone in Congress agitated. It was the reconfirmation of Alan Greenspan as Chairman that was at issue. The administration had orchestrated a package deal, wrapping Alice and me with the Chairman, mainly as a way of protecting me from possible opposition in Congress. This was not a formal package, but an attempt to have the three nominations considered at the same time—to go together before the Senate confirmation hearing and to be voted on at the same time on the Senate floor.

Democratic senator Tom Harkin had the same view as the President and Felix Rohatyn—that the Fed had been unnecessarily restraining the economy. He wanted a full day or two of floor debate on the subject before releasing his hold and allowing a vote on the nominations. The Republicans, the majority, had no interest in such a show by Harkin on the Senate floor. As a result, the nominations were going nowhere.

By mid-June, however, cooler heads prevailed. A deal was made for a half day of floor debate and then a vote on the nominations. Greenspan was confirmed by a vote of 91–7. Alice Rivlin was confirmed by an unexpectedly narrow margin of 57–41. Everyone loved and respected her. She wasn't the issue. But voting against her allowed some Republican Senators to send a signal of displeasure to the administration about some pending issue before the Senate. This is the way messages are often sent and received in Washington.

I was confirmed 98–0. That's unanimous, by the way. The last time I was unanimously confirmed for anything was as the leader of a Cub Scout pack, at age eight, and even then I had to twist a few arms. I'd come a long way.

But before I leave the subject of getting there, let me thank Senator Harkin. He did make my future more uncertain during the period he held me hostage. Nevertheless, he deserves some credit. These days, it seems that most senatorial holds are orchestrated to provide leverage for a deal involving pork for a Senator's state or some reward for the special interests that backed his or her campaign. Tom Harkin put a hold on the nominations because he was concerned about the direction of monetary policy. And all he demanded in exchange for lifting the hold was an old-fashioned debate on the Senate floor.

I didn't agree with him on the issues, and I didn't and still don't think that nominees should be subject to the long delays caused by such actions. But it's comforting to see passion on occasion over real issues, rather than partisan spin and bickering. And to tell the truth, it all worked out for the best, at least as far as I was concerned. The long hold gave me time to negotiate the sale of my interest in my consulting firm to a St. Louis–based brokerage. That transaction helped make life a little easier financially for my family during my years on the Board. So, Senator, thanks.

—∾—

THERE WAS ONE final concern as I made my way to the Fed. In February 1996, an article in *The New Yorker* described in gory detail the unhappy experience of Alan Blinder as Vice Chairman of the Board.[1] The article detailed Blinder's many complaints, including his relationship with the Chairman and a Fed staff that sometimes infringed upon the authority of the Board members and did not always provide Board members with an adequate flow of information.

Alan's discontent worried me. I knew Alan quite well, liked him personally, and admired him as an economist. Moreover, we shared many of the same opinions about economics and monetary policy. If Alan Blinder did not have a happy experience navigating between the powerful Chairman and the powerful staff, I wondered if I would fare any better.

That Alan was the first Democrat appointed after twelve years of Republican appointments might have contributed to his problems. He was perceived by some, and perhaps on occasion by himself, as a possible and even likely successor to Greenspan as Chairman. Such an impression, even if unintentional, would not win Alan many friends among the staff or his colleagues on the Board.

Alan also assumed that his position as Vice Chairman would entitle him to a special relationship with the Chairman. This was not consistent with the style of the Chairman or with the experience of past Vice Chairmen. I would learn that Alan Greenspan, though a very cordial person and a superb leader, is not someone who builds personal relationships with fellow Board members or who forges a special relationship with Vice Chairmen.

Blinder was not alone in his concern about the relationship between the staff and Board members. Some of the same issues that were first revealed in the article in *The New Yorker* were further explored in an article by John Berry titled "At the Fed, a Power Struggle over Information" that appeared in *The Washington Post* in July 1996.[2]

In particular, the article described a meeting among four governors and the Chairman at which the governors aired their grievances about certain staff practices. The governors complained that they were not kept informed about staff activities on a wide range of international matters, including contacts between the staff and foreign central banks. Blinder had objected to the governors' exclusion from the staff's work on the forecast. He wanted to attend and actively participate in the staff meeting where the issues were discussed and debated, though not necessarily be involved in the meetings where the forecast was actually hammered out.

Some of the governors also objected that the staff withheld information about their forecast from Board members. For example, when the staff delivered the Greenbook, the report that details and discusses the staff's forecast, it did not include some significant hard details, specifically the projected paths of the federal funds rate, long-term bond rates, or equity prices.[3] The staff said they didn't feel the FOMC members needed the precise paths for these variables—ones that if leaked would have the greatest market effect—to make their decisions. They argued that a qualitative discussion of the paths in the Greenbook were sufficient. Some of the governors, on the other hand, felt that the staff's decision to withhold critical information amounted to a slap in the face.

The staff at the Fed, it must be noted, hold a great amount of power. The staff members involved in preparing the governors for FOMC meetings and in providing guidance to the Committee at its meetings are highly qualified economists. Many have spent their entire careers at the Fed and have seen many governors and Reserve Bank presidents come and go. In recognition of their status, importance, and indeed power, the very top staffers—the division directors for research and statistics, monetary affairs, and international finance—were called "the Barons," and they often lived up to their billing.

These were the tensions that existed as I took my final steps toward the Fed. Of course, I didn't want to find myself in conflict with the staff, as was Blinder's fate. So when I returned to St. Louis after my nomination, one of my first calls was to Mike Prell, director of the Division of Research and Statistics. Prell was responsible for leading the forecast efforts. I told him that one of the reasons I was so pleased to be nominated for a position on the Board was the respect I had for the staff. Before joining the FOMC, I had visited with the staff a couple of times a year to offer my assessment of the economic outlook and always enjoyed my interactions with them.

I added that when the President nominated me, he didn't make me any smarter and that I therefore hoped I could count on the staff to be as intense and engaged in their interactions with me as a Board member as they had been in our earlier encounters. There was a pause at the other end of the line, and then Mike responded: "Well, actually, it will be different."

Now I was wondering if I was about to jump from the frying pan into the fire.

REGARDLESS OF THE FIRE AHEAD, there were preparations to be made. First I needed an assistant, a position I was fortunate to fill with Anne Kannellopoulos, who had been an assistant to the former Vice Chairman. She taught me the etiquette of the Board—including which meetings were mandatory and which were optional, which invitations I could accept and which should be deferred to Public Affairs for approval. She even got my children to call me their "honorable" dad. My wife, Flo, showed up one day at my office, early in my term. We were headed out of town that afternoon, and I was in a meeting when I should have been on my way. Flo moved to the door to knock. Anne interceded, telling Flo, "Let me handle this. I'm the office wife!" Flo and Anne got along great.

Next was an office, in which I was similarly lucky. My predecessor, John LaWare, bequeathed the Board a beautiful desk, table, couch, and chair. Everything looked in pretty good order to me, but the staff insisted on reupholstering the couch and the chairs. I was told that all the new governors receive a small budget for redecorating. I didn't protest. After all, apparently, I was special. I was getting used to it. Even the guards began to call me by my new name. I was Governor Meyer now. I parked in the governors' parking garage, rode the governors' elevator, and worked on the governors' floor.

My last decision was whether or not to ask for someone from the pool of talented Fed staffers—whose specialties spanned from economics to the regulatory and supervisory issues related to banking—

to be assigned directly to me or to rely on the senior staff for my research and other needs. This was a politically loaded decision. A few of the former governors had suggested that having a staff member assigned directly to me would facilitate my being an independent force on the Board. Their view was that the senior staff gave priority to the Chairman and could not be counted on to provide the same level of service to the other governors. Furthermore, the input from the staff would come as a consensus view, not with a range of opinions. If I wanted to get objective, untainted information and complete political loyalty, they said, get your own private sidekick.

But when I indicated that I was planning to go in this direction, the senior staff persuaded me otherwise. They'd spend the time with me, they pleaded, and the level of experience, expertise, and other resources they would offer would surpass that of a single, more junior assistant. I do believe the *The New Yorker* article, and the unhappy experience of Blinder, had persuaded them to make an example of happiness of me.

In the end, I took the advice the senior staff offered and never regretted it. Interestingly, the staff and I often wound up with similar views on the outlook, views that were often different from those of the Chairman. On more than a couple of issues, the staff and I were both wrong. But misery loves company, so we got along famously.

WHEN I WAS PREPARING to leave the Fed after my five and a half years, my friends at the Federal Reserve Bank of San Francisco created a pamphlet celebrating my accomplishments and foibles as governor. It included a column entitled "Lost Name." They asked those who had known me before I became a governor to try to recall my first name—and if they could, to please tell me, because I'd need it again soon. They were right. Now I'm just Larry again.

2

COME WITH ME TO THE FOMC

When I was sworn in as a governor on June 20, 1996, the economy was in the sixth year of an expansion. The Dow Jones Industrial Average was up more than 20% for the year, manufacturing was picking up steam, and home sales were hitting their highest marks in a decade.

But in the cool confines of the Federal Reserve, the celebration was muted. Already, many staffers were worrying that the strong growth and low level of the unemployment rate would soon encourage workers to demand higher wages. Those demands, in turn, would begin fueling inflation, which had burned through the economy with such destructive force in the 1970s and 1980s.

With the economy growing strongly and already near full employment, the mission of the Fed was to encourage a "soft landing." In economic terms, a soft landing occurs when growth slows—just as the economy reaches full employment—so that the unemployment rate remains steady. If inflation is also low enough, at this point, then the FOMC has achieved its two primary objectives: full employment and price stability.[1]

It's analogous to an extraordinarily smooth aircraft landing, so perfect that you want to applaud the pilot: In this case, the pilot is the FOMC, the airplane is the actual output of the economy, and the runway is the maximum sustainable output of the economy.

In the best of all worlds, the FOMC pilot should be able to bring a soaring economy right down onto the firm surface of the maximum sustainable level of output—without blowing out all the tires. Unfortunately, as I learned over the next few years, it takes a lot more luck to land an economy than it does an airplane.

Nevertheless, it was the issue of bringing the economy down to earth that dominated my first FOMC meeting on July 2 and 3, 1996. Walking into the Fed, you get the feeling that important business is being done here. And so it was that day.

—m—

AS ALICE RIVLIN and I entered the room, we were welcomed warmly into the club. I had already met the other Board members—Mike Kelley, Larry Lindsey, Susan Phillips, Janet Yellen, and, of course, Alan Greenspan—but I had previously met only a few of the Reserve Bank presidents.

The senior Fed staff members were also milling about—including Mike Prell, in charge of preparing the staff forecast of the U.S. economy; Ted Truman, director of the Division of International Finance, in charge of monitoring developments in foreign economies; and Don Kohn, director of the Division of Monetary Affairs, in charge of providing guidance about policy options. Prell, Kohn, and Truman played an important role in preparing the Board members for FOMC meetings. They also provided guidance to all the Committee members during meetings. As a result, they wielded considerable power. For that reason, as I have mentioned, they have been dubbed "the Barons."

A few minutes later, Greenspan entered the room and walked immediately to his place at the imposing mahogany meeting table, signaling everyone else to take their respective chairs. He already had his game face on, that inscrutable expression behind reflective glasses. The Chairman, I noted, entered from a door that connects to his office. The rest of us entered through the main door of the boardroom.

—~—

I FIRST MET the Chairman in December 1994, when I was invited to sit on a panel of academics and present my views on the outlook and monetary policy to the Board. I had seen him three times since then, once at another academic panel discussion at the Board, again at the ceremony for my nomination as governor, and finally at my confirmation hearing. But I had never been in the inner circle before. Now I was about to learn the secrets of the temple.[2]

—~—

AS WE SAT DOWN for my first FOMC meeting, I noted that Norm Bernard, the deputy secretary of the FOMC, was seated to the Chairman's right. He was there to keep the agenda on track, help the Chairman determine whose turn it was to speak next, read the proposals as they came up for a vote, and conduct the roll call vote. To the right of Bernard was William McDonough, president of the Federal Reserve Bank of New York, the Vice Chairman of the FOMC, and a permanent member of the Committee.[3] To the left of the Chairman was Alice Rivlin, the new Vice Chair of the Federal Reserve Board.

The remaining governors of the Board were seated relative to the Chairman according to their seniority on the Board. Just so they didn't get it wrong, their names appeared on little plaques on the chairs. The other Reserve Bank presidents also sat around the table in a prescribed order, for which no one could seem to remember the logic. The staff Barons also had a place at the table, while the other members of the staff were seated in chairs on all four sides of the room.

Now I noticed a green light come on in front of the deputy secretary, indicating that the meeting was being recorded. First, Alice Rivlin and I were formally welcomed by the Chairman. Then Peter Fisher, the manager of the system's portfolio[4] and an officer of the Federal Reserve Bank of New York, briefed the Committee on developments in the financial and foreign exchange markets, using an array of charts to drive his points home. He also reviewed the operations conducted on behalf of the Committee in the government securities and foreign exchange markets.

The core of the meeting began when Mike Prell, thin, bearded, and intensely devoted to the Fed's mission, presented the staff forecast for the U.S. economy. He began by noting that the economy had grown at about a 3% rate in the first half of the year, while potential output[5] was growing at a 2% rate. (Figure 1 in the appendix depicts the level of output [measured by the real Gross Domestic Product (GDP)] and the level of potential output. Figure 2 in the appendix depicts the growth rate of real GDP from the second half of the 1990s through 2003.) This disparity could turn out to be a problem: If the economy was actually growing faster than its maximum sustainable level, the unemployment rate—which was already low—would fall still further. If so, workers would be increasingly successful in their demands for higher wages, which could raise prices and ignite an upward spiral of inflation.

As Prell continued with his forecast, nothing he said came as any great surprise to us at the table: We had already received the forecast in what is called the Greenbook, a report (with a green cover) that is traditionally delivered to Committee members toward the end of the week before the FOMC meeting. I had had my nose buried in my copy of the Greenbook all weekend, in fact.

The numbers in the Greenbook offer probably the best and most worked-over economic forecast available. The Fed's own staff economists, who are certainly among the best and the brightest forecasters in the land (and have the most extensive resources on which to build their forecasts), put it together. Although each of the governors and Reserve Bank presidents comes to the table with his or her own forecast, the Greenbook plays a dominant role in shaping the Committee's views. For that reason, I began to call the Greenbook the thirteenth member of the FOMC.

Before I joined the Board, I wondered whether the Greenbook was really the staff's independent judgment of economic trends or if it was the Chairman's personal forecast, rubber-stamped by the staff. By the end of my very first meeting—after I had seen Greenspan disagree with the staff's forecast for inflation and productivity growth—I realized it was theirs alone.

As the meeting got under way, the staff and some of the Committee members voiced their concern that the economy was "overheating"—reaching the point of growth and low unemployment that would trigger rising inflation. They based this opinion on the view that unemployment was already below its "full employment"[6] level and might be poised to decline further.

But others at the table disagreed. Certainly the unemployment rate was low. But perhaps it wouldn't spark inflation this time. Could some fundamental economic change be under way that would alter the traditional rules? Perhaps there was a boost in productivity—allowing for faster growth and lower unemployment, without an upward trend in inflation.

Productivity refers to the amount of output produced per hour of work, on average, in the nonfarm business sector of the economy. The higher the level of productivity, the higher the level of output that can be produced (for example, when the economy is operating at full employment). And the faster productivity grows, the higher the maximum sustainable rate of growth of output—that is, the faster output can grow without the threat of overheating and triggering higher inflation.

As was generally the case, the debate moved calmly and thoughtfully from one member to another. No one was pontificating. We were struggling with these issues both individually and as a group.

For his part, the Chairman was especially supportive of the productivity explanation. In particular, he believed that computers and other communications technologies might be giving the economy the ability to grow faster and to operate at higher output levels than ever before—without triggering an increase in inflation. The phrase hadn't been coined yet, certainty not in capital letters—but was this a New Economy?

I knew that Congress and the administration had been raising this very issue. Politicians, in general, liked the idea that a "New Economy" might have arrived, one that allowed the economy to grow faster than ever before. This was good for the country, in their opinion, and also, let's be honest, good for their political careers. Not surprisingly, these politicians wanted the FOMC to believe in the New Economy, too. If we did, then we would be far less inclined to raise interest rates and dim the lights on their party.

I expected this from the politicians. But what surprised me was how strongly the Chairman (whom some members of Congress had frequently criticized for resisting the New Economy concept) was now passionately supporting the idea.

For myself, I was not convinced that there was a New Economy. I saw the economy in a more traditional way, one in which continued above-trend growth and further declines in the unemployment rate would threaten a rise in inflation. But I had to admit that, even though the unemployment rate was already at a level that, in the past, might have been expected to trigger higher inflation, inflation was not a problem. In fact, inflation was declining. So while I was not sold on the idea that the economy had fundamentally changed, I still recognized that something out of the ordinary might be under way.

When Prell had finished with the discussion of the forecast for growth and employment, he turned to the prospects for inflation. The overall inflation rate, as measured by the Consumer Price Index (CPI), was running at around 3%, he said, and core inflation—the rate for goods and services other than food and energy and the measure of inflation that the FOMC tended to focus on most—was slightly above a 2½% rate.[7] Furthermore, he said, according to their forecast, core inflation would likely rise in the near future, to about 3% in 1997. (Figure 3 in the appendix depicts the core CPI inflation rate in the second half of the 1990s through the end of 2003.)

That remark drew concerned looks from most of the governors and Reserve Bank presidents around the table. The 2½% rate for core CPI inflation was already above their comfort zone. And now Prell was telling them it might climb even higher.

—∾—

TO UNDERSTAND THE LOGIC of the staff forecast, you need to understand the NAIRU. This has been called one of the most powerful influences on economic policy in modern times. It is also central to how the FOMC staff forecasts inflation.

According to the NAIRU model, inflation will remain steady if the unemployment rate is just equal to a critical threshold, which is called the NAIRU. At this point, there is an equilibrium in the labor market—a balance between the supply of workers and the demand for workers. At this balancing point, there is neither pressure for wages to rise faster nor pressure for them to rise more slowly.

However, if the unemployment rate falls below the NAIRU, there will be an "excess demand" for workers. As a result, wages will start to rise more sharply.[8] A faster pace of wage increases, in turn, will push up inflation.

In the NAIRU model, it is helpful to view the relationship between the unemployment rate and inflation as a seesaw. There is a balancing point, where unemployment and inflation are both stable. That balancing point is the NAIRU. As unemployment descends, according to the seesaw analogy, inflation rises.

But the NAIRU model is like a seesaw with a bad attitude. If the unemployment rate falls below the NAIRU, and stays there for very long, inflation will rise in a self-reinforcing spiral, rising further and further. You don't want to be on that seesaw. Neither did the FOMC.

If overheating and higher inflation threaten the economy, the FOMC is supposed to swoop in and raise interest rates. That's what the textbooks say. But we were around the FOMC table, not in a classroom. The question we faced was whether the rules had changed: Whether there really was an imminent threat of inflation—and whether the time had come to cool the economy in order to prevent a rise in inflation.

This leads to another problem about the NAIRU: The concept is about as controversial as global warming and possibly as emotional. Some economists believe passionately in the NAIRU. When unemployment threatens to fall below the NAIRU, they demand preemptive action from the Fed to avoid a rise in inflation. Others, just as passionately, argue that the NAIRU is a myth. They claim that there is no particular rate of unemployment which results in a faster pace of wage increases and no set relationship between unemployment and inflation.

A lot of people fall in between. Many believe in the concept of the NAIRU but are uncertain where it is. That uncertainty made it difficult to marshal support for a preemptive attack on inflation—that is, for raising interest rates in anticipation of a rise in inflation.

When I joined the Board, I came with a strong commitment to the NAIRU concept. In my private consulting business, we had won awards for the accuracy of our forecasts. I always noted the contribution of our NAIRU-based model, in particular, to the accuracy of our inflation forecasts. What surprised me, once I joined the FOMC, was the extent to which my belief in the NAIRU was challenged, not only in terms of my estimate of the NAIRU, but in terms of the validity of the NAIRU model itself.

Indeed, my beloved NAIRU was not working as it should: Although unemployment had been below the prevailing estimate of the NAIRU for nearly two years, inflation had not reared its ugly head. My NAIRU paradigm had predicted a rise in the core inflation rate, but inflation was stable, even declining slightly. Something was amiss.

We were now grappling with a seductive proposition: If economic growth could be stronger than previously imagined—and the unemployment rate could fall to a level that in the past would have triggered higher inflation without triggering inflation—then the FOMC might not need to raise rates as hurriedly as it had in the past. Could the economic expansion we were experiencing in the summer of 1996 be sustained without the FOMC tapping on the brakes? We didn't know. We were fumbling around in the dark, wondering what would happen next.

AFTER THE COMMITTEE had the opportunity to ask the staff questions about their forecast, we were ready to begin the outlook "go-around." In this segment of the meeting, each member of the Committee had an opportunity to make a brief presentation on the outlook. By tradition, the presidents go first, reflecting the fact that they bring a rich supply of anecdotal information gleaned from interactions with businesspeople and community leaders in their districts.[9] Anecdotal information delivers a different perspective from that of the data and is especially valued in that it arrives fresh and without the time lag of the data.[10]

Reserve Bank president Al Broaddus from the Richmond Fed began the go-around, noting that his inflation forecast was similar to that of the staff. For that reason, he was arguing for a tightening of monetary policy. Bob Parry, president of the San Francisco Bank, agreed, noting that the risk of rising inflation was "alarming." Presidents Mike Moskow from Chicago, Cathy Minehan from Boston, and Tom Hoenig from Kansas City all said that they saw upside risks to both growth and inflation.

I knew that Greenspan was less concerned with rising inflation at this time and was also inclined to keep rates as they were. So I was surprised to see the Reserve Bank presidents so openly laying their cards on the table. They were not afraid to challenge the Chairman. This meeting was going to be more interesting, I mused, than I had imagined.

Others around the table disagreed with the first group of Reserve Bank presidents. President Edward Boehne of the Philadelphia Fed, for one, noted that inflation was in fact falling, not rising. The Committee needed to be "watchful," he said, but didn't need to tighten rates at this meeting. Presidents Jack Guynn of Atlanta and Jerry Jordan of Cleveland agreed.

While the presidents begin the outlook go-around, the order of presentations is otherwise set through what I call the "wink" system. When a Committee member wants to make his presentation, he winks at the deputy secretary, who then puts the member on the list, in the order of the winks.

I also learned that FOMC meetings are more about structured presentations than discussions and exchanges. This surprised me. Each member spoke for about five minutes, then gave way to the next speaker. Many read from a prepared text or spoke from a detailed outline, diverging only occasionally to include a comment on what was said earlier in the meeting. To my surprise, what evolved was not a spontaneous discussion, but a series of formal, self-contained presentations.[11]

After the presidents had spoken, and my wink had come to the top of the list, I was able to address the Committee for the first time. I was a bit nervous, but very energized.

I began by noting that the staff and I had the same number in mind for the NAIRU, about 5¾%. That said, I quickly conceded that the unemployment rate had been below my NAIRU estimate for nearly two years—without any broad-based evidence of an acceleration in inflation. Indeed, core inflation had declined in 1996.

That suggested that my estimate of the NAIRU might be a little too high, I said. But that did not justify abandoning the NAIRU model, I continued, a model that (in my view—and the staff's) had previously been so useful in forecasting inflation. My defense of the NAIRU must have made an impression, for from then on, I would be tagged as the NAIRU guy, both inside the FOMC and out.

—∾—

AFTER THE OUTLOOK go-around was completed, the Chairman turned to another topic, the meaning of the FOMC's price stability objective.[12] In other words, what level of inflation should the FOMC shoot for—and why? This discussion turned out to be one of the most interesting ones I participated in during my time on the FOMC.

Janet Yellen, who had taught economics at Harvard, the London School of Economics, and most recently at Berkeley, was the first to address this question. She was very much respected by the members of the Committee, the staff, and the Chairman. I soon became her biggest fan on the Committee.

There is no doubt that low inflation is advantageous, Governor Yellen began. But, she argued, there are also significant costs to very low inflation. If there is zero inflation, for instance, then monetary policymakers cannot lower the "real" interest rate below zero.[13] A little inflation, therefore, gives monetary policymakers a greater degree of latitude to stimulate the economy, permitting them to drive real short-term rates into negative territory, if necessary, to stimulate the economy.

Furthermore, she said, a little inflation "greases the wheels" of the labor market. Relative wages across different industries and occupations must be free to change, thereby signaling workers to migrate from one industry or occupation to another. If there was no inflation, some wages would rise, but others would have to fall.[14] There is, however, some evidence that workers are reluctant to accept outright declines in their wages. In this case, it might be impossible for relative wage rates to vary enough to ensure an efficient allocation of labor across industries and occupations. If there was a little inflation, however, and therefore a higher average rate of wage increases, some wages would rise more slowly than the average, but none of the workers would have to experience an actual decline in their wages.

In arguing that inflation could be too low as well as too high, Yellen anticipated the deflationary problems that Japan would face in the second half of the 1990s. The FOMC's definition of price stability, she was saying, should be true price stability—plus a cushion. It should first allow for the upward bias in measured inflation rates (perhaps ½ to 1 percentage point for the CPI) and then add an additional amount, perhaps another percentage point, to provide that extra latitude for the FOMC to ease, if necessary, and to grease the wheels of the labor market. Today her comments would pass as conventional wisdom, but at that time the case for a positive inflation target had not been articulated so clearly.

Yellen concluded that a cut in inflation from the current 3% rate to 2% would "very likely, but not surely" yield net benefits. This reflected her assessment that the "grease the wheels" argument would not be very significant at a 2% inflation rate, but would be more compelling as inflation fell below 2%. She added that she would be increasingly skeptical of any net benefits as inflation declined to a level below 2%.

When she was finished, Greenspan looked over and said, with a tone of surprise and implicit criticism: "You did not even accept . . . price stability as a goal." The Federal Reserve Act states explicitly that the Fed should promote price stability, yet Janet had called for a positive inflation rate.

She thought for a moment. "I would simply respond to that by saying that the Federal Reserve Act directs us to aim for both maximum employment and price stability. . . . I do not read the Federal Reserve Act as unambiguously telling us that we should choose price stability and forgo maximum employment," she replied with a cool smile. If there was a conflict between the two objectives, Yellen believed it was up to the Committee to reconcile them. She concluded that she would opt for a 2% rate of inflation and maximum sustainable employment as the FOMC's objectives.

Although I was unaware of it then, this was an unusual exchange. Yellen was directly challenging the Chairman's views. She was getting away with it, I suppose, because of her style and great smile. Of course, as I would come to appreciate later, the Chairman never shied away from a good intellectual battle.

"Mr. Chairman, will *you* define 'price stability' for me?" Yellen asked.

The Chairman considered for a moment and then responded

with a characteristic, vague definition: "Price stability is that state in which expected changes in the general price level do not effectively alter business or household decisions," he said. That is, price stability existed when inflation was so low that people didn't pay attention to expected changes in the price level in their household and business economic decisions. This definition allowed the Chairman to assert the importance of price stability, and his commitment to it, without ever having to name a numerical inflation target.

Although I suspect that most of us were dissatisfied with that answer, only a few would have dared press the Chairman further. But Yellen was on a roll. "Could you please put a number on that?" she asked boldly.

Before the Chairman could respond, he had to wait for the laughter to subside. But he was surprisingly willing to do so. "I would say the number is zero, if inflation is properly measured," he said.

This was the only time in my years at the Board that anyone successfully baited a number out of the Chairman. Yellen countered, saying that she preferred 2%, imprecisely measured. That was precisely the number that I would have named.

Now the debate spread across the table. A few members said they didn't believe that inflation could be too low. They preferred a target of zero inflation—price stability, pure and simple. I said I supported Yellen's analysis and choice of 2% as the FOMC's inflation objective. Other members—most, in fact—favored holding core inflation to the prevailing 3% rate and then moving slowly to reduce it to 2%. The Chairman later summarized the discussion: "We have now all agreed on 2 percent."[15]

Now that the Committee had reached a consensus on the implicit inflation target, it could identify whether inflation was above or below its objective. Since core CPI inflation was about 2½%, inflation was running modestly above the Committee's preferred target. The next question was whether monetary policy should follow a "deliberate" or "opportunistic" strategy toward reducing inflation over time.

The "deliberate" strategy judges the success of policy exclusively by whether it lowers inflation toward its target whenever inflation is above the target. The "opportunistic" strategy calls for policy initially to encourage full employment and trend growth, hopefully preventing a further increase in the inflation rate, and, over time, to take advantage of "accidents" that would lower inflation toward its target (for example, an unexpected and unavoidable recession).

I preferred the opportunistic approach and, indeed, before joining the Board had coined the phrase *opportunistic disinflation* to describe this strategy. Most of the Committee members had said they wanted to hold the line on inflation—or at least prevent inflation from rising above a particular ceiling. The ceiling, as I noted earlier, was generally considered to be 3%, although most of the members wanted to see inflation reduced gradually over time until the 2% target was achieved.

The following morning, the Chairman reminded us of "the highly confidential nature of what we talk about at an FOMC meeting." He looked at us around the table and said quietly, "The discussion we had yesterday was exceptionally interesting and important. I will tell you that if the 2 percent inflation figure gets out of this room, it is going to create more problems for us than I think any of you might anticipate."

Greenspan did not elaborate on his concerns. But I suspect he worried that the discussion might be interpreted by some, including members of the Congress, as suggesting that the FOMC would henceforth focus its attention more single-mindedly on inflation, thereby paying less attention to its obligation to promote full employment.

In any case, the transcripts have been out for about two years now, and I have yet to hear much outcry about the discussion. Of course, that may be because no one reads the transcripts.

—~—

FOLLOWING THIS WARNING, our discussions turned to monetary policy—the setting of a target for the federal funds rate. The federal funds rate is the interest rate that banks pay when they borrow reserves from one another. It, in turn, affects mortgage rates, bank loan rates, and rates on commercial paper and corporate bonds. The federal funds rate also sways equity prices, which in turn affect consumer spending (through the effect on household wealth) and business investment (through the effect on the cost of financing the purchases with new issues of equity).

The FOMC tries to achieve its objectives—full employment and price stability—by adjusting the federal funds rate to influence the level of aggregate demand—that is, the spending by households and businesses. If output is below the level consistent with full employment, the FOMC will lower or ease interest rates to stimulate spending of households and firms, encouraging firms to raise production and hire more workers. The Taylor rule—which I found to be a useful set of guidelines for making monetary policy while I was on the FOMC—suggests that policymakers lower the federal funds rate by 50 basis points (½ percentage point) in response to a 1-percentage-point decline in output relative to potential.

If the economy is overheated and inflation begins to rise, the FOMC will raise or tighten interest rates to restrain spending by households and businesses. This then restores production and employment to levels that are consistent with stable inflation. Of course, to ensure that the "real" federal funds rate rises, the FOMC must raise the federal funds rate by more than the increase in inflation. This is the most important rule for central bankers to follow. In this case, the Taylor rule calls on monetary policymakers to raise the funds rate by 150 basis points in response to a 1-percentage-point increase in the inflation rate. This would raise the real federal funds rate by 50 basis points in response to a 1-percentage-point increase in inflation.[16]

We now had some policy decisions before us. First, we had to decide whether to tighten policy, ease policy, or keep policy unchanged. Second, we had to choose the Committee's "policy bias"—in other words, the direction in which we were leaning for future policy decisions. This was to give the financial markets some warning of where we were heading.

The FOMC's policy bias at the time was either "symmetric" or "asymmetric." Although symmetric meant there was an equal chance of tightening or loosening rates in the future,[17] in practice, a symmetric posture implied there was little prospect for a change in rates in either direction in the near term. An asymmetric bias, on the other hand, meant that the FOMC was leaning in one direction or the other, either toward raising or lowering rates.

An asymmetric directive was sometimes interpreted as a license for the chairman to hike rates or lower them between FOMC meetings. Technically, the Chairman, at that time, had the authority to change policy in between meetings whenever he wanted and without consultation with the Committee. Some chairmen took advantage of this power, although during my term Greenspan always chose to consult with the FOMC members before intermeeting moves, with the governors assembled in the boardroom, and with the presidents connected by phone.[18]

The asymmetric directive also played a role in providing financial markets with a heads-up. The FOMC does not like to surprise the markets, so moving to an asymmetric directive prepares them for a possible policy change. It also allows the markets to more confidently price the expected course of monetary policy into long-term interest rates.[19] The effectiveness of monetary policy, I learned, depends not only on decisions taken about the funds rate at each meeting, but also on the expectations that monetary policymakers convey to the markets about the future course of monetary policy.

Finally, an asymmetric directive allowed the Committee to shift gradually from no change in policy to a tightening or loosening of rates. It provided a middle ground—a compromise—that often helped the Committee reach a consensus. If the Committee believed there was a strong possibility that a policy move would be needed in coming months, but could not reach a consensus on the timing of that move, an asymmetric directive could serve as an acceptable solution.

—𝔪—

DON KOHN, always calm and thoughtful, and perhaps the staff member the FOMC members relied upon most frequently for guidance at meetings, now led us to the various policy options that might be appropriate in light of the outlook. In this endeavor, the staff never provided a specific recommendation on the appropriate policy direction for the Committee. Instead, its role was to help the Committee understand the policy options, given the prevailing economic conditions and uncertainties.[20, 21]

We'd already seen these options outlined in what is called the Bluebook, which had been circulated to us earlier. The Bluebook generally suggests the two most likely policy options, given the economic landscape, and provides a coherent rationale for each.

The first option in this case was to hold the funds rate constant. This option rested, in Kohn's views, on two arguments: first, that policy was already restrictive enough to keep inflation from rising much, if at all; and second, that there would be relatively little cost in waiting to get a clearer picture.

The first argument was based on the relationship between the federal funds rate and its neutral value. The concept of a neutral rate plays an important role in the Committee's thinking and is the final component of the Taylor rule. The neutral rate is the rate that would provide neither stimulus nor restraint to the economy. This rate would be appropriate when the economy is sitting happily at both full employment and price stability.

The federal funds rate at the time was about ½ percentage point above the staff's estimate of its neutral value.[22] So policy could be interpreted as already being slightly restrictive. This meant that policy might already be consistent with slowing growth, as projected by the staff, and consistent therefore with achieving a soft landing.

Second, Kohn noted that even if the unemployment rate was already below the NAIRU, it was unlikely that it was far below the NAIRU. In this case, if inflation rose, the rise would be small and gradual. There would be little damage in holding rates unchanged, therefore, even if the staff estimate of the NAIRU was correct. This would allow us more time to assess whether or not the unemployment rate was in fact below the NAIRU.

Kohn then provided a rationale for the second option on the table, which was raising the federal funds rate. The case for a tightening, he told us, rested on the notion that "short-term rates likely will need to be tightened at some point to keep inflation in check." He also noted that "waiting risks complicating the conduct of policy down the road;" in fact, "the longer the adjustment is postponed . . . the larger it will have to be." In other words, the rate would ultimately have to rise enough not just to contain inflation, but to reverse any increase in inflation that occurred because of the delay in raising rates.

This was a clear argument for preemptive monetary policy. It could stop a rise in inflation, or at least minimize the increase. And it would also reduce the total amount of tightening that might otherwise be required.

Finally, Kohn turned to the policy bias. Should the Committee remain symmetric, or should we move to an asymmetric posture? If the Committee chose not to raise rates at this meeting, Kohn counseled us, but saw the risks as decidedly skewed toward the need for a tightening, we might consider the asymmetric directive. Kohn's suggestion immediately provided a formula for a consensus—holding policy unchanged but explicitly recognizing the risk of higher inflation and leaning toward a possible subsequent tightening.

—∾—

THE PREVIOUS DAY, as was his custom, Greenspan chose not to participate in the outlook go-around. He preferred to wait for the policy go-around before initially addressing the Committee. I soon came to understand why: This arrangement gave him the final word on the outlook and, simultaneously, the first opportunity to set out a policy recommendation. This made it easier for him to build a consensus around his own positions.

The anticipation built as Greenspan prepared to speak. We all knew that he would disproportionately influence the outcome of the policy decisions. In fact, he would almost certainly define them. His remarks would also often bring new data and a unique perspective to the table. But what surprised me most was that regardless of how obscure the Chairman was in his public declarations, he was much clearer and to the point when speaking to the FOMC.

This was always the case when he presented his recommendation for the target for the federal funds rate. He always made a specific recommendation. He also usually indicated his preference for the policy bias—whether he wanted a symmetric or asymmetric posture. On occasion, however, he left this decision to the Committee. When he did so, it seemed to energize the Committee. Indeed, members sometimes got giddy with the prospect of actually having an opportunity to debate some aspect of the policy decision at the meeting and decide on it, as opposed to accepting the Chairman's recommendation.

The Chairman began by noting the tension between the incoming data and the staff's forecast. "We obviously are viewing an economy that at the moment does not resemble most of our textbook models," he said. "The unemployment rate is low and has remained low for quite a while. Anecdotal evidence continues to indicate tight labor markets, but . . . broader measures of price inflation are, if anything, still declining."

Despite this tension between the data and the conventional NAIRU model, the Chairman took a balanced view. He was not suggesting that we abandon the old model, but that we recalibrate it to account for a higher level of sustainable output and employment than we had previously imagined.

In terms of the outlook, he voiced his skepticism about the staff's forecast for higher inflation, arguing that an acceleration in productivity might be allowing the economy to grow faster than previously and operate at a lower unemployment rate without rising inflation. At the same time, he expressed concern about the tightness of the labor markets and suggested that a further tightening of those markets could trigger higher inflation.

This was characteristic of the Chairman's stance throughout the second half of the 1990s. He understood that there were new possibilities (higher productivity growth and a lower NAIRU) to take into account, as well as old regularities (labor markets that were already tight and likely to get tighter) that would at some point reassert themselves. By keeping a foot in each camp, he was able to argue either way—either that the economy was sound, and it would be prudent to hold policy unchanged, or that the economy was beginning to overheat, and it was time to raise rates to avoid higher inflation.

While Greenspan was a NAIRU skeptic at this time, he was not an atheist. He saw the decline of the NAIRU as a "onetime move of the goal post." In fact, he said: "Inflation is not dead. As we get closer to the new goal line, the old inflation pressures will reemerge." In this, he was noting a change in the parameters of the paradigm, not in the paradigm itself.

When it came to the policy, the Chairman said he believed we had "the luxury of waiting." He added, "Accordingly, I would hope that this Committee, while accepting alternative 'B' [holding the funds rate unchanged] to give us an opportunity to assess what is going on, would nonetheless accept an asymmetric bias toward tightening. . . . My judgment is that in all likelihood, if the Committee does not move at this meeting or during the intermeeting period, we probably will do so at the August meeting or later. It seems quite unlikely to me . . . that we will luck out and find the economy expanding at a pace that would not necessitate moving."

A debate followed the Chairman's remarks—not a noisy debate, as some outside the room would later imagine it, but one that studiously posed the alternatives before us. Some members said they would prefer an immediate tightening. Others agreed with the Chairman: It would be better to wait for additional data.

For my part, I was very comfortable with the Chairman's recommendation, although I was not as convinced as he was that we would have to raise the funds rate by the time of the next meeting or two. First, if the staff forecast of a slowdown to trend proved correct, the danger of significant overheating would be quite small. Second, I was not convinced that we were already below the NAIRU.

At this point in my term on the FOMC, the Chairman and I were on opposite sides of the policy debate (as President Clinton had expected when he appointed me). For the Chairman's part, he appeared to be preparing the Committee for a possible near-term increase in the funds rate. For my part, I believed that an immediate tightening was premature and quite possibly unnecessary in the near future. Ironically, as you will see in the coming chapters, the Chairman and I would soon trade places.

At the end of this discussion, the Chairman presented a proposed "directive" for the Committee to vote on.[23] Norm Bernard read it to us: "In the implementation of policy for the immediate future, the Committee seeks to maintain the existing degree of pressure on reserve positions. In the context of the Committee's long-run objectives for price stability and sustainable economic growth, and giving careful consideration to economic, financial, and monetary developments, somewhat greater reserve restraint would or slightly lesser reserve restraint might be acceptable in the intermeeting period."

As I listened, I wondered what that statement had to do with the discussion we had just concluded. Where was the decision to maintain an unchanged federal funds rate target of 5¼%? Where was the decision to shift from a symmetric to an asymmetric directive?

These decisions were in the message but concealed by the code. "Maintaining the existing degree of reserve pressure," for example, was code for leaving the federal funds rate unchanged. The Committee, at this time, did not even officially admit it had a target for the federal funds rate.[24] Meanwhile, the woulds and mights were code for an asymmetric directive. Those who read the sentence carefully enough might find the message that the Committee was more likely to raise the funds rate over time than lower it.[25]

Finally, we voted. There was no suspense in the outcome. The Chairman's recommendation would prevail.

THE CHAIRMAN'S disproportionate influence on FOMC decisions, his efforts to build consensus around his policy recommendations before FOMC meetings, and the strong tendency for Committee members to support the majority view—all these were secrets of the temple that I learned at my first FOMC meeting.

All of this was for a reason. The Chairman, by tradition, is always expected to be on the winning side of the policy vote. Indeed, while this is not written anywhere, the Chairman is expected to resign if the Committee rejects his policy recommendation. For this reason, and since the Chairman also votes first, he prefers to know in advance that he has the support of the majority of the Committee.

To ensure he has the votes to support his policy recommendation, the Chairman visits with the members of the Board in advance of FOMC meetings. When I began my term, the Chairman would meet individually with the other governors during the week before FOMC meetings. His assistant would call to make an appointment, and he would then come to the office of each of the governors. He would sit down and explain his views on the outlook and his "leaning" with respect to the policy decision that would be considered by the Committee at the upcoming meeting.

Some governors found this rather offputting. They interpreted the Chairman's visit as his way of informing them in advance of the outcome of the FOMC meeting rather than an opportunity to sound them out about their own views and to work with them to build a consensus. I was just happy to have the opportunity to visit one-on-one with the Chairman and to talk economics and monetary policy. I always used these meetings as opportunities to engage him in a discussion, to let him know my own views and how they differed from his—and to reveal my own comfort or discomfort with his policy recommendation.

After a while, the Chairman abandoned the private talks before the FOMC meetings and instead used the Monday Board meeting (the day before the FOMC meeting) to share with us his views on the outlook and indicate where he was leaning with respect to policy.

Unlike the FOMC meeting the next day, the discussions at the Monday Board meeting did not consist of prepackaged presentations. They were a much truer give-and-take, a serious exchange of ideas, with each of us questioning one another along the way. I often used the pre-FOMC Monday Board meetings as an opportunity to engage the Chairman in a discussion of the outlook and monetary policy, as I had previously done in the individual meetings.

While we may not have always explicitly voiced our support of his policy recommendation at the end of the individual meetings, and later, at the end of the pre-FOMC Monday Board meetings, there was, in my view, an implicit commitment to support the Chairman the next day. Of course, if you were not prepared to support the Chairman at the FOMC meeting the next day, you had the obligation to tell him so at the Monday Board meeting. During my term, no governor dissented in the vote at an FOMC meeting.

Thus, by the time the Chairman enters the FOMC meeting, he is virtually guaranteed the support of the members of the Board, who are, in turn, the majority of the voting members of the Committee. In my five and a half years on the FOMC, never once did the Chairman fail to secure a vote in favor of his initial recommendation. In fact, within recent memory, there has never been the case of a chairman losing a policy vote at the FOMC.

WHILE THE RESERVE BANK PRESIDENTS are not part of the premeeting discussions at the Board, they have their own devices for influencing the policy discussion in between meetings. They do this specifically through requests to change the discount rate.

The discount rate is the interest rate banks pay when they borrow from Federal Reserve Banks. Discount rate requests are formally made by the board of directors of the Reserve Banks—not by the Reserve Bank presidents themselves. The view of a Reserve Bank's board of directors on the appropriate level of the discount rate, however, is generally shaped by its interaction with the bank's research staff and the bank's president.

I therefore view requests for changes in the discount rate as a source of information about the policy preferences of Reserve Bank presidents, specifically as a noisy indicator of the bank presidents' preferences for a change in the federal funds rate at the next FOMC meeting.

If a relatively large number of Reserve Banks request an increase in the discount rate, for example, this would suggest potential support among those presidents for an increase in the federal funds rate at the upcoming FOMC meeting. This hint of wider support for a tightening, in turn, can give leverage during the pre-FOMC discussions to a governor, for example, who preferred to tighten (while the Chairman preferred to hold policy unchanged). The influence of the discount requests are perhaps reinforced by the fact that the pre-FOMC Board discussions of monetary policy come at the time the Board reviews the Reserve Bank requests for discount rate changes.[26]

—~—

WHILE THE CHAIRMAN clearly does wield disproportionate power in the FOMC, he does not necessarily always get his way. It was the Chairman's responsibility, for example, to count heads to ensure he had a majority supporting him. He might on occasion find himself moving sooner than he would otherwise prefer to ease or tighten in response to the strong consensus within the Committee for such a move. He sometimes would lead by persuading others of the merits of his argument and sometimes perhaps by skillfully adopting as his own view what had become the consensus of the Committee. With a skillful Chairman, as Greenspan certainly is, you never knew whether he had to alter his position to lead the consensus. Indeed, I ended my term not sure I had ever influenced the outcome of an FOMC meeting. This was one of the frustrating aspects of serving on the Greenspan FOMC, but it never stopped me from trying.

Once the majority view (which, as I've already mentioned, is that of the Chairman) is apparent at FOMC meetings, the Committee is expected to rally around it. This means that most votes are unanimous—and when there are dissents, they are typically limited to one or two opposing votes. This is sometimes referred to as a system of "collective responsibility" for decisions, in which the majority view is adopted and supported by the entire body.

There are, nevertheless, occasional dissents. Indeed, while most votes are unanimous, one or two dissents are not unusual. A third, however, would be viewed as a sign that the FOMC is in open revolt with the Chairman's leadership. The dissents, rather than the policy decision itself, would become the story. This would be disruptive to the process of monetary policymaking and unsettling to the financial markets.

Because of this, I came to think of the voting process as a game of musical chairs. There were two imaginary red chairs around the table—the "dissent chairs." The first two FOMC members who sat in those chairs were able to dissent. After that, no one else could follow the same course.[27]

I never dissented during my term as a governor. I differed on occasion with the Chairman's recommendation but, after making clear my reservations, joined the consensus. I believe that dissents are an important part of the process. They allow the public to appreciate when the decisions are particularly difficult without undermining the consensus process. This is the case as long as there are no more than one or two dissents. Because I was often visibly identified as someone who disagreed with the Chairman, I believed that my dissents would draw special attention and divert focus from the issues to personalities. So I talked about the issues and, as I said, voted with the consensus.

—ɱ—

SO WAS THE FOMC MEETING merely a ritual dance? No. I came to see policy decisions as often evolving over at least a couple of meetings. The seeds were sown at one meeting and harvested at the next. So I always listened to the discussion intently, because it could change my mind, even if it could not change my vote at that meeting. Similarly, while in my remarks to my colleagues it sounded as if I were addressing today's concerns and today's policy decisions, in reality I was often positioning myself, and my peers, for the next meeting.

I could not contain my enthusiasm for being part of the Committee and part of the process of making monetary policy. Toward the end of the first day, I even had to interrupt the meeting to say: "Gee, this is even more fun than I thought it was going to be!" You didn't hear laughter spilling out of the Committee room too often, but this was a memorable exception.

3

HAWKS AND DOVES

Following the July 1996 meeting, the American economy continued to climb higher. Most surprisingly, amid this robust growth, rising inflation was nowhere to be seen. For that reason, at our August 20 meeting, the FOMC decided not to raise rates.

But the tension within the FOMC was continuing to build. Some of us believed we should move preemptively to slow growth, convinced that the unemployment rate was already so low that inflation was bound to begin to rise. That's what the traditional NAIRU model had predicted, and most of us still believed it. Others were less sure where the NAIRU was located. They preferred to allow the economy to continue to grow robustly and the unemployment rate to continue to fall until inflation began to rise, definitively signaling that the economy had moved beyond the NAIRU.

The pressure to tighten rates was coming from Reserve Bank presidents Broaddus, Gary Stern (Minneapolis), Parry, Minehan, Hoenig, and Tom Melzer (St. Louis), who were urging an immediate tightening. Disagreeing with them were presidents Jordan and Boehne and Governor Rivlin, who felt that the funds rate should remain unchanged.

For my part, I was beginning to make a significant crossing in my point of view. Up until then, I was willing to hold rates as they were.

But as the unemployment rate continued to decline and finally closed in on 5%—without the slowdown projected by the staff—I became increasingly convinced: We needed to tighten monetary policy to prevent an overheated economy and a rise in inflation.

This, of course, put me on the other side of the debate from the Chairman. He knew that the pressure to tighten was building, and he continued to talk about tightening. But he seemed reluctant to do so. One reason, he said, was that this would be a "first move"—a change in the direction of policy.

In the Chairman's playbook, a "first move" would have a disproportionately great effect on the financial markets, so it had to meet a higher standard. At the July meeting, the Chairman had explained it for us: "We have to be aware in this particular context that to reverse direction requires a somewhat higher hurdle of evidence than would be required if we were merely continuing a previous trend of monetary policy moves." Then he argued that that higher hurdle had not yet been cleared.

The first-move edict also reflected the Chairman's reluctance to tarnish his reputation (and the FOMC's) with a move that, if wrong, might need to be quickly reversed. "If we are perceived to have tightened and then have been compelled by market forces to quickly reverse," he had said at the July meeting, "our reputation for professionalism will suffer a severe blow. This will weaken our ability to raise rates in a dramatic, preemptive fashion in order to contain inflationary forces at an early stage."

THERE WAS ALSO the upcoming presidential election to consider, the race between Clinton and Dole. The Fed thinks of itself as apolitical and does not want to become a political issue. The fact that an election was nearing meant that the Committee preferred to avoid any decisions that might draw critical fire. That, I expect, discouraged us—and particularly the Chairman—from tightening rates immediately before a presidential election. That said, concerns about the election—while perhaps weighing on our minds—were never raised around the FOMC table, formally or informally, while I was there.

As for myself, I was too consumed with questions about the

NAIRU and productivity to worry much about the election. Of course, I may be somewhat politically naive. As proof of this, it was in September 1996, in advance of the FOMC meeting immediately preceding the election, that Janet Yellen and I chose to visit the Chairman in his office and urge him to recommend that the FOMC tighten rates. We both said that we would not be able to support the Chairman much longer if he didn't recommend a move. It was not an ultimatum, but it was a message that our patience was running out. We continued with a brief chat about the outlook, then left without receiving any commitment from him.

Later, I understand that the Chairman referred to me as "politically tone-deaf." If he did say that, it simply confirms my view that he is a very good judge of character. For the sake of the Fed's independence, I was quite happy to be politically tone-deaf. And I'm also pleased that the Chairman, in contrast, was politically savvy.

—ꟽ—

BY SEPTEMBER, the economy was still showing no signs of slackening. The stock market was up and so was consumer confidence, reaching its highest point in five years. Most important, the news arrived in early September that the unemployment rate had finally dropped beneath 5½%, where it had been hovering for more than a year.

As a result, the debate within the FOMC was vigorous enough to be heard outside the Committee room. "A rift at the Fed has already developed," *BusinessWeek* noted in its September 9 issue. "Squabbles among Fed bankers are not unheard of, but they are rare enough to raise eyebrows."[1]

In the eyes of the media (and the markets), the debate was increasingly between the "hawks" and the "doves" at the FOMC. This was the media's way of separating the debate into personalities as well as ideas.

Hawks worry most about inflation. They believe there are high costs associated with it. So when hawks spy inflation, they argue for preemptive tightening. To ensure that inflation remains low and stable, they are willing to take the risk that the unemployment rate may not always be at its lowest sustainable level.

Doves, on the other hand, worry more about unemployment. They want to see monetary policy positioned to ensure that the economy achieves the highest sustainable level of employment. They might, for example, be willing to tolerate inflation above the level associated with price stability for a while to avoid disrupting an economy already at full employment. And they might be more willing to risk some upturn in inflation to make sure that they had driven the unemployment rate to its lowest sustainable level.

Some hawks and doves are fixed by their economic and political beliefs. Driven by these beliefs, they remain adamant in their positions regardless of the circumstances. I call these "constitutional" hawks and doves. But other hawks and doves switch roles depending on their reading of the latest data and forecasts. They are pragmatic. I call them "circumstantial" hawks and doves.

Hawks and doves, furthermore, are separated by where they draw the line on inflation. A hawk might prefer a zero inflation objective—true price stability—believing that the best economic performance is achieved by wringing every last ounce of inflation out of the system. A dove might settle for a less exacting objective.

Finally, hawks and doves are distinguished by their degree of confidence in the traditional NAIRU model. In 1996, hawks were generally more likely to be proponents of the NAIRU. They were concerned that the current unemployment rate would trigger inflation. Doves either rejected the NAIRU model altogether (and hence didn't worry about lower unemployment triggering higher inflation) or accepted the NAIRU model but were willing to let the unemployment rate descend until a twitch in inflation revealed the NAIRU's true location.

Ed Boehne was the most consistent dove at this time, but he was often joined by Alice Rivlin, Bill McDonough, and Jack Guynn from the Atlanta Fed, and later Bob McTeer from Dallas. Initially, the hawks included Tom Melzer, Al Broaddus, Bob Parry, Cathy Minehan, Gary Stern, and Tom Hoenig—with Mike Moskow leaning in their direction. Over time, as confidence in the NAIRU model waned, the ranks of the hawks thinned out.

The Chairman was harder to nail down. The media often characterized him as a hawk, and no one doubted his commitment to price stability. He also preferred a target of zero inflation, measured correctly. That was the signature of a constitutional hawk. On the other hand, the Chairman was skeptical of the NAIRU model, and he was reluctant, therefore, to tighten rates preemptively based on the traditional NAIRU formula. That put him, in one FOMC meeting after another, with the doves.

Talking like a hawk, worrying aloud about tighter labor markets triggering higher inflation, and suggesting an imminent need to tighten policy, yet making policy again and again that pleased the doves: The best description of the Chairman was a hawkish dove.

As for myself, over time I would become labeled as a hawk. That's because I believed in the NAIRU model and was prepared to tighten preemptively if the unemployment rate fell below my estimate of the NAIRU. But I was considered a somewhat dovish hawk, I believe, since I was prepared to tolerate some inflation rather than drive it down to the point of true price stability.

In the second half of 1996, the Chairman and I played out our assigned roles, although neither of us was the most ardent bird in the respective flock. Greenspan played the hawk, arguing that a near-term tightening really might be needed (while dragging his feet on an immediate move). I played the dove, believing that a tightening at this time was premature (while worrying that the unemployment rate might be headed in the direction that threatened an overheated economy).

As I mentioned earlier, the Chairman and I would trade places in the coming year. He would become increasingly dovish, owing to his belief that productivity was permitting the economy to grow faster and operate at a lower unemployment rate without triggering higher inflation. I, on the other hand, while grudgingly adjusting my NAIRU estimates to some of the new structural changes, soon became convinced that the time had come to raise rates, slow growth, and prevent the unemployment rate from falling further.

Of course, the more the Chairman became a dove, the more I was seen as a hawk, at least in the eyes of the press.

—~—

THE MEDIA SOON divided us into warring camps. They were particularly interested in exploring any situation that might be interpreted as a "challenge" to the Chairman's leadership. As a result, we all realized that we had to start speaking with increased caution.

Markets are especially sensitive to any comments made by FOMC members immediately before and after FOMC meetings. For that reason, a voluntary guideline discourages members from giving speeches or talking to the media during the "blackout" period, which extended from the week before an FOMC meeting to the end of the week of the meeting. I thought that this was a very sensible rule and followed it scrupulously.

Still, at one of our FOMC meetings, the Chairman said he thought too much "chatter" was going on between FOMC meetings. By that he meant that the press was attributing too many opinions on the outlook or monetary policy to specific FOMC members or to unnamed Fed sources. These comments invariably heightened speculation about impending policy actions and often increased market volatility. The Chairman preferred Committee members to talk as little as possible about the outlook and monetary policy.

At one meeting, the Chairman asked the Committee how it might discipline itself to avoid such occurrences. Several members had suggestions for the rest of us offenders. One said that when delivering speeches, he always tried to be as boring as possible. I responded that I was always only unintentionally boring. Another remarked that he limited his comments to topics that were unrelated to Fed responsibilities. I responded that I talked only about issues that were directly related to Fed responsibilities.

Someone suggested that Joe Coyne, head of public affairs at the Board, develop guidelines that specified what Committee members should and should not talk about. The Chairman encouraged this. I replied that as far as I was concerned, that suggestion was way over the line. I would take into consideration any personal criticism about my comments, I told the Committee, but had no intention of being bound by a consensus-driven decision on appropriate speaking topics. The guidelines would not apply to me, I made clear. Nevertheless, the Chairman asked Coyne to prepare the guidelines and circulate them as soon as possible for discussion. They were never circulated.

THE FACT WAS, I had decided early on in my term to give regular speeches on the economic outlook and monetary policy. I have to admit that in making this decision, I wasn't fully aware that it was the Chairman, not the governors, who was expected to provide this kind of regular communication. As it turned out, however, no one else on the Committee, including the Chairman, spoke as regularly and explicitly on these issues as I did. So I believed my speeches served a useful purpose. But when I aired my views on challenging issues and controversial decisions, I discovered that my words had turned me into a lightning rod.

Perhaps I should have been better prepared for this, particularly in dealing with the media. When I first joined the Fed, a few former governors had warned me that Joe Coyne would try to discourage me from making many speeches and, most of all, from saying anything substantive if I did. So I was suspicious of Coyne before he even uttered a word. Over time, however, I came to value his experience in dealing with the media. And he worked hard to keep me out of trouble.

Coyne told me that Committee members should try to avoid saying anything that would move the markets, and he lectured me about the importance of maintaining the confidentiality of materials circulated in preparation for FOMC meetings, as well as the importance of protecting the confidentiality of FOMC discussions.

FOMC members, of course, have the right to discuss their views in both public speeches and press briefings, he said. Nevertheless, Committee members should not make their comments so explicit that their votes could be inferred from their comments. I called this "keeping your options open" and found it to be good advice. From then on, I spoke explicitly about my interpretations of recent events and my past votes, but far less explicitly about my expectations of future developments. And I was downright vague about how I might vote in the future.

Coyne then took me through a bewildering taxonomy of various terms used during interviews—on the record, on background, off the record, not for attribution, and deep background. "On the record" meant that everything said in the conversation was usable and quotable. "For attribution but with no direct quotation" meant that your remarks could be paraphrased and attributed to you. "Not for attribution" meant that the information could be used but the source should not be directly identified. Typically, the comments would be attributed to "government officials" or, in the case of the Fed, "senior Fed officials."

Talking "on background" meant that the material gathered in the discussion could be used by the reporter but not attributed to me as an individual or to the Federal Reserve. However, the information could be attributed to "government officials." Sometimes the press would make reference to "Fed sources." The next degree of detachment was "deep background." In this case, the information could be used, but the source should not be identified. The final possibility was to talk "off the record." In this case, the reporters could not use the information in any way that indicated they got it from you or your organization.

To further complicate matters, Coyne told me that this list of terms was interpreted differently by different reporters and that, in any case, I shouldn't trust any reporter to abide by the ground rules I might put into place. "They are paid to report," he warned me. "If you give them information, no matter what the ground rules, they will try to find a way to use it."

AFTER SOME THOUGHT, I decided that these rules of engagement weren't relevant to the way I wanted to interact with the media. So I developed my own set of ground rules—and reviewed them with reporters when we first met.

My first rule was that I was going to talk only about my views and never speculate on what the Committee was thinking—and certainly not about what the Chairman was thinking or planning to do. In addition, I would never comment on what went on inside the FOMC room, since that information is clearly privileged. Until the transcripts of the meeting are published five years after the fact, it is never appropriate—indeed, it is a violation of confidentiality rules—to talk about what goes on around the FOMC table. If reporters wanted to find out what a particular Committee member thought, they should ask that member, not me. If they want to better understand the Chairman's views, they should talk to the Chairman.

Second, without my explicit approval, nothing that I said could be quoted or otherwise attributed to me. And they could never attribute my words to "a senior Fed official," "Fed sources," or some imaginary person. It was much more disagreeable, in my view, to have my words attributed to a "senior Fed official" than directly to me.

Third, when I allowed one of my opinions to be quoted, I wanted it attributed directly to me, as my personal point of view, I did not want to be interpreted as speaking on behalf of the Board or the FOMC. The Chairman was particularly insistent upon this rule, and rightly so. The Chairman is the only member of the FOMC with the authority to speak for the Committee. To underscore that, I usually began my speeches by explaining that I was speaking only for myself.

With Coyne's help and my own set of rules, I thought engaging with the media should be easy. But it wasn't. In fact, my very first opportunity to meet with the media after joining the Board taught me an important lesson.

This lesson came when I was in Boston to speak at the annual meeting of the National Association of Business Economics. I'm a member of the NABE and indeed have been elected a Fellow. I picked this venue for my first talk because it guaranteed me a friendly audience, a strategy that has served me well during my years as a speaker.

After the speech, the press requested some time for an interview. I didn't see any reason why not, so we moved to an area where they had set up several rows of chairs for them and one lone one for me. The press had lots of questions. No problem; I had lots of answers. To tell the truth, I was having fun in the limelight, fielding one question after another.

That night, however, I awakened in a cold sweat. What had I said? I wondered aloud. How would it be interpreted? How would it affect the markets? As I looked back, I imagined them luring me, a member of the Federal Reserve Board, into all kinds of overtly provocative responses. What would they report tomorrow in the papers? What was already out on the wires?

As it turned out, by some miracle, I had not said anything regrettable. Nevertheless, I was more cautious thereafter about subjecting myself to such an unstructured press conference. I wanted the opportunity to put each comment into the appropriate context and to attach the appropriate qualifiers to each comment. After that experience, I typically reserved my direct contact with the press for meetings in my office or on the telephone, using the rules of engagement that I had painstakingly developed. I thought I had fixed the problem. But there was more trouble with the media ahead.

—m—

ON SEPTEMBER 17, 1996, a story written by Isabelle Clary appeared on the Reuters newswire revealing that "eight of the twelve district banks in the Federal Reserve System have requested a hike in the discount rate amid mounting evidence that the pace of the expansion is likely to remain brisk in the second half of 1996, a senior Fed official said. . . ."[2]

Clary went on to say that the Fed source had confirmed that a consensus was forming for a 25-basis-point increase in the federal funds rate. If this was true, it was a remarkable nugget of information for the markets to work on. But it was more than that: This was a leak of sensitive and highly confidential information, a serious breach of Fed rules, and indeed a criminal offense.

Committee members are supposed to know the rules, but just to remind them, each January every member receives a set of rules and operating procedures for the FOMC. This includes a stern statement about the confidentiality of materials related to the FOMC process and the discount rate. To emphasize the sense of confidentiality, the FOMC materials are color coded. There are, for example, tan- and salmon-colored reports (tan signaling the highest level of confidentiality, salmon less so) along with the Greenbook and the Bluebook. The message is clear: Keep your mouth shut. This means not only in your communications with people outside the Fed, but even in speaking within the Fed to people who may not have been cleared for a certain level of sensitive material.

In the case of the Clary article, the leak was a bad one. It suggested wider-than-expected support among the Reserve Banks for tighter policy. This, in turn, signaled the possibility of an impending increase in the federal funds rate.

The Chairman was very upset. The possibility that the leak was intentional, and designed to influence the outcome of the upcoming meeting, made it even more worrisome. The next day, Greenspan informed the Board that he had asked the Board's inspector general to initiate an investigation. He would try to determine who was responsible for the leak.

The media began to hint at an uprising within the Committee. Some of the news stories referred to the leak as "political hardball inside the Fed"[3] and "a shot across the bow from one of the hawkish Federal Reserve Bank presidents to Alan Greenspan."[4] Some postulated that the surmised uprising would cause Greenspan, who had been resisting the hawks, to beat a tactical retreat and accede to a ¼-percentage-point increase in the funds rate.

That was bad enough. But then it got worse. On September 25, the *New York Post* published an article written by John Crudele with the headline "Could This Be the Fed's 'Deep Throat'?" and a picture of . . . me! Crudele suggested "that investigators start looking at Fed governor Laurence Meyer as the chief suspect. . . ."

Crudele explained my motive by quoting from Clary's article: "Some of the Fed governors known for their moderate views on monetary policy—such as Laurence Meyer—were sympathetic to the bank presidents' concerns that the economy may be overheating." I was not the source of the leak, had never heard of John Crudele, and was livid at having been accused on the basis of wild speculation.

Crudele laid out his reasoning for singling me out. He said that "it is not unusual for a reporter to express the view of a source by name in one part of the story while hiding that same source's identity in another part of the story." Hence, the fact that I was quoted in the Reuters article, perhaps more than any other Fed official, in Crudele's assessment, immediately cast suspicion on me as the source of the leak. The final "proof," as far as Crudele was concerned, seemed to be that I had an opportunity to meet with Clary during the Boston NABE meeting and that, based on previous stories, it was "obvious that Clary is friendly with Meyer" and would likely have talked with me at that meeting.

Indeed, Clary and I had talked on the phone before I was confirmed. And we did meet in person for the first time at that meeting. Crudele noted that the previous June, Clary had written a lengthy feature about me, one that Crudele characterized as a "gushy profile" and a "suck up piece that was bound to pay off some day." Gushy? I just thought she captured the real essence of me!

The leak was a major event at the Fed. Now investigations were under way by both the FBI and the Board's inspector general. Both wanted to interview me. I decided to visit a lawyer.

In the end, however, the Board's general counsel felt that I didn't need an attorney. Relax and let the story fade, he said. He also suggested that I go see the Chairman and seek his advice. I did. The Chairman said that he had full confidence in me. He said to ignore the story and go about my business. And that's what I did.

To my knowledge, the source of the leak was never uncovered—though it is possible that the source was uncovered and the Chairman dealt with this person directly and quietly.

—ↀ—

REGARDLESS OF THE SUPPOSED insurrection as reported in the *New York Post*—and regardless of the visit that Janet Yellen and I took to the Chairman's office to urge him to raise rates—the Committee decided not to boost rates at the September 24 meeting. In fact, the staff argued that the decline in unemployment was a mere aberration and, furthermore, that growth would soon slow to trend. No tightening might be necessary if that forecast was correct.

While the pressure had been building in September and October 1996 to tighten rates, in November the pressure backed off. The reason for this was not any slackening in the economy, but the fact that the staff, at the November meeting, announced they had lowered their estimate of the NAIRU from 5¾% to 5.6%.

This adjustment, they said, reflected lower-than-expected readings on recent core inflation, which in turn suggested that structural changes in the economy had, indeed, lowered the minimum sustainable unemployment rate. This adjustment turned out to be just the first in a series of downward revisions to the NAIRU that the staff implemented in response to continuing evidence of better-than-expected inflation performance.

Now the Chairman felt he had confirmation for what he had been suggesting for quite some time. To be sure, the staff continued to expect an upward drift in inflation (because the unemployment rate was still judged to be below the downward revised estimate of the NAIRU). Nevertheless, because growth was apparently slowing to trend and inflation was still declining, the Committee now realized that it might be able to avoid a tightening.

Parry, who had been arguing for an immediate tightening, now supported an unchanged policy. Even Broaddus, who had been urging a 50-basis-point tightening, mellowed and called for only a 25-basis-point move.

The vote in favor of an unchanged policy was now unanimous. The situation remained about the same at the December meeting: The vote was unanimous for no change in the funds rate, with an asymmetric directive just to hedge against the remaining inflation concerns.

—w—

BY JANUARY 1997, however, the data clearly showed that the economy was not slowing to trend. In fact, it was on a roll: Manufacturing was up, and software was flying on Internet time. Consumers were buying, and home builders were building. The stock market was up almost 30% over the last year.

By now, many on the Committee had become impatient with the failure of the economy to slow in line with the staff forecast. The consensus was starting to swing again in the direction of a tightening. Even the Chairman was molting before our eyes from a dove into a hawk.

To be sure, the state of the economy had not really changed that much. The economy was projected to grow near trend in 1997 and 1998. The unemployment rate was still hovering about 5% and expected to remain close to 5% over the next two years. Because the staff still believed that the unemployment rate was below the NAIRU—even after acknowledging some adjustments due to the "new structure" of the economy—they projected a gradual increase in inflation. But the Committee was less inclined to assume that the economy would slow without a tightening of monetary policy. I was also leaning toward the need to tighten.

Of course, the Chairman was still cautious about what would be a "first move." Moving today "would really shock the market in a way that would be destabilizing and not advance our goals," he said. He wanted to give the markets enough notice.[5]

But Greenspan left little doubt about where he thought we were headed: "I think we are getting to the point—March may be the appropriate time—when we will have to move unless very clear evidence emerges that the expansion is easing significantly." While the Chairman was once again holding off pressure to tighten, he had now signaled the possibility—indeed, the likelihood—of a tightening at the next meeting. There clearly seemed to be a consensus to move in that direction.

Greenspan also said that if the economy was not seen to be slowing before his testimony before the Senate Banking Committee on February 26, he would then underscore in his testimony "not only . . . our intention to hold the line on inflation and to take preemptive action as needed . . . but we would have to prime the markets to anticipate that we might be moving quite soon even in the absence of clear evidence of upward movements in wage or price inflation."

He urged the Committee to "be prepared to move if we have to at the next meeting." That was not the same as saying we necessarily would—he was not locking the Committee into a decision, he added. But it meant not only that we would stay at an asymmetric directive, but that this one would be a "real" asymmetry, one that would trumpet an imminent tightening (unlike the weaker "notional" asymmetry, in place at the last few meetings, which says that the risks are tilted toward higher inflation and that the next move in fund rates is more likely to be up than down).

SHORTLY AFTER THE JANUARY MEETING, I spoke to the Charlotte, North Carolina Economics Club. It was my first major speech on the economic outlook, and in it I hoped to balance my desire to be forthcoming with the Chairman's admonition not to move markets.

In the speech, I described the economy as being "at the top of the mountain." This was my way of saying that economic performance was as good as it could get, that we had achieved a close approximation to the fabled but rarely experienced soft landing. It followed, then, that once you got to the top, all roads led down. The only questions were how long could we linger near the top—that is, with output near potential and growing close to potential—and what road the economy would take going down.

The most likely route, judging from historical experience—and the one I worried most about once I joined the FOMC—was that the economy, starting at full employment, would continue to grow robustly and overheat, resulting in rising inflation. Typically, efforts by the Fed to contain and then reverse the inflation end with a recession.

My attempt to avoid moving the markets was not entirely successful in this case. When I returned home, my wife said it best. "Well, now you finally did it. You really trashed the market." To this day, we have a bit of a debate about whether she said "trashed" or used some more colorful language. But I got her point.

The next day, the *Atlanta Journal-Constitution* had a rather amusing way of describing the incident. The article noted that the Dow dropped 30 points "in a wink" after I had given the impression in a speech that faster growth could force the Fed to raise rates. But the article began with an interesting observation: "Laurence Meyer is not Alan Greenspan. Which helps to explain why the Dow Jones Industrial average recovered from a bout of Meyer-induced jitters to finish with another record."[6] So I had a momentary effect on the markets, but no staying power. That, at least, was a relief.

Still, when I returned to the Board, the Chairman asked me to pay him a visit in his office to discuss my violation of his "don't move the markets" advice. I acknowledged that my remarks had affected the market and vowed to try to avoid such effects in the future. But I also indicated that I could not let this desire "not to move markets" gag me and prevent me from expressing my views on the outlook and the challenges for monetary policy. I promised only to try harder; I didn't promise never again to move markets.

—∾—

AS AN ACADEMIC and forecaster, I had plenty of experience speaking to audiences and the press. I recall once complaining about being misquoted in the press to my friend and colleague at Washington University, Murray Weidenbaum. Murray is a former chairman of the President's CEA and someone experienced in dealing with these issues.

He counseled me not to call and complain to the reporter. Better, he said, to call and thank the reporter for quoting me. All anyone would remember within a day or two, he noted, was the fact that I was quoted, not what I said. That was fine when I was an academic and a private forecaster. But now it was different. My words could move markets and create impressions of dissension within the Committee. It was not enough to get the substance right. The tone—indeed, every word—had to be right.

—w—

SHORTLY AFTER THIS INCIDENT, *The Wall Street Journal*'s David Wessel asked if he could accompany me to one of my talks. He wanted to write a story on the difficulty FOMC members have in giving talks about the outlook and monetary policy without moving the markets. Wessel may have been thinking especially about the wire service reporters, who had the ability to put my words immediately into the public arena.

Indeed, the wire reporters were especially challenging for me to deal with, as Joe Coyne had warned me they would be. They would follow me like groupies to talks all around the country. That was fine, but I felt they had a very different approach to reporting from that of newspaper reporters. A newspaper reporter has time to think about his or her story. Indeed, some newspaper reporters would call me after a talk to seek clarification before they wrote about it. But wire services trade in instant analysis. Speed is their competitive advantage.

They also seemed, as a rule, to try to be especially provocative or, more precisely, to make my remarks appear as provocative as possible—or even more provocative than I thought possible. My interpretation was that there was so much competition among the wire service reporters that each had to demonstrate some unique value added. That value added came, in turn, from a unique interpretation of what a governor might have said. With so many wire service reporters filing at virtually the same time, there would always be an instant jumble of opinions about what I said immediately after I said it. Sometimes I would ask myself if I really could be so unclear.

I also sometimes suspected that wire service reporters got paid a commission proportional to the effect their stories had in moving markets. They seemed to expressly want their stories to move the markets, and they therefore were prone to interpret whatever you said in whatever manner had the most chance of doing so. This motivation resulted in an obvious conflict with the Chairman's sound advice to governors and other FOMC members to avoid moving the markets.

One of the most stressful events for me at the Board, then, was in having to read the wire service accounts immediately after my speeches. You had to put up with a variety of interpretations attached to a single statement, even a single sentence in a statement, that were sometimes everything but the one you intended. After suffering a few wounds, I tried not to take it personally. Every time I was misinterpreted, I accepted some of the responsibility myself for not being clearer.

So I thought that Wessel's idea was an interesting one. It would be useful for me to contribute to a story on the challenges of an FOMC member talking about the economy and monetary policy, trying to convey a message, but also trying to avoid "moving the markets." I thought that the story, titled "When Fed Governor Talks, People Listen; But Do They Hear?," turned out well. The subtitle was "How Hard Mr. Meyer Tries Not to Move Markets; Why He Failed Yesterday."[7]

Wessel reported that "[Governor Meyer] wince[d] at media accounts that greet him after every one of his speeches." He quotes me as saying: "Preparing the speech is a joy. Giving the speech is fun. Dealing with the aftermath is the only thing where there's stress." That is exactly as I said it—and precisely what I felt.

—~—

BY MARCH 1997, the strength of the economy was becoming ever more evident in data that was pouring in. Consumer spending, factory orders, housing, and nearly every other aspect of the economy all were pushing skyward. Some pundits were wondering if the old rules no longer applied, whether the business cycle, as we once knew it, might have passed on. That was clearly an exaggeration, but one thing was for real: The economy was not slowing down.

Inside the FOMC, the case for a tightening had become compelling, even to those who had been in the wait-and-see camp. The staff now expected continued above-trend growth and an unemployment rate that would fall to 5% or less through 1998. The Greenbook projected a slight acceleration in inflation in 1997 and then a rise in the inflation rate to 3¼% for the CPI measure in 1998. While this was not a dramatic acceleration, Prell said it was "a change in direction of the underlying trend" and suggested "the risk of a building inflationary momentum."

Now, at our March 27, 1997, meeting, Don Kohn reminded the Committee that, earlier in the day, Mike Prell had counseled that we might have to tighten rates at some point. Was the time now? "Put another way—you've had an asymmetrical directive for about nine months," he said, abandoning his usual sense of evenhandedness. "Is it time to deliver?" This question set the tone for the policy discussion. Of course, the governors had all met with the Chairman previously. So we all knew the answer.

Kohn continued his discussion. He tried to show both sides of the debate, as was his obligation, but there was little doubt where his sympathies lay. "If tightening is needed," Kohn went on, "the longer it is delayed—that is, the longer the economy operates beyond its sustainable potential—the more substantial the offsetting correction in economic activity required if the Committee is to keep inflation from ratcheting higher." This was always a key argument in support of tightening.

Kohn also noted that a 25-basis-point increase had already been built into market expectations. In this case, a 25-basis-point tightening would neither surprise nor upset the markets. To the contrary, "not tightening could unsettle financial markets as participants reassessed their reading of the signals coming out of the Federal Reserve." In other words, if you already signaled the market about an upcoming move, you will confuse the markets if you don't deliver.

Kohn then turned to the question of whether to remain asymmetric or return to symmetry. An asymmetric directive would suggest that the Committee was likely to tighten further and probably soon. On the other hand, a symmetrical directive would suggest a more cautious approach, in light of recent favorable inflation performance.

THE COMMITTEE MEMBERS noted that it was hard not to be impressed with the economy's across-the-board momentum. Even those who had been resisting calls for tighter policy now joined the consensus favoring a rise in rates. I agreed. I now expected the unemployment rate to decline to 5% later in 1997 and to below 5% in 1998. Although inflation continued to surprise us on the downside, the greater near-term momentum in growth and the lower unemployment rate projected for the remainder of 1997 and in 1998 encouraged me to revise my inflation forecast upward for 1998 and led me to support a tightening at the March 27 meeting. (Figure 4 in the appendix depicts the unemployment rate and an estimate of the NAIRU in the second half of the 1990s and through 2003.)

The Chairman summed it up: "It is quite evident that we have come to a point where . . . as Don put it, . . . we have to deliver. . . . The proposition that inflation has stopped falling is not readily provable. . . . The reason is very clearly that productivity is badly underestimated and indeed may actually be accelerating. . . . We are not at this stage moving into . . . an overheated boom. . . . There is [no] particular urgency to move in a very aggressive way. We are not behind the curve. . . . But it is crucial to keep inflation low."

He concluded that we needed to move 25 basis points today. (Figure 5 in the appendix depicts the path of the federal funds rate from the second half of the 1990s through 2003.) He noted that moving 50 basis points would suggest to the markets that we thought we were behind the curve. He also urged the Committee to return to a symmetric directive, adding that such a move wouldn't constrain our future actions: If we felt we needed to tighten, of course, we could do so, even from a symmetric directive. But asymmetry would "establish a presumption that we would probably move again in May," he said. We might have to move again in May, but the "issue is basically whether we want to convey that notion in advance. . . ."

If the Committee did convey that message to the bond markets, longer-term interest rates would begin to build in expectations of further increases in the funds rate in the future. The Committee was not sure this was the time to encourage such expectations.

—~—

THERE WAS, IN FACT, a "love-hate" relationship between the FOMC and the bond market. The Committee loved it when the bond market priced into longer-term interest rates the expected changes in the funds rate that the Committee thought might be required. This sped the effect of monetary policy on the economy, multiplying the power of monetary policy. The market and the FOMC were working in tandem.

But the FOMC also disliked being constrained by the bond market. It hated it when the bond market built expectations about policy actions at the very next meeting into current long-term interest rates, when the Committee was uncertain whether or not it would prefer to move that soon. In such a case, the Committee might be forced at the next meeting to disappoint the same market expectations that it had encouraged, perhaps confusing the markets about the Committee's forecasts and intentions (or the Committee might feel pressured to change rates earlier than they would have preferred).

In this case, I strongly supported the 25-basis-point move but noted that I could have been persuaded to stay asymmetric. But the Chairman preferred to return to a symmetric position, and the Committee obliged.

The choice of symmetry and asymmetry was virtually never a deal breaker, incidentally. Combining a tightening with a move to a symmetric directive was a way of ensuring a stronger consensus, making it easier for those who preferred not to move to join in what could be interpreted as a one-time-only move.

—ɯ—

IMMEDIATELY FOLLOWING THE VOTE, the head of public affairs passed around the table the statement that would be released to the public at the conclusion of the meeting.[8] To my surprise, I learned that these statements were written before the meeting by the Chairman, with input from the director of monetary affairs and sometimes, the head of public affairs. As such, they did not reflect a shred of the discussion we had just concluded.

We discussed the statement, and some of us suggested a few minor revisions, which were ultimately left to the discretion of the Chairman. Perhaps that was as it should be—committees do not do well in finite time writing such statements. But the fact that the statements were prepared by the Chairman without any real input from the Committee, created a degree of tension over the matter that never diminished during my term.

In any case, we released the statement at 2:15 p.m. Finally we had moved to tighten rates. And now the real firestorm began.

THE FIRST TIGHTENING is almost always controversial, especially when it is preemptive. The shock of investors, in this case, was based not on any concern that this little increase would threaten the expansion, but rather on the concern that this would be just the first of a series of tightenings.

That prospect definitively alarmed some people, including many in Congress. Because I had spoken in defense of the March move, and was seen as likely supporting additional moves, a lot of attention focused on me. Again, I was the lightning rod.

On the morning of May 20, I was having breakfast and fine-tuning the remarks I would make at the FOMC meeting that morning. I took a break from my work to glance through the newspapers, just in case there were stories speculating on the outcome of the meeting. I picked up *The Wall Street Journal* and, for some prescient reason, turned directly to the editorial page. There, staring back at me, was a line drawing that looked vaguely like me, although, I felt, not nearly as handsome. Wrapping the illustration was an editorial that consumed two-thirds of the page, entitled "The Meyer Fed?"

I was about to be flogged by the ultraconservative editorial board of *The Wall Street Journal*, which in my circles, at least, is the equivalent of receiving a shiny medal for heroic endeavors. Still, it was a rough ride.

The editorial began: "Laurence H. Meyer joined the Federal Reserve Board only last June, but the new governor has attracted an unusual share of attention. He knocked a half point off the long bond with a speech to the Forecasters' Club of New York in April, for example, saying things such as 'the economy appears to be growing at an unsustainable above-trend rate.' "

They translated my statement that "I am a strong and unapologetic proponent of the Phillips curve and the NAIRU concept" into the proposition that "inflation is caused by too many people working," vividly demonstrating that the NAIRU model is politically incorrect. I would translate the editorial writers' position into "There is no limit to how low the unemployment rate can go without triggering higher inflation." Oh, to live in a world without limits.

The editorial went on to note that the bond market had since recovered from the "Meyer shock" and that the economy could absorb the ¼-point increase in the funds rate at the March meeting. Their concern was the possibility of a series of further rate hikes that I might support.

Now, I have to admit that the *Journal* editorial writers, while ideologues, to be sure, are not stupid. They appreciate the power of the Chairman. "Trouble is," they wrote, "Mr. Greenspan today sounds a lot like Mr. Meyer." They quoted the Chairman as saying, "While there is scant evidence of any imminent resurgence of inflation at the moment, there also appears to be little slack in our capacity to produce." Right on, it seemed to me! They interpreted this as suggesting that what was bothering the Chairman was low unemployment and tighter labor markets. They were not entirely wrong. They believed that the Chairman was, in a less explicit and more oblique fashion, to be sure, falling into the same NAIRU-speak that I was so clearly guilty of.

After I had read through the editorial—and had taken some time to smooth my hawkish feathers—I was, of course, due at the FOMC meeting.

I walked in and greeted my colleagues, who never mentioned the editorial. Then, as always, Greenspan walked in from his separate entranceway. He looked cool and confident, as usual, and certainly not in any danger of losing control of the Greenspan Fed. As he walked by me, he turned and winked. I read it as saying: "I saw the editorial and had a good laugh. I hope you did, too!"

That afternoon, I shot a note off to the *Journal*. I limited my comments to what I objected to most—the line drawing, which I referred to as a "caricature assassination." The note must have made an impression. That picture never appeared again. The new illustration, which adorned future articles, pictured a trimmer and far more handsome fellow.

—∾—

TO BE SURE, the media delighted in separating us into hawks and doves, to see the feathers fly (which happened occasionally around the table, in vigorous debate). But when it came to the vote, the tendency was to join the majority view. In this way, we remained birds of a feather.

4

TEMPORARY BLISS OR PERMANENT BLISS

"Ah, to be a fly on the wall in the room with the big oval table," *BusinessWeek* reported following our decision in March 1997 to raise rates. "The meeting place of the Federal Reserve's policymaking committee was undoubtedly the site of some tense discussion on March 25, amid heavy anticipation of the first interest rate hike in two years. . . . So for now, analysts can only speculate about what went on, what happens next, and what it all means for the outlook."[1]

The truth was, none of us on the FOMC knew what would happen next either. My guess was that we would raise the federal funds rate at least another 25 to 50 basis points over the next several months. But as winter melted into spring, and then continued into summer, we hesitated again and again.

To be sure, we did return to an asymmetric directive in May 1997, signaling our possible intention to raise rates. But every time we got close to tightening rates, evidence came pouring in that inflation was not only well contained, but actually declining. Needless to say, we were surprised. We had never seen anything like this before.

For a few months, the Committee was willing to reconcile the phenomenon by assuming that there had been a modest decline in the NAIRU. But as the unemployment rate declined still further in 1997—from about 5¼% early in the year to below 5% by midyear and below 4¾% by the end of 1997—without triggering higher inflation, we began a renewed search for other suspects.

The Chairman continued to suggest that higher productivity growth could be the answer to the puzzle. But as before, the Chairman's insight played to an unresponsive audience. The staff and most of the other Committee members, not convinced, continued to seek another explanation.

Eventually, two theories began to assert themselves around the committee table: Either this was a temporary situation ("temporary bliss," as I termed it), which meant that the economy would eventually settle back into its traditional ways of operating, or this was "permanent bliss," a profound, fundamental, and permanent change in the way the economy worked. If so, this permanent bliss not only ushered in a new relationship between unemployment and inflation, but introduced to the American economy a new horizon of remarkable prosperity.

Those in the temporary bliss camp argued that the economy was luxuriating in a number of favorable but short-term conditions that would soon fade away. Chief among these was a dramatic slowdown in labor costs, which existed despite a very tight job market. Usually, when labor is tight, employees demand higher wages—and that ignites inflation. But by the spring of 1997, there was another factor afoot: globalization. Many people believed that workers were not demanding increased compensation, mostly because they feared that their jobs would be sent overseas.[2] But this could change, the temporary bliss camp argued, as the labor market tightened further.

There were other "temporary" enhancements to the economy: Oil prices were declining through 1997. Imported goods were cheaper, thanks to an appreciating dollar. And health care costs were holding relatively steady, thanks to a new innovation, the HMO (health maintenance organization). Finally, there was a rapid decline in the price of computers and other high-tech products, due to a burst of innovation in information technology.

Together, these "favorable supply shocks" were causing the bliss that we were experiencing, advocates claimed. But when the benefits passed, they warned, the economy would be back to where it was before.

The permanent bliss advocates, on the other hand, argued that the economy had crossed into new territory, where the old rules didn't apply. This was the beginning of the New Economy argument, although we didn't know it at the time.

There were two parts to the argument. One was that recent developments in the labor market had lowered the NAIRU. For example, a paper by Lawrence Katz, a professor at Harvard, and Alan Krueger, a professor at Princeton,[3] provided support for the possibility that an increase in the prison population[4] and an increase in the share of temporary workers in the labor force,[5] among other things, had lowered the NAIRU in recent years compared with the mid-1980s. The cumulative effect of these developments was ¾ to 1½ percentage points, they said. The second part of the permanent bliss story was, as I have noted earlier, the idea that the rate of productivity had accelerated thanks to computer and telecommunications innovations. This was the Chairman's long-standing argument.

I had some sympathy with the possibility that there had been a modest decline in the NAIRU, along the lines of what Katz and Krueger were espousing, though not nearly so large. But at this point in 1997, I was still skeptical of the Chairman's story about a productivity acceleration. There just wasn't enough supporting data.

Whichever theory was right—permanent or temporary bliss—it would have significant implications for monetary policy. If temporary bliss was the right explanation, then policymakers had to recognize that the economy would eventually overheat and inflation would begin to rise.

But if permanent bliss was correct, then policymakers could relax and enjoy—the economy could operate at a higher rate of growth indefinitely and perhaps at a lower unemployment rate (without rising inflation) than previously imagined. In this case, monetary policymakers needed to stand back and give the economy the opportunity to reap the benefits of the structural changes (stand back, at least, until the economy showed signs of growing faster than even the new rules allowed and moved to an unemployment rate even lower than the new, lower NAIRU).

Since the Chairman had already staked out the permanent bliss story—based on his belief in the acceleration of productivity—I decided to stake out the opposite side of the argument. It was not that we were not both wrestling with the possibilities on the other side of the argument, but since the Chairman was focusing so much of his passion on permanent structural changes, I found myself driven to balance his argument with a sharper emphasis on the temporary answers (and the possibility that the economy might overheat once they faded). I also felt that my focus on the temporary bliss story would help ensure that the threat of overheating would remain on the table at the FOMC.

I don't think this irritated the Chairman. In fact, I suspect that he appreciated my choice of the cautionary counternote, so that he could concentrate more fully on the optimistic structural change story. Of course, my point of view made me inclined to favor an earlier tightening of rates, and his, toward being more patient. But in reality, we were never quite as far apart in our theologies as our sparring positions made us seem to be.

—∞—

THE MEDIA QUICKLY attached feathers to the bliss debate. Those who believed that the economic situation was temporary were hawks. After all, they wanted rates to rise in preparation for what they saw as a return to routine. The doves, though, saw in permanent bliss an economic situation that would not change in the immediate future. They were in favor of holding the current rates, at least for the time being.

At the May 1997 FOMC meeting, the staff again played the hawk. Mike Prell told the Committee, "You'll probably need to raise interest rates further if you wish to keep inflation in check." Don Kohn reinforced Prell's message: "If you share the staff forecast . . . tightening would seem to be called for before too long."

But the staff were already blending some dovishness into their message. For the last few months, after all, their forecast had overstated inflation. Now they were worried that they had overstated it again. There was also a concern that if the Committee tightened further, it might shock the markets and send what was a sunny economy into a funk. Seeking a happy medium, Kohn suggested that the Committee merely announce an asymmetric directive, rather than raise the funds rate.

For his part, the Chairman was talking hawk—but acting dovish. At the meeting, he suggested that another 25 basis points would likely be warranted before the end of the year—but once again, perhaps in response to the reaction to the March move, he recommended no change in the funds rate at this meeting. I was ready to move another 25 basis points but accepted the Chairman's recommendation in the interest of supporting the consensus. I expected our difference was a matter of timing and that the Chairman would soon support a further preemptive tightening.

Several other members indicated that they would have preferred to tighten at that meeting. Only Al Broaddus dissented. The asymmetric directive, which held the prospect of a near-term tightening, once again allowed the FOMC to reach a consensus.

FOR THE REST OF SPRING and into summer, the FOMC played the same game. The staff forecast would suggest the need for a tightening, and the FOMC members would part into hawks and doves. And then the Chairman would come in, as always, speaking like a hawk and walking like a dove.

This seemed to fall into a pattern: The Chairman would ask for no change in the funds rate, suggest that the time was approaching for action, and indicate that there was a high probability of a move at the next meeting. Then at the next meeting, he would explain that the data did not yet provide a credible basis for tightening, and in any case, that the markets didn't expect a move. However, he would conclude that he expected the Committee would be forced to move at the next meeting.

While it may look as though the Chairman was promising near-term tightenings merely to mollify the hawks, in retrospect I think he was genuinely waiting for inflation to at least stop declining before making a move.

Of course, Greenspan continued to suggest that there was a fundamental change under way, driven by an acceleration in productivity. But we still weren't buying it. Indeed, at the July 1997 meeting, the staff once again concluded there simply was no evidence to support the view that there had been a fundamental acceleration in productivity.

THAT SPRING I LEARNED another secret of the temple, and it had to do with my personal finances. Each spring, I discovered, I was required to fill out disclosure forms detailing my assets and liabilities, the interest, dividends, and capital gains earned on my assets, and all the purchases and sales of stocks and bonds during the previous year. When I arrived at the Board, I thought I had to do this only once, before my confirmation, not once a year. This turned out to be more painful than doing my taxes.

Now, I knew that my salary at the Fed was public information (I started at about $125,000, and my salary had increased to $150,000 by the end of my term). But I didn't know that the value of my financial assets would also become public information and that my personal investment skills would be on display as well. There was one year in which my investments did better than the other members of the Board, and having to reveal that was not so bad! What a savvy investor, everyone (no doubt!) was thinking. But the next year, wouldn't you know it, I had the greatest decline of anyone on the Board. It hurt doubly to know that my embarrassingly poor investment performance was public.

In financial matters, governors face several restrictions. Of course, governors have to avoid conflicts of interest and so must sell their shares in banks and other firms where there might be conflicts. There are also restrictions, believe it or not, on the amount of government debt a governor can hold—presumably out of concern that a governor might steer policy to make a bundle. Of course, if that was the concern, it was silly to limit the restriction to the holding of government securities, since Fed decisions indirectly but assuredly affected interest rates on other securities and equity prices as well. Fortunately, I did not have the Fed ethics office to blame for this silly rule. It was imposed by the Justice Department. A more sensible restriction—in this case, a "voluntary guideline" from the Board's ethics office—was that governors should not buy or sell financial assets in a window around the time of FOMC decisions.

The Chairman, of his own accord, did not invest in the stock market. But most of the rest of us did, riding the roller coaster up and down in the latter part of the 1990s and into the first few years of the new millennium. I definitely shared in the euphoria—and in the pain.

ALL THROUGH THE SPRING and summer of 1997, the Fed took heat from Congress for the March rate hike. The Democrats were particularly incensed, and several of them decided they wanted to hold hearings to express their concern. Traditionally, only the Chairman testifies before Congress on monetary policy. This is generally as it should be. The Chairman is the only one who should speak on behalf of the entire Committee, and he alone should defend Fed policy before the Congress.

But this time, the Congress didn't want just the Chairman. They wanted to hear from other members of the FOMC as well. When we received the welcoming letter from the House committee running the hearings, they said they weren't sure yet which of the governors they wanted to testify. But they did indicate that regardless of the others, they definitely wanted me.

This was going to be interesting. From my first days on the FOMC, I had appreciated the sense of political insulation and independence afforded to Committee members. The Clinton and George W. Bush administrations, during the time I was on the Board, were extremely respectful of the independence of the Fed. There were no occasions, to my knowledge, of any pressure put on the Fed to alter its own assessment of the appropriate course for monetary policy.

Members of the Congress, on the other hand, often commented publicly on monetary policy and sometimes wrote letters to the Board. Such letters virtually always recommended that the FOMC either refrain from tightening or ease rates. I cannot recall an instance during my tenure, in fact, when anyone in Congress asked the FOMC to tighten policy!

Even though the Congress has granted "operational" independence to the Fed, there are opportunities for the Congress to exert influence on the conduct of monetary policy. For example, the U.S. Congress sets the objectives for monetary policy—in the case of the Fed, full employment and price stability. The members of the Board are nominated by the President and have to be confirmed by the Senate, allowing some further political influence on monetary policy.[6] Still, the Congress respects the operational independence of the Fed. This does effectively insulate the day-to-day conduct of monetary policy from political interference—especially interference motivated by pressures to deliver short-term political gains irrespective of longer-term costs.

Still, I wasn't looking forward to testifying. I knew that some members of Congress were as eager to berate me for my conservative views on the NAIRU—and my insistence that monetary policymakers had to be alert to the possibility of overheating and higher inflation—as they were to praise the Chairman for his willingness to allow the economy to reap the full benefits of what was now being hailed as the New Economy. I was the party pooper.

So be it. When I accepted my nomination for the FOMC, my wife and I had already decided that one term would be enough.[7] So I felt that if the Congress, or the administration, didn't like my views or the way I voted, that was not my problem. I was going to be independent to the maximum degree.

Still, I stopped by to see the Chairman and asked him whether we should somehow coordinate our testimonies, so as not to further encourage the idea that there was a major split on the Committee. I was a little surprised that the Chairman wanted no part of such a coordinated effort. Still, I respected the fact that he wanted the full freedom to express his passion about the productivity acceleration—and that he wanted to ensure that I had the same freedom to present my own perspective. In any case, he said he wanted to do his thing, and he encouraged me to do mine.

THAT AFTERNOON I sat at my computer and hammered out my testimony. The theme was "Balancing Possibilities and Regularities." I used the term *possibilities* to capture the idea that structural changes might now allow the economy to grow faster and operate at a lower unemployment rate without triggering higher inflation. *Regularities* was intended to capture the role of traditional considerations, the balance between aggregate demand and supply, the importance of respecting the economy's speed limits, and the continuing relevance of the concept of the NAIRU.

The Chairman, of course, was Mr. Possibility—and I was Mr. Regularity, at least in broad caricature. I wanted to emphasize the importance of both considerations, but I appreciated that there was also a division of labor between the Chairman and me: He provided the passionate case for the new possibilities, above all else, and I emphasized the old regularities. Together we balanced the view of the economy—rather than split it apart.

I was a bit irritated, then, by some of the comments I received from Congress. Barney Frank, in particular, had been giving long speeches on the House floor (to an empty chamber, I suspect) expressing strong disagreement with my speeches.

For example, on April 29, Frank made a speech on the House floor that referenced me specifically: "The Federal Reserve Open Market Committee a couple of weeks ago decided that we were creating too many jobs too rapidly in America and, fearing that this would be destabilizing, they raised interest rates," he began. "The [FOMC] will meet again in May and July, and there is a very real prospect that they may do this again. . . . I wish we could have [a] hearing and I hope the chairman [referring to Congressman Jim Leach, chairman of the House committee] will reconsider. . . . But until that time, we have no other option but this. I say that because I am about to engage in a one-sided debate with Mr. Laurence Meyer. . . . I would much prefer to have Mr. Meyer in before us . . . so we can engage in a two-sided debate."[8]

Congressman Frank singled me out, obviously, because I said that increasing unemployment is sometimes necessary. Such a view, I admit, is politically incorrect. But stable inflation at a higher unemployment rate is clearly better than a continuing and, in time, accelerating rise in inflation at a lower unemployment rate. At the time that Congressman Frank made this statement, I was prepared to try to explain this to him. Now I would have that opportunity. In fact, I wrote my testimony with Mr. Frank's comments in mind. Maybe that's why it came out sounding so combative.

When the staff gathered in my office later that day to review my speech, they expressed strong support. They saw it as an "in your face" challenge to those in Congress who did not appreciate the importance of placing monetary speed limits on the economy's growth. They told me that this was a message that needed to be delivered—and they applauded me for delivering it in such a bold manner.

Then the Board's head of public affairs and the head of the Board's congressional liaison office joined the party. They had a very different response to my draft. "You will never get to finish this testimony," they told me. "The members of the committee will be screaming at you before you finish. You can get your message across—but tone it down, be gentler."

I tried to be gentler in the next draft—while still making the points that I thought needed to be made. There was one glitch, however. In the confusion, I sent the much tougher version over to Congress. The Board's congressional liaison had to rush over and collect the copies, replacing them with the gentler version before any damage was done. Once again, the staff worked overtime to keep me out of trouble.

On the first day of the hearings, I tuned in to the Chairman's testimony on the radio. I was particularly interested in the Q&A portion. This would allow me to better anticipate the questions I might be asked—and perhaps avoid responses that would suggest more of a difference between the Chairman and me than I perceived existed.

The Chairman took a balanced position. He began by noting, "The key questions facing financial markets and policymakers are What is behind the good performance of the economy and Will it persist." He credited the exceptional performance to a combination of "temporary factors that have been restraining inflation" and "basic improvements in the longer-term efficiency of our economy." This, of course, was a combination of the temporary and permanent bliss stories.

He went on to passionately describe the possibility of a productivity acceleration, noting how important it was for monetary policymakers to give the economy room to achieve maximum sustainable growth. But he balanced that view with the recognition that there were still limits and specifically noted the unsustainability of a continuing decline in the unemployment rate. He defended the March

1997 tightening as an effort to counter the "perceived . . . probability of demand outstripping supply" and emphasized the importance of preemptive monetary policy.

The Chairman, by the way, is a master at testifying. His forte is not the opening statement. This can be wandering and obscure. But he excels at the question-and-answer phase, where the premium is for thinking fast on your feet. The Chairman is especially skillful at making every member of Congress look like a genius for asking a particular question, even when the question is truly idiotic. And he is, above all else, incredibly calm. No matter how vitriolic and loud the personal attack may be against him, the Chairman never raises his voice. That I could be so calm, or so incredibly good on my feet. But I do write a very good opening statement.

—w—

THE NEXT DAY at the hearing, I was joined on the panel by Bill McDonough, president of the Federal Reserve Bank of New York and Vice Chairman of the FOMC, and Alice Rivlin, a fellow governor and Vice Chair of the Board. It was a day of spirited discussion and some amusement.

The members of the House committee began, as is traditional, with opening statements. I thought Congressman Ken Bensten best captured the set of topics of central interest to the committee: "This hearing dealing with the conduct of monetary policy requires us to look at . . . whether or not the business cycle has been repealed or extended; whether or not the Phillips curve has been denied; whether or not we can increase growth beyond current levels and still maintain a stable economy; whether or not we are in a transitory period, as the chairman of the Fed testified yesterday, and as I know some of you all have in your statements as well."[9]

Congressman Maurice Hinchey then cut to the heart of the hearing: "Yesterday we had the chairman here, and he talked about his views of monetary policy, as he always does, somewhat enigmatically. . . . What concerned me about the chairman's testimony yesterday . . . was the hint that it may be necessary to raise interest rates again next year. I hope that that is not the case."

Transparency is to be admired, by members of Congress as well as by the Fed. That was indeed the point of these hearings: to make it clear that many members of the Congressional committee did not see grounds for further tightening. Indeed, they made clear their expectations that members of the FOMC, especially those like myself who seemed more inclined in this direction, would not take that action without clear and definitive evidence that inflation was in fact picking up.

After the opening statements by the members of the House committee, we each had about five minutes to make our statements, which were followed by questions from the members of the committee. There is a green and red light staring at the members of the panel to remind them when to start and when to stop. It is really bad etiquette to ignore the red light. But I always have had an unusual ability to cram a lot into my opening statement. I think it has something to due with the speed with which I deliver it!

In my opening statement, I presented the theme of balancing possibilities and regularities. Then I pointed out that my estimates of the NAIRU and the maximum sustainable growth were well within the mainstream of economists outside the Fed, including scholars who had spent their lives estimating these parameters—and including the Congress's own nonpartisan think tank, the Congressional Budget Office, and the President's own Council of Economic Advisers.

I also defended the FOMC's decision to raise the funds rate on March 25: "The history of business cycles has repeatedly taught us that the greatest risk to an expansion comes from failing to prevent an overheated economy," I explained. "The best way to insure the durability of this expansion is, therefore, to be vigilant that we do not allow the economy to overheat and produce the inevitable rise in inflation. . . . The policy action on March 25 was clearly a preemptive one, not based on inflation pressures evident at the time, but on inflation pressures likely to emerge in the absence of policy action. . . . Monetary policy should not sit on interest rates and wait until the economy blows by capacity and inflation takes off. . . . A small, cautious step early is the recipe for avoiding the necessity of a sharper destabilizing move later on."

With the testimony from each of the panel members completed, we now faced the questioners. An interesting question came almost immediately from Bernie Sanders, an independent from Vermont.

Mr. SANDERS. *The United States has the most unfair distribution of wealth in the industrialized world. The richest 1 percent own 42 percent of the wealth, more than the bottom 90 percent. Mr. Gates makes a billion dollars more every day, and people down below are having a hard time surviving.*

What are you going to do about the unfair distribution of wealth, so that we do not have that dubious distinction of, on the one hand, having a proliferation of millionaires and billionaires and, on the other hand, having the highest rate of child poverty in the industrialized world?

I loved the question. I reacted like a schoolkid and raised my hand, indicating that I wanted the first shot at answering it. I was given that honor.

Mr. MEYER. *I would like to answer that question, and I don't mean to be disrespectful, and I hope this will not seem too sharp, but I am going to give you a very simple answer. What am I going to do as a member of the Board of Governors of the Federal Reserve System voting on monetary policy? What am I going to do about income inequality? The answer is—nothing.*

I paused for dramatic effect—and to make sure Congressman Sanders had not risen from his seat to pay me a personal visit. Then I went on:

One of the most important things that you have to understand as a policymaker is what you are capable of achieving and what you are not capable of achieving. I envy you the position that you have as a Member of this body and as a Member of Congress, because these are the very issues, the heart of the problems that we are facing today.

And . . . I think you are right on in your comments. And I apologize for focusing on some of the issues that macroeconomists focus on—inflation and the low unemployment rate—and not giving attention to the slow rate of growth in productivity, the slow average rate of increase in the standard of living, and the fact that, in that context many people are falling behind . . .

The only thing I want to do is throw it back to you. Monetary policy has one instrument and two goals. Some people think that we have too many goals already, and you want us to do something about the income distribution. Frankly, I don't know how to do that.

I suspected he would not take this answer well, but I thought it needed to be said. But he took my response surprisingly well. He immediately engaged me in a discussion about what the Congress should do. He started by asking whether I would support a $6.50 minimum wage. The minimum wage is the lowest hourly rate that employers can pay employees. At the time, it was $4.75.

I responded that we were now moving in a potentially more fruitful direction, but that, no, I could not support that specific proposal. I noted that there is evidence that a higher minimum wage might discourage the hiring of the workers directly affected. As a result, I preferred an expansion in the earned income tax credit, a policy that lowered the tax rate for workers with very low incomes. This rewarded work rather than discouraged employment.

Then Sanders went on to ask my opinion about a variety of other fiscal policy issues, as well as my view on other government programs.

Mr. SANDERS. *Will you then suggest that we should raise taxes on upper-income people to put more money in education to make college affordable for everybody?*

This irritated me. After all, the session was supposed to be about monetary policy. While Alan Greenspan loved to be asked and to give his views about fiscal policy and other government policies to the Congress, I felt that this distracted the monetary policy oversight committees in the Congress from their responsibility to oversee the conduct of monetary policy.

Mr. MEYER. *I am simply not going to take positions on every single matter of fiscal policy. . . . I don't go around the country and give speeches about fiscal policy, about education, about these things. I go around the country talking about what I spend every single day focusing on, and that is economic outlook, monetary policy, bank regulation, financial modernization, consumer protection, and so forth.*

I told the committee that I did not have time to develop positions on all the economic issues that came before them and that I thought fiscal policy was their business, not mine.

The answer drew chuckles from some members of the committee, but it did not deflect them, that day or ever since, from continuing to ask the Chairman more questions about fiscal than monetary policy during monetary policy oversight hearings.

This exchange on fiscal policy highlighted a concern that I had about the effectiveness of the congressional oversight process. I felt that the congressional oversight committees often showed remarkably little interest in monetary policy and used the oversight hearings as a way to get the Chairman to comment on fiscal issues of more interest to the committee. I also came to be distressed that the Chairman would encourage this direction by offering his own views on a range of fiscal issues, even without the encouragement of the committee.

Then it was Barney Frank's turn. I shuddered a bit but knew I was prepared for him. I planned to remain calm, like the Chairman, during the interrogation. But when Congressman Frank began to scream at me, I immediately returned the favor. It was like a Ping-Pong match, back and forth, louder and louder.

At one point, after a rapid-fire exchange, Congressman Frank made a wonderful admission: "I find it much more interesting when I speak than when I listen." He seemed to be reminding me that I was merely a prop at the hearings, allowing him to make the points he wanted to make. Still, the Congressman obviously thrives on vigorous interchanges, loving every second of it.

> Mr. FRANK. *Here is my problem . . . I believe, by the Fed's own acknowledgment, the March increase was wholly unnecessary. I hope it wasn't damaging, but it was clearly based on assumptions about growth which turned out not to be true. Mr. Greenspan acknowledged that. You voted for the March increase, and I think it clearly was proven to be unnecessary. Things began to drop in the second quarter, and nobody thinks that the March increase caused that.*
>
> *Here is the problem. Yes, price stability is a good thing. There is a lot of empirical evidence of the last couple of years that we can sustain more growth than we thought without endangering price stability. And you are*

acting to some extent as if that didn't happen and wasn't true, and you are telling us that you have to err on the side of caution.

Well, Mr. Meyer, [h]ow long have we been under the NAIRU, then, by your estimate, and what negative consequences have happened? And are you convinced that there are going to be negative consequences?

Mr. MEYER. *Your point is well taken. You ought to have less confidence in this model, less confidence in the estimate of NAIRU, because of everything that has gone on. . . . I agree with you. I have less confidence in it, too. But I believe, because of the extraordinary value and reliability of this concept and estimate earlier—*

Mr. FRANK. *How long have we been under it?*

Mr. MEYER. *I have said . . . that I thought NAIRU might be 5.5 percent. We averaged 5.4 percent in 1996. We have been significantly under the estimate of NAIRU, in my judgment, for about three months. The lags involved in monetary policy are very long. We will not have a test of whether we are below NAIRU until about the middle of 1998. . . .*

Let me make it a little bit more interesting for you. You say that we should certainly not have made the move in March, because what we worried about didn't happen, because growth slowed down. I completely disagree with that. I have called that monetary policy action "just-in-time monetary policy." I believe it was worthwhile.

When we were making that decision, the unemployment rate was 5.3 percent. My judgment was that the momentum in growth was so strong that I believed that the unemployment rate was going to move down to or below 5 percent over the next 6 months. It moved down to 4.8 percent. Now it is up to 5 percent, but the point is, it did move down. It was utilization rates that were the issue here. In my judgment, monetary policy should result in interest rates being pro-cyclical. When the economy is growing above trend and utilization rates—

Mr. FRANK. *First of all, what I am saying is that I think you are disregarding evidence that the trend is better than it has been, and specifically when you talk about the slowdown. But it did slow down. You are now telling me that we are not significantly below the NAIRU. Do you think that the March increase is the reason that we didn't grow faster?*

Mr. MEYER. *No. Monetary policy—*

Mr. FRANK. *Let me say two things. It is one thing to say, "At the time I made the right decision," but I think in retrospect the explanations given for it were simply wrong, that the growth rate didn't continue at the high level that it was at then and it didn't stop the growth rate.*

Further, if you knew in March what unemployment and inflation and growth rate figures were going to be for the succeeding months, you still would have voted for the increase?

Mr. MEYER. *That is correct.*

Mr. FRANK. *Why?*

Mr. MEYER. *Because the issue wasn't the growth rate. The fact of the matter is, the growth rate in the first half of the year was stronger than I anticipated when the decision was made in March.*

Mr. FRANK. *But if the issue wasn't the growth rate, why did you raise interest rates?*

Mr. MEYER. *The issue was the expectation that utilization rates would rise further from already high levels. The expectation, by the way, was realized immediately. It was done in anticipation of an increase in utilization rates, which, indeed, happened immediately.*

Mr. FRANK. *Are utilization rates, and have they been in this quarter, at an unsustainable high level?*

Mr. MEYER. *We will only know that over time.*

Mr. FRANK. *You don't have an opinion on that?*

Mr. MEYER. *I have given my opinion on it.*

Mr. FRANK. *I missed it. Give it to me again—slower.*

Mr. MEYER. *I am concerned that the utilization rates may already be so high—*

Mr. FRANK. *My problem is that this is a confirmation of what I thought. . . . I reject the notion that you are supposed to err on the side of caution, because all the errors are on the side of slowing down. Nobody ever thinks about erring on the side of maybe avoiding some unemployment, and I think that adds up to a bias that is unfortunate.*

I am not saying that you are biased against growth. Obviously, you are not. You are biased against, in my judgment, the interpretation of the most recent set of statistics that suggest that we can sustain more growth than we have been. I think it is cultural lag, rather than bias, that is our problem.

Thank you, Mr. Chairman.

Chairman LEACH. *Thank you. The time of the gentleman, who has implicitly acknowledged that he speaks faster than he listens, has expired.*

This incident does highlight the difference in style between Alan Greenspan and myself: The Chairman, as I noted earlier, is always calm, never gets ruffled, and never raises his voice, no matter what the provocation. But shout at me, and expect to get shouted back at. I once commented to the Chairman about our differences in style. He admitted that he had noticed. He confided that he sometimes wanted to respond the way I did but felt it was not appropriate in his role as Chairman. He did not encourage me, however, to change my style.

When I returned to my office after the hearing, my phone was ringing. It was the Chairman. "You did a great job. I am proud of you for standing your ground." After all that, I really appreciated the call.

—ɯ—

AT THE AUGUST 1997 MEETING, the Chairman resumed his standard practice of pointing to the need to tighten soon but recommending no change. "Signs are beginning to emerge that suggest we are finally running out the string," he said, referring to the ever-tightening labor market. He noted that you didn't have to even bring in the "NAIRU issue" or "go through a Phillips curve analysis" to reach this conclusion. The simple fact was that the number of people left in the labor force who were available to work (those unemployed and those who were potentially available to work but were not at the moment looking for work) was diminishing at a rapid pace. "When you run out of a product—in this case labor—its price goes up," he declared.

The Chairman was clever. This was the same argument the staff and I were making with the NAIRU and the Phillips curve, but without a commitment on his part to those politically incorrect concepts. So instead of talking about the unemployment rate, as is the spirit of the NAIRU analysis, he simply focused on the physical limits to additional employment, using up all the available workers. This was a kinder way of expressing the same thought.

But he concluded, "With disinflation probably still going on, there is little reason to move today. . . ."

BY THE TIME of the September 1997 meeting, the staff had revised upward their estimate of productivity growth and hence the maximum sustainable rate of growth in output. But they still emphasized the importance of respecting the economy's speed limits. Mike Prell noted that if the New Economy was about faster potential growth and a lower NAIRU, we didn't need a new paradigm. Instead, we could incorporate these themes of the new era view into the existing paradigm "in which supply-demand imbalances can occur and give rise to inflationary pressures. . . . Despite our flirtation with the new era view, our forecast conveys a rather clear message that risks are tilted toward higher inflation in the absence of some restrictive policy action." Don Kohn added, "Growth that is accompanied by rising utilization rates is, by definition, unsustainable, even in a new era."

But there was still the problem that the markets did not expect a tightening at this meeting. Kohn suggested the markets "need to understand the concerns of the Committee," and that could be "clarified in the Minutes and elsewhere without precommitting the Committee to particular policy actions." Once again, the Chairman gave the now predictable conclusion: "I do not think we should move today, but I do think the probability that we will be forced to move at the next meeting has gone up quite considerably." He put the odds of a November move at 50/50.

When I walked out of the September meeting, I felt the next tightening would come at the next meeting, in November. We seemed to be set in that course, and when the FOMC is set, it takes data in the intervening period that clearly *disconfirms* the need to take action to cancel the move. It seemed to me that this was one of those occasions.

But we didn't want to be in the position at the next meeting, as we had in the past, when the Chairman said that the markets were unprepared for the move. This time, several of us urged the Chairman to begin to lay the groundwork now. "I encourage you to seize an opportunity in a speech or congressional testimony or some other avenue where you can lay out the line of thought that you just gave," said President McDonough. ". . . That has to be done by the Chairman. . . . Others can . . . be supportive, but it really is only the Chairman who speaks for the Committee. Therefore, I think it is important that you do that before the next meeting."

—∾—

THE CHAIRMAN HAD SEVERAL ways of signaling upcoming policy action. The policy bias—such as shifting from a symmetric to an asymmetric posture—was the first and most standard way. Second was a speech or testimony, which could signal, for instance, that the bias had moved from a "notional" asymmetry to a "real" one.

But the Chairman didn't give many speeches on the outlook, and the timing of testimonies (which were scheduled by the Congress) did not always fit the need for signaling a change in policy. So the Chairman needed a third route, and that he found in talking to the press.

The use of reporters as part of the Fed's signal corps is not official Board or FOMC doctrine. The public affairs staff and the Chairman like to pretend it doesn't happen. I expect that the Chairman generally expects reporters to read between the lines or somehow sense the signal in his body language. He typically relies on a small group of reporters for the purpose. John Berry, longtime reporter for *The Washington Post* and now at Bloomberg, is most widely recognized in this role. But *The Wall Street Journal* reporter covering the Fed—it was David Wessel, then Jake Schlesinger, and most recently Greg Ip during my term—was also a regular member of the signal corps.

There is one Board guideline, however, that makes this process more difficult: the blackout period. During the blackout period, which stretches from the week before an FOMC meeting to the Friday of the week of the meeting, Committee members are not supposed to comment on monetary policy or the economic outlook. This means not giving speeches and not talking with reporters. The bond and equity markets are particularly touchy during this period, and any FOMC "chatter" could increase their volatility. I thought this was a very sensible rule and tried always to abide by it.

I was surprised, then, one Monday before an FOMC meeting, to pass John Berry coming out of the Chairman's office. I believe that Berry and I would have been shot on the spot (perhaps by the Chairman himself) if we had been discovered together in my office during the blackout.

Berry's job is to report, so he gets an A plus for his access. The question was whether or not the Chairman should have been talking to the press at this time, when other members of the FOMC were discouraged from doing so. The answer to that question is not as obvious as it seems, given that the Chairman is the head of the signal corps and has a unique role in speaking for the Committee.

The problem with signaling through Berry or another reporter, however, is that the source of the signal (the reporter) carries a lot of noise with it. Was the journalist's report a misinterpretation of the Chairman's typically oblique words, or had the Chairman successfully planted the message in *The Washington Post* or *The Wall Street Journal*? We never knew.

I like to differentiate between sanctioned and unsanctioned signaling. Sanctioned signaling is when the Committee has reached a consensus and encourages the Chairman to find a way to signal it to the markets. An example was the mandate the Chairman received from the Committee to signal the markets at the end of the September 1997 meeting that a near-term tightening was likely, perhaps by the time of the next meeting.

Unsanctioned signaling occurs when any Committee member, including the Chairman, tries to signal a move without prior approval of the Committee. It is clearly inappropriate for anyone other than the Chairman to signal without the Committee's consensus (because only the Chairman should speak for the Committee). But is it appropriate for the Chairman to signal before the Committee has voiced its support? That is a gray area.

To be sure, there are times when circumstances change so rapidly between meetings that an intermeeting move or a move at the next scheduled meeting may become necessary, even though there had been no discussion of this possibility at the previous meeting. In this case, the Chairman could unilaterally prepare the markets for a possible move, so that the Committee could then make the move without fearing that the markets were unprepared.

The danger, however, is that the Chairman could prepare the markets for a move that the Committee might consider premature. That would put the Committee in the uncomfortable position of having to surprise the markets by not moving, or contradicting the signal and confusing the public about the Fed's reading of the economy and the direction of its policy. Of course, these consequences make it possible for the Chairman to occasionally use unsanctioned signaling to pressure the Committee into agreeing to a policy action when there otherwise might not be an overwhelming consensus for it.

IN ANY CASE, the Chairman clearly had the Committee's blessing at the September 1997 meeting to signal an upcoming policy move. So when I walked out of that meeting, I felt pretty confident that the Committee would "deliver" at the November meeting. I think many of my colleagues felt similarly. Little did we know, however, how a convulsion in the global economy would suddenly change our plans.

5

GLOBAL FINANCIAL TURBULENCE

While we were busy arguing whether the New Economy was permanent or temporary—or even new—events on the other side of the world were conspiring to put an end to our party.

Like the beginning of so many cataclysmic events, this one began quietly. On May 10, 1996, the Bangkok Bank of Commerce, Thailand's ninth largest bank, collapsed. Although investors lost millions of dollars, the damage seemed to be limited. Before long, most of the regional analysts were writing off the collapse as an unfortunate but isolated event.

But they were wrong. In March 1997, we learned that Finance One, Thailand's biggest finance company, also packed with bad debt, had collapsed as well. That was followed by the failure of additional Thai banks. At the same time, capital was flowing out of the country. The Thai government, meanwhile, was intervening in the foreign exchange market to try to defend its fixed exchange rate regime (the Thai baht was pegged to the dollar at the time). When it was clear it was about to run out of reserves, the Thai government had no choice but to allow its currency to float. Unfortunately, the Thai currency didn't really "float." It sank—and the wave it produced swept across the global markets, shaking up stocks across Asia and even into Latin America.

As the crisis unfolded, the Fed staff were busily monitoring developments. Staff members clearly were sensitive to the criticism they had received during the Mexican financial crisis of 1995, when they were accused of failing to keep the Board properly informed. This time, through memos, presentations, and discussions, they kept us abreast of the situation.

But while we were kept informed, the Fed was still just an observer to these overseas events. Thailand was just too small to affect the U.S. economy, let alone the global economy. Its problems just did not enter into the calculus of our monetary policy decisions.

SO IT CAN BE UNDERSTOOD that by the time of our annual economic conference, hosted by the Kansas City Federal Reserve at Jackson Hole, Wyoming, in late August 1997, the events in Asia were not of overwhelming concern. To be sure, the conference was titled "Maintaining Financial Stability in a Global Economy," and yes, we spent a great deal of time discussing the role of central bankers in defusing such crises.

But in general, times were good. The U.S. economy was sailing ahead, and there were no clouds in the sky. As *USA Today* noted, "A half-dozen research papers were presented [at the meeting], but the idyllic setting seemed to be the highlight of the conference."[1]

Beth Belton, in the *USA Today* article, captured the true essence of the Jackson Hole conference: "Fed Governor Larry Meyer, his wife, Flo, and about 70 conference attendees spent Friday afternoon navigating the rapids along an 8-mile stretch of the Snake River. Others took off for a few hours of trout fishing, horseback riding, hiking or sightseeing. . . . Despite forecasts of thunderstorms, the weather was warm and sunny." She continued: "And why shouldn't we have three sunny days in a row, considering a 4.8% U.S. unemployment rate, low inflation, and a Dow near 8000?' asked Martin Feldstein, director of the National Bureau of Economic Research."[2]

If that were the complete story, however, I wouldn't be writing this chapter.

—෴—

WORSE EVENTS WERE TO COME. In the space of a few weeks in the autumn of 1997, the Thai crisis spread to the economies of Indonesia, Malaysia, the Philippines,[3] and finally Hong Kong.[4] The repercussions sent the Asian financial markets crashing and investors into shock.

"Global contagion," exclaimed John Roque, chief international technical analyst at Lehman Brothers, while the collapse was still rolling through Asia. "Those were the words on everyone's lips at this morning's meeting."[5]

This time, the U.S. markets were not immune. On October 27, the Dow fell a record 554 points, as investors worried that the Asian crisis would soon undermine the profitability of U.S. firms.

—෴—

TO THOSE UNFAMILIAR with the Fed, it might seem that the FOMC would spring into action at this point. To be sure, the Chairman was in the middle of the global financial developments, attending the G-7 meetings of finance ministers and the heads of central banks. He discussed the crisis with the Secretary of the Treasury during their weekly meetings, which were now even more frequent. The Chairman was also an alternate governor to the International Monetary Fund (IMF) for the United States and so played a role in shaping the IMF's response to the Asian situation.

But the Congress, in establishing the Fed, did not conceive any role for the institution as an international policymaker. The Fed's mandate was to promote full employment and price stability in the United States. Period. That meant it was to make policy decisions to achieve the best possible outcomes in the United States. It was certainly not to assume any risks to the U.S. economy in order to lighten the burdens on other countries or regions. In any case, it was the Treasury that was to determine how the United States should aid other countries in times of financial crisis, not the Fed.

Yes, we did have some discussion around the oval table of the Asian events and the toll it had taken on global stock and bond markets. And certainly we recognized that we had to be prepared, in the event that the Asian contagion spread to the United States. In my case, I participated in several regional meetings and bilateral discussions with a number of Asian countries during this period (as part of a delegation led by the Treasury Department). But the Board never met to chart out a "Fed view" of what should be done.

Besides, we felt that the Asian contagion would probably not reach the States or have much impact on the economy. In its forecast, in fact, the staff assigned little drag to the economy from the Asian crisis—just a couple of tenths subtracted from the GDP in the coming year.[6] No one could predict how dominant the Asian crisis might become, Mike Prell noted, but "it would have to be a large one to override the momentum in domestic demand in the near term."[7]

But if the Asian crisis itself didn't compel us to lower rates, it also halted the momentum that had been building to raise them. The markets had been battered, and now we could see in the futures markets and financial surveys that investors expected the FOMC to deliver some kind of relief, at least in a forgoing of rate hikes. A tightening of rates would come as a complete surprise, we realized, and would likely precipitate a much sharper and more disruptive effect on global financial markets, especially in the crisis countries, than would otherwise have been the case.

Under these circumstances, Governor Edward (Ned) Gramlich suggested that a sense of "international citizenship" might compel us to defer a tightening. Another Committee member suggested that if the Asian crisis didn't obligate the FOMC to adjust policy to support the global economy, then perhaps it should at least influence *the timing* of any tightening.

For myself, I agreed that we should not take any immediate action that would further disrupt the global financial markets. The fact was that if we did raise rates, global investors would rush to buy U.S. assets, forcing the sickening economies to raise their own rates, which would only plunge them more deeply into despair. On the other hand, I did not believe that the Asian financial crisis should prevent the FOMC from raising rates in coming months, once the intensity of the global financial turmoil had abated.

The bottom line was this: I believed that the United States could best help control the crisis by being the anchor in an unsteady world economy. We would play this role best, I felt, by maintaining the maximum sustainable and noninflationary growth possible in our own country. This was precisely the role intended for the Fed, and that was the most the rest of the world could reasonably ask from us.

I think the Chairman agreed with that view, and this certainly must account for why he began his comments on November 12 with the issue of productivity. Of course, by now we should have been accustomed to the fact that the Chairman *always* began his remarks with a discussion of productivity.

Indeed, I remember this meeting today less for the discussion of the crisis in Asia than as the time when the Chairman's conviction about the productivity acceleration strengthened to the point where he stiffly began to resist a further tightening of rates.

But this time, the Chairman had something new to show us—evidence that the new paradigm in productivity was finally showing up in the macro data. This further raised the Chairman's confidence, if that was possible, in the productivity acceleration and increased the weight he assigned to it in his assessment of the appropriate course for monetary policy.

At our last meeting, the Chairman conceded that he had suggested a 50/50 probability of a move. But now, with this new evidence in hand, he was changing his mind. The new data made the chances of inflation even more remote, he explained. Indeed, if productivity was gaining, then businesses would find cost savings due to productivity gains. And those savings would allow them to offset the rising wages caused by the ever-tightening labor markets.

So even in the absence of the Asian financial crisis, he confided to us, he would not have argued for a tightening at this meeting. And with the current financial instability, which could be exacerbated by a tightening, he certainly wouldn't.

As we sat around the Committee room table absorbing this, I offered a different perspective. While I agreed that we shouldn't tighten rates at the November meeting, I felt that the Chairman had thrown up a potential roadblock to tightening, even if the Asian financial crisis was to subside, and I wanted to keep that option alive.

I argued that in the absence of the Asian financial crisis, it would have been appropriate to raise the funds rate by ¼ percentage point at this meeting. This would have been consistent with the concerns raised at the last meeting, concerns that should only have been strengthened by the stronger-than-expected growth in the third quarter and the further decline in the unemployment rate in October. While there was no question in my mind that delaying such a tightening was the correct decision in November, I said that we should remain alert to the need to raise rates once the turbulence subsided.

The Committee accepted the Chairman's recommendation: No change in the funds rate and retention of the asymmetric directive.

—w—

AT THE FED, the governors have several opportunities to represent the Board at domestic and international meetings and, in a few cases, can specialize in a specific region of the world. The plum international assignments are, of course, taken by the Chairman and Vice Chairman. The most interesting of these, I believe, are the now bimonthly meetings of the G-10 central bank governors. Most of the meetings are held at the Bank for International Settlements in Basel, Switzerland. During my term, Greenspan did not want to attend all the meetings, which were then more frequent; so he would split the assignment with the Vice Chairman. Occasionally other governors got to go, and I attended three of them.

There were other interesting assignments though. I represented the Board on the Economic Policy Committee of the Organization for Economic Cooperation and Development (OECD). This committee met twice a year in Paris to discuss the global economic outlook and assess the appropriate policy responses around the world. My participation at these meetings was one of the occasions I most looked forward to during my term. I also represented the Board on the Financial Stability Forum, begun in the aftermath of the global financial turbulence in the latter part of the 1990s, which focused on assessing financial vulnerabilities around the world and making recommendations for the improved regulation of financial institutions and markets.

But my most interesting international assignment during this period was as the Fed's Asia Pacific governor. It gave me new insight into the region and a unique perspective into Washington's methods of hammering out its overseas policies.

My first assignment, in early 1997, sent me to a meeting of the

Six Markets Group in Tokyo.[8] I kept Ted Truman awake most of the way there, so that he could brief me on the sources of instability in the region and help me understand how we could keep the lid from blowing off. After Tokyo, I went immediately to a meeting of APEC (Asia-Pacific Economic Cooperation) in Cebu, Philippines.[9] In both Tokyo and Cebu, I was surprised to find that the crisis-inflicted countries were in full denial. They just failed to accept the seriousness of the situation, and we couldn't convince them otherwise.

By the time of my trip to attend the Manila Framework meetings in November 1997, however, the problems in the region had become more acute. There was far less denial. Now the crisis countries that gathered around the table—including most of the Southeast Asian nations and Korea—realized how bad things had become.[10] Many of them were at the meeting, in fact, specifically to ask Japan for help. Expecting this, Japan had proposed an Asian Monetary Fund, one that would pool funds in the region, including a large contribution from Japan, to provide immediate liquidity.

The United States didn't like the idea, however, because it feared that Japan would not attach the right "conditionalities"—provisions for how the countries should reform their economic policies and supervisory and regulatory practices—to the loans.[11]

This disagreement reflected different views about the source of the crises in the first place. The United States felt the crises were due to fundamental structural vulnerabilities (such as weak financial systems, fixed exchange rate regimes, and an overreliance on short-term and foreign-denominated debt) in the afflicted countries. The Japanese, and many other Asians, on the other hand, largely blamed the investors, who had arguably pulled their capital out of the Asian markets in a blind panic.

Given our view of the source of the problem, the United States felt that the loans had to have conditionalities. Given their view on the basic causes, the Japanese did not. In addition, the United States favored providing multilateral financial packages through the IMF, where the U.S. had a strong influence. U.S. officials saw the Japanese proposal as a potential duplication that not only undermined the ability of the United States to shape events, but also would not likely have the desired disciplined conditionality. The Asian countries, of course, favored the Japanese proposal because it had so few strings attached.

But they were in for a surprise. The meeting's key moment took place the first night, when the head of the Japanese delegation, Eisuke Sakakibara, Vice Minister of Finance for International Affairs (and the counterpart to Larry Summers, Deputy Secretary of the Treasury and head of the U.S. delegation), suddenly informed the group that Japan, given its own problems at home, would not be able to meet its previous commitment to the Asian Monetary Fund. He asked the Asian countries to listen carefully to the U.S. proposal, because that was the best offer they were going to receive. That quickly changed the attitude of the Asian delegates in the room. Suddenly everyone was more receptive to the idea of conditionalities.

There was still a good deal of negotiating to be done, of course, but the basic direction was now set. Tim Geithner, now president of the Federal Reserve Bank of New York and then Assistant Secretary of the Treasury for International Affairs, was charged with getting the details straight. Negotiations went on into the early hours of the morning.

When I awoke the next morning, a bleary-eyed Geithner told me that an agreement had been reached, and he shared the communiqué with me. It wasn't everything that Treasury wanted, but it was close enough. And in this situation, with Geithner standing before me exhausted, and me having a good night's rest and sipping my coffee, I was glad that international affairs are the domain of Treasury and not the Fed.

THEN, ON NOVEMBER 22, 1997, South Korean president Kim Young-sam announced that his country was on the verge of a financial collapse. The message sent shock waves through Washington and every other Western capital. South Korea was no small economy, like Thailand, the Philippines, or even Hong Kong, but rather the world's eleventh largest. In addition, South Korea was the last standing battlefield of the cold war, with thirty-seven thousand U.S. troops stationed in country.

A few days earlier, *Washington Post* columnist Robert J. Samuelson had written: "All that can be said is that the economic crisis that began quietly in Thailand in July has now spread to much of Asia—

including Japan, Korea, and Hong Kong—and moved on to Brazil and even Russia. It could snowball into a broader economic downturn that would drag much of the world with it. Will it? The prevailing view is 'no.' Federal Reserve Chairman Alan Greenspan told Congress last week that Asia's problems, though serious, won't trigger a U.S. recession."[12]

But now, after the crisis had spread to Korea, no one was sure.

—∞—

NEVERTHELESS, INSIDE THE CONFINES of the FOMC, everyone remained cool. Yes, the Asian crisis now topped the agenda at the meeting on December 16, 1997. Although Peter Fisher described the events as "not just a bad thunderstorm, but something more like a 100-year flood," we were not yet seeing any damage to the U.S. economic machine. In fact, Mike Prell reported that he still felt the economy faced the possibility of overheating. "My gut tells me that the pressure is building in this labor market pot to where the lid could blow off."

To be sure, the Asian crisis had encouraged a downward revision in projected export growth for the United States. But this forecast was not so different from the previous month's forecast—except that the slowdown in growth and well-contained inflation could now be attributed to the anticipated spillover effects from Asia, rather than from a further tightening of monetary policy.

Furthermore, the Asian crisis was causing the dollar to appreciate against Asian currencies. This put downward pressure on the dollar price of imports from Asia, which in turn put downward pressure on consumer prices in the United States, further reducing inflation. This was one of those "favorable supply shocks" that lowered inflation, if only temporarily.

For these reasons, at our December meeting, the staff reintroduced an easing option into the Bluebook—a dramatic turnaround from the previous meeting, when the staff had assumed a 75-basis-point tightening over the coming quarters in its forecast—and suggested the Committee reconsider whether it wanted to stay at its current asymmetric posture (leaning toward a tightening), since a tightening now seemed very unlikely.

The Chairman, true to form, took up where he had left off in November. "There is no way of getting around the fact that . . . productivity has been accelerating over the past several quarters," he said, noting that we "keep getting reams of ever lower CPI readings that seem outrageous in the context of clearly accelerating wages and an ever tighter labor market."

But despite this, he also hinted at a possible tightening in the near future. Did this sound familiar? For those enamored with the New Economy, the Chairman offered up his praise for the productivity acceleration and its argument against further tightening. For the NAIRU crowd and others worried about an overheated economy, he held out the prospect of an early tightening, especially if the Asian crisis proved not to be a problem for the United States.

In the end, the Chairman recommended a return to a symmetric posture—and the Committee obliged.

ON DECEMBER 22, 1997, New York Fed president Bill McDonough, with the urging of Treasury Secretary Rubin and Chairman Greenspan, held a meeting with U.S. bankers to sound out their views on Korea. Two days later, McDonough convened top executives from America's six top banks. There, he warned them: Either they rescheduled South Korea's debts, or the Korean economy, and their loans, would go into default. The banks knew the G-10 governments would not provide additional financial assistance unless the banks cooperated in rescheduling their loans to Korea. Within a week, the banks agreed and rescheduled some $22 billion in debt.[13]

Rubin and McDonough undoubtedly facilitated this outcome by making the alternatives completely clear and certainly helped convince the few banks that needed a bit of convincing to join in the agreement. While the Board was not directly involved in these negotiations, the Board and the FOMC knew by December what was happening. For their parts, McDonough and the Federal Reserve Bank of New York were operating under the close supervision of the Chairman and the senior staff at the Board. In addition, they were operating at the request of the Treasury.

In the end, the banks extended the loans, and the immediate crisis was avoided. But it would be a long time, and a few more scares, before the Asian crisis would cool down completely.

—m—

BY THE END OF 1997, it appeared that the overall U.S. economy would not be damaged by the Asian crisis. Net exports did decline significantly, as expected, but the surprise was that domestic demand picked up the slack, allowing the economy to continue to expand at a 4%–4½% rate. This demonstrated not only the resilience of the U.S. economy, but the fact that capital from elsewhere in the troubled world was now flowing into the United States, pushing down our longer-term interest rates. Both consumers and businesses in the United States could borrow easily, at extremely favorable terms.

The American stock markets also continued to soar. The Dow climbed to record heights, and the NASDAQ rose beyond even the wildest imaginings. The Dow Jones and NASDAQ increased by about 30% and 35%, respectively, in the year ending in October 1997. Even with the Korea crisis thrown in, equity prices for the year were up about 25% from the end of 1996. The rise in the U.S. stock markets reflected the feeling that there was only one safe haven in the world, and that was America.

Yet among some lone observers, pessimism was beginning to rise. Could the United States really escape the world contagion?

In December 1997, after the stock market had declined from its earlier peak, Robert J. Samuelson once again offered some prescient thoughts in an article titled "The Asian Connection: It May Be More Threatening to Our Economy Than We Complacent Americans Would Like to Think."[14]

Wrote Samuelson, "But now I'm uneasy with the recent swing of economic opinion toward boundless optimism. And I doubt its latest conclusion: that Asia's economic breakdown will hardly disturb the super-charged U.S. economy. You can see the optimism in the stock market's recovery since late October. Or you can hear it in the reassuring statements of Treasury Secretary Robert Rubin and Federal Reserve Chairman Alan Greenspan.

"Perhaps they are correct," he continued. "But anyone even slightly familiar with history will find unsettling parallels between the present situation and the onset of the Great Depression. Then, as now, stock markets worldwide crashed; then as now, banking crises depressed production and employment; then as now, government officials professed optimism."

Samuelson was wrong in terms of the final impact of the Asian financial crisis. But he was right in one sense: There were even bigger crises to come.

IN FACT, THE NEW CRISES were already building. Beginning in the spring of 1998, the Russian economy began to stagger. The problem had many of the ingredients of earlier financial crises: a large fiscal deficit, escalating external debts, a fixed exchange rate regime, and steadily declining international reserves. In the first quarter of 1998, in fact, foreign investment fell by 14.5%, compared to the year earlier—evidence that foreign investors were pulling out their money. By July 1998, the IMF had worked out a $22.5 billion IMF-led bailout. It had stabilized things to some degree, but it had not been able to stop the outflow of funds.

Because of this and its inability to get more outside aid, Russia suspended payments on its outstanding debt on August 17 and sharply devalued its currency. Needless to say, this was a substantial additional adverse shock to the global economy, following on the earlier Asian developments.

Indeed, the devaluation and default precipitated a sharp reaction in global financial markets around the world. Even in the United States, which had previously seemed to be a safe harbor, spreads opened between interest rates on corporate and government bonds.[15]

By the time the FOMC met on August 18, the Russian crisis had shown its full potential for damaging the global economy. Now we were projecting a slowdown through 1999 to a below-trend rate. This forecast, and rising concerns about the future, convinced the Committee to return once again to a symmetric posture.

BY AUGUST 27, 1998, we were back at the Jackson Hole conference. The previous year we had discussed Thailand, expressing intellectual interest in the developments there. This year, we were dealing in fear—fear that the financial collapses could spread worldwide.

While the formal topic of the conclave was "Income Inequality Issues and Policy Options," the off-the-table discussions were consumed by the escalating global crisis. This was the only topic of conversation, in fact, outside the formal conference, at meals, and on the hiking trails. How bad might it get? Might the global financial turmoil finally spill over to the United States and other developed economies? Was it time to make an adjustment in the domestic monetary policies of the United States and other developed economies?

If we needed a further sign of the concern and pessimism sweeping the markets, we got it when the Dow Jones Industrial Average dropped 512 points on the day the conference began. Other markets around the world slid dangerously as well.

Greenspan used the occasion to speak to the FOMC members present (five other Board members and seven of the Bank presidents were in attendance) individually and privately. In my case, we stepped away to the far corner of a crowded room to talk.

To my knowledge, the Chairman had never before asked the FOMC members to meet with him at Jackson Hole to discuss monetary policy (and never did again, at least while I was on the Board). In fact, even among themselves, FOMC members rarely discussed the outlook and monetary policy at the August meetings. Jackson Hole was supposed to be our opportunity to mingle with other policymakers, private sector forecasters, and academics.

But this meeting was different. The global financial crisis had intersected with Jackson Hole. The Chairman needed to use the opportunity to speak to each one of us, individually.

Greenspan wanted us to know that his upcoming speech in Berkeley, California, would be a dramatic one. He wanted to confer with us before that speech. After more than two years of reluctance to raise rates, he would now abruptly turn around, signaling to the world that the Fed would try to ease what was approaching near panic in many financial markets. Once again, the Chairman was preparing the markets carefully for an upcoming move.

On September 4, during his speech at the University of California, Berkeley, Greenspan commented that "it is just not credible that the United States remain an 'oasis of prosperity.' " In this way, the Chairman was signaling that the Fed was no longer leaning toward a rate hike and indeed would be prepared to ease rates, if necessary, to offset any turbulence that reached U.S. shores. Greenspan's words could not have come any sooner. More trouble lay ahead.

ON SEPTEMBER 17, 1998, New York Fed president McDonough received a call from LTCM, a hedge fund that, at its peak, had an incredible $100 billion in assets in its portfolio and lines of credit with some of the biggest banks in the world. LTCM had spoken with McDonough several times the previous month, mentioning that the Russian crisis was causing it problems. Now, following the Russian default and devaluation, LTCM said its problems were getting much worse.[16]

Hedge funds are lightly regulated investment pools, typically operated as limited partnerships. They make their money using a wide variety of investment strategies, including taking short positions and investing in such exotic financial instruments as derivatives.[17] Some, like LTCM, take on added risk by borrowing heavily to finance the investments.

Hedge funds were initially designed to make money independent of the direction of the overall market. LTCM used a typical strategy for such "market neutral" investing, called "relative value" trades. The principle was to find temporary pricing disparities between pairs of securities—short-term and longer-term securities, government and corporate securities, and the debt of emerging and industrial market countries—and then go long and short on them simultaneously, making money as the pricing disparities disappear.

If the spread between interest rates on risky and safer bonds is wider than normal, for example, they might buy the riskier bond (because it's underpriced relative to normal) and sell the safe bond (because it's overpriced relative to normal). When the spread between the risky and safe bonds narrows toward the normal, the price of the asset they are long in (the risky asset) would rise relative to the price of the asset that was shorted (the safe asset), resulting in a positive rate of return.

For three years prior to its collapse, LTCM had been extremely successful in playing this game. John Meriwether, who had founded the fund, built its operations and reputation on two star-quality Nobel Prize–winning academics, Robert C. Merton and Myron Scholes.[18] David Mullins, another partner, was a well-respected former professor at Harvard, who had served as Assistant Secretary of the Treasury for Domestic Finance and later as Vice Chairman of the Federal Reserve Board of Governors.

LTCM was phenomenally successful at first. In 1994, its first year of operation, it earned 28%, posting impressive returns the next two years. By the end of 1996, its asset holdings had ballooned to $100 billion.[19] But as more competitors came in, it became harder for LTCM to find the pricing disparities that could create a nice profit. LTCM tried to compensate by moving into trades with which it had less experience and expertise, many involving directional bets, including, in time, going "long" on bonds in Russia.

Unfortunately, it was the wrong bet. When Russia defaulted on its debt and devalued its currency, the world ran from unsafe holdings—such as Russian government bonds—to safer ones. LTCM took a bad hit, which began to unravel the highly leveraged house of cards it had built. By the time Peter Fisher, who was head of the markets division at the Federal Reserve Bank of New York, and other staff from the New York Fed and Treasury, visited LTCM at their Greenwich, Connecticut, offices on September 17, 1998, the firm's capital was down from $7 billion to about $1.5 billion.

If that $1.5 billion was wiped out, the large commercial and investment banks that were LTCM's creditors and counterparties would be forced to liquidate LTCM's enormous positions, likely incurring very substantial losses in the process. If LTCM went bust, in other words, a wave of destruction would burst through America's biggest financial institutions, posing a serious threat to the sustainability of the expansion.

It became clear that the Wall Street banks and securities firms had an interest in trying to orchestrate a rescue, but none appeared ready or able to initiate a collaborative effort. If the collaboration was to have a chance of success, it appeared that the Fed would have to play the role of facilitator.

As Roger Lowenstein describes in *When Genius Failed,* his riveting account of the LTCM debacle, the New York Fed's Peter Fisher asked three of Wall Street's largest financial institutions—Goldman Sachs, Merrill Lynch, and J. P. Morgan—to breakfast at the New York Fed.[20]

According to Lowenstein, Fisher informed the three that he wasn't really worried about the bankruptcy of LTCM or even the losses that would result for the major Wall Street banks and securities firms. They had sufficient capital and could weather the storm. But he was concerned about systemic risk—the possibility that the failure of LTCM would trigger further problems for the global financial markets, already reeling from the Asian financial crisis and Russian default and devaluation.

Soon thereafter, Bill McDonough met with the major banks and security firms that were the primary creditors of LTCM. His role was to facilitate the meetings of the private creditors, not shape the outcome of their deliberations.

It didn't require genius for the banks and securities firms to realize what was in their best interest: In the end, they each put about $300 million into a pot that finally equaled $3.5 billion. This gave LTCM the ability to hang on long enough to benefit from the ultimate narrowing in spreads. The creditors took a 90% interest in LTCM after the bailout, but the original partners continued to be active in the operations of the firm.[21]

—w—

AFTER THE DEAL became public on September 28, 1998, a firestorm of controversy ensued. What was the Fed's role in the rescue of a private hedge fund? Why was it involved in the problems of a nonregulated, nonbank organization?

To be sure, the role of the Fed as a central bank goes beyond monetary policy and supervision of banks and their holding companies. Its role is also to defend the integrity of the U.S. financial system and markets in order to maintain macroeconomic stability. In the past, that had sometimes included bailing out failing banks, as was the case repeatedly during the S&L crisis of the late 1980s and early 1990s. But even that activity came under fire: In 1991 the Federal Deposit Insurance Corporation Improvement Act imposed considerable restraint on the ability of the Fed to bail out failing banks.

That legislation was intended to encourage the Fed to balance its responsibilities for maintaining financial stability, with the recognition that bailing out banks could undermine future market discipline (in the sense that it would lessen the consequences for private creditors and investors of their risk taking). Thus, even the Fed's limited role as a facilitator in the rescue of LTCM might be construed as creating what is called a "moral hazard."

The government creates a moral hazard when it signals a willingness to bail investors out of their financial woes. That leads other investors to rush in, perhaps more bailouts, and a vicious circle of events. It's like a car owner being less careful in leaving the keys in the ignition because he or she has theft insurance. In the case of LTCM, observers wondered if the Fed had inadvertently encouraged future investors to take risky positions, on the assumption that the Fed would bail them out if necessary.

Was the Fed out of line? Or did the LTCM rescue simply allow the orderly liquidation of a financial firm—one that avoided the chaos that might have resulted from a fire-sale bankruptcy?

WHAT DO I THINK? In defense of the action, I will say that the role of the Federal Reserve Bank of New York was limited to being only a facilitator of a meeting of private parties, at which a private solution was fashioned for LTCM. No money was provided, and no promises were made to encourage the banks to participate in the rescue.

Furthermore, the rescue did prevent what might otherwise have been a serious deterioration in financial conditions around the world. It's easy now to fret about the moral hazard that might have been encouraged by the rescue. But at the time, with the danger of escalating financial turmoil and a possible recession, the trade-off between facilitating the private rescue of LTCM and facing the dark unknown was much harder to assess.

To be sure, in the middle of a crisis, the unknown always looks daunting. A line will ultimately have to be drawn, but the point is that the near-term risks put a very heavy pressure on policymakers. I therefore won't second-guess the decision to act. Given the limited nature of the intervention, the fact that, in the end, it was a private sector rescue of LTCM, and considering the exceptional turbulence in the global financial markets at the time, I believe the judgment of the Federal Reserve Bank of New York, in this case, was sound.

But that doesn't settle everything. There is also the question of *how* the situation was handled, in terms of the Board and the FOMC.

I felt I was left in the dark. What I know about the negotiations and the terms of the agreement, I learned from media contacts during the episode and officially only afterward. I believe that I, and my fellow Board members, should have been better informed about the progress of the negotiations and, indeed, had some say in determining whether the New York Fed should have acted as a facilitator in the first place. Actually, if David Wessel of *The Wall Street Journal* had not called me regularly with updates, I would have been even less informed during this episode than I was.

I suppose I could rationalize that there was no time for Board meetings (although the discussions at the New York Fed went on for several days, and as I recall, I was available for discussions throughout this period). I can't even tell you if the Chairman was kept adequately informed, though my suspicion is that he was not as involved as he ought to have been. Whether or not he was involved, I certainly felt left out.

When the affair was over, I paid the Chairman a visit to register my displeasure. He listened patiently but did not admit that he or the Federal Reserve Bank of New York had handled the process of decision making improperly. And I alone brought up the issue at the next FOMC meeting. It was not, however, a subject the other members of the Committee seemed interested in pursuing, at least at that time and place.

So that's my take on the LTCM affair. I was an outside observer, during, after, and now. Thus, if nothing else, my remarks are completely objective.

BY THE END OF SEPTEMBER 1998, we assumed that the weak economies in Asia and Russia would drive down U.S. exports, bringing the problems to the U.S. market at last.

This was not necessarily undesirable. Indeed, the FOMC had refrained from tightening earlier because of the conviction that the Asian financial crisis would slow growth in the United States (and substitute for at least some of the tightening that otherwise would have been necessary). The only question now was whether growth would slow more dramatically than we would feel comfortable with.

Given the mounting downside risks, this seemed to be the appropriate time to take out some insurance. The Chairman recommended a ¼-percentage-point cut at the meeting on September 29, 1998, and the Committee backed him unanimously. The rate cut was not just in response to a downward revision to the forecast for growth in real GDP. It also reflected an appreciation of the strains in the financial markets and the growing sense of risk aversion, to the point where it was becoming difficult for firms to arrange financing and roll over existing financing. This was the first cut in rates since July 1995. I enthusiastically supported the move.

At the time, some observers suggested that the rate cut was a lifeline thrown to the international financial markets, perhaps as a prelude to a globally coordinated interest rate cut. But this was not so. The FOMC was never interested in coordinating its policy actions with other central banks. We always wanted to be free to move as aggressively and as quickly as we thought appropriate, without having to build a consensus for action with other central banks.

While we all agreed on the rate cut, there was less agreement about the bias. A narrow majority favored moving to an asymmetric directive, with a bias toward easing. This in fact is what we did. We felt this directive would signal the Committee's readiness to respond promptly to conditions that threatened the sustainability of the expansion. We were poised to go. In fact, we even discussed convening by phone for further discussion if global economic conditions deteriorated further during the intermeeting period.

WHEN WE CUT THE RATES, I thought it would calm the markets and receive approval as a welcomed change in thinking at the Fed. This turned out to be wrong. Instead of celebrating, the Dow Jones index declined by 210 points on September 29, after having tumbled by 237 points the previous day. "That's the best you can do?" the markets seemed to be telling us. "You just don't get it."

In *The Wall Street Journal,* David Wessel described how Edward Boehne, president of the Philadelphia Federal Reserve Bank, learned "that the Fed had goofed. When he checked into a hotel in a small town in Pennsylvania, the clerk looked at his title and said, 'You didn't do enough.' "[22]

That sentiment was widely shared. Rather than calming the markets, the small size of the rate cut raised doubts that the Fed appreciated the severity of the growing financial panic. Said the *Financial Times:* "There was also a palpable and very scary sense in the financial markets that the move suggested, for perhaps the first time, that Mr. Greenspan had failed to grasp the scale of the problem." Whatever the cause, between the furor over the LTCM bailout and the slight rate cut by the FOMC, Greenspan was now under attack. Asked the *Financial Times:* "Was this the week Alan Greenspan's gilt-edged halo slipped?"[23]

AS WE SAW THE MARKETS losing some confidence in our leadership, we became increasingly concerned. The Chairman did not want the markets to doubt our recognition of the severity of the financial turmoil overseas. He decided to implement a 25-basis-point cut in the federal funds rate target on October 15. This was the first intermeeting cut in four years and served to sharply rally the bond markets.

I generally dislike intermeeting moves. They give the Chairman more power than he otherwise has because he can make intermeeting moves on his own, without consulting with the Committee or asking for a vote. However, during my term, the Chairman always convened with the governors in the boardroom with the presidents connected by secured phone lines to discuss the move he was contemplating. Sometimes, but not always, he asked for a vote. Despite my dislike for intermeeting moves in general, I thought his decision was a good one and endorsed it immediately. We hoped it would change the market's perception of what we were prepared to do. Fortunately, it did: The markets rallied immediately, recognizing that we would support the economy, stabilize the financial markets, and prevent an excessive slowdown.

The markets were happy. Indeed, the sun was breaking through all over. By the time of the November 17, 1998, FOMC meeting, the financial markets and the economy looked much healthier. Third-quarter GDP growth had turned out to be unexpectedly strong, and incoming data on consumer and business spending showed a significant degree of resilience. The resurgence in equity prices and the overall reduction in stress in the markets suggested that we had avoided the downside risks that had been earlier feared.

This left the policy decision as a close call. We decided to cut the funds rate another ¼ percentage point but to return to a symmetric posture, signaling the likely end of the easing cycle.

In hindsight, I regret having supported the further cut in the funds rate. The first two rate cuts were very much called for by the intensity of the turbulence in the bond market, regardless of the continued robust economy. But with just a little more patience, we would have seen that the economy didn't need the boost of another loosening of rates.

By the December 22, 1998, meeting, the data were signaling that the economy was continuing to expand at a "brisk pace." Indeed, Committee members expressed confidence that the economy would expand over the coming year at a rate near potential growth. The global financial crisis was receding. Before long, the Committee would be back to wondering whether the continued solid growth and very low unemployment rate would prove sustainable.

For now, at least, we were leaving the financial storms behind us.

6

IT'S PRODUCTIVITY, STUPID!

While we were forging our way through the year of global turbulence, the resiliency of the U.S. economy continued to surprise us. Moreover, we were beginning to realize that this performance was heavily reliant on the very same phenomenon the Chairman had identified at least two years earlier. "It's productivity, stupid!" he'd been telling us. Of course, the Chairman never called anyone stupid and always encouraged each of us to present his or her own views around the table. But it was an acceleration in productivity, pure and simple, that he kept pressing on us as the fundamental driver behind the New Economy.

If so, this was important. Productivity is perhaps the most important measure of the economic well-being of a society. Productivity itself determines the maximum sustainable level of output of an economy, while the *growth* of productivity determines the maximum sustainable rate of growth of an economy—how fast an economy can grow without lowering the unemployment rate and ultimately triggering higher inflation. If productivity was indeed accelerating, as the Chairman was asserting, then it changed the whole economic universe in which we at the FOMC worked.

Why had the Chairman discovered this first? For one, Greenspan spoke with more businesspeople than did the other governors. They were telling him that new information technologies (computers and networking) were enabling them to squeeze more output out of their existing workforces—thereby boosting productivity. They were pleased with the return on their invested capital and were planning to increase their orders for new equipment. This indicated that a productivity acceleration was not only under way, but that it was building momentum.

For another, the Chairman was a student of history. He often used historic precedents to frame a current issue. He was particularly passionate about the work of economic historian Paul David, who, in studying the Industrial Revolution, had shown that newborn technological innovations take years to become productivity-accelerating tools.[1] Greenspan told us that this was exactly what was happening now, as computers and the Internet were boosting factory-floor performance.

Also, Greenspan was (and still is) a master of macroeconomic data. Like a scientist silently at work, he sought to uncover inconsistencies between the data and what he saw in the real world. At my very first FOMC meeting, in fact, Greenspan had remarked that the macro data on productivity made no sense. Something was wrong. He noted that the incoming data kept describing a decline in productivity outside the corporate sector—but he found that hard to believe. This was a distorted view of the economy, he asserted. In order to confirm his suspicions, he began to dig beneath the macro data, into the more telling details of the disaggregated data.[2]

His doubts were reinforced by the fact that productivity was said to be accelerating in such easily measured sectors of the economy as manufacturing, but falling in such hard to measure sectors as services. The Chairman suggested an ingenious experiment: Pencil in a zero wherever the data indicated declining productivity, then average the productivity across all the sectors. This would provide an adjusted measure of overall productivity (for nonfarm business). By counting the high numbers and ignoring the low ones, you would, of course, raise the average. There was a logic to his approach, and the analysis was intriguing, even if it didn't convince many of us at the time.

The most fundamental reason for the Chairman's belief in the productivity acceleration, however, was the plainest of all: It was just the simplest and most direct explanation for the anomalies in the data, specifically for the apparent contradiction between the faster-than-expected growth and lower-than-expected inflation.

You have to give Greenspan credit. He got it right before the rest of us did. Not only that, he worked out his theory in near isolation. The staff were skeptical, and they didn't mind saying so. For example, at the August 1996 meeting, Mike Prell bluntly told the Committee: "There simply isn't any statistical evidence to suggest that productivity is taking off." I wouldn't say the staff abandoned the Chairman in this matter, but they came close.

Greenspan did have some support on the Committee. Cleveland Fed president Jerry Jordan was an early convert to the Chairman's view. So was Philadelphia Fed president Ed Boehne, who disputed the staff's skepticism. By July 1997, Alice Rivlin also agreed that "circumstantial evidence" pointed to an acceleration in productivity, although she cautioned that the data still didn't support it.

Over time, an increasing number of Committee members acknowledged that something was up with productivity. But no one was as passionately convinced as Greenspan.

DESPITE THEIR SKEPTICISM, the staff initiated a study to learn what would happen, hypothetically, if there was a productivity acceleration in the future. They presented their findings to the FOMC at the July 1997 meeting.

The first conclusion was that an acceleration in productivity would ignite a surge in aggregate demand. This was counterintuitive—who would have thought that an increase in the rate of growth of supply would end up increasing demand by so much that it outstripped the growth in supply?

The staff simulations, nevertheless, predicted precisely this chain of events: The faster the rate of growth of output from a given labor force (with unchanged nominal wages), the greater the surge in profits. The greater the surge in profits, the more optimism on the part of investors and firms. The greater the confidence of investors, the higher the value of equities. And the higher the price of equities, the greater the investment on the part of companies that were blessed with soaring stock values. In addition, the higher the value of the equities, the more consumers would spend. The model, we were surprised to see, was replicating what was already happening in the real world.

And what about inflation? Why was inflation falling, despite the fact that the unemployment rate was declining to a level that should have caused the economy to overheat? The simulation had an answer to this puzzle as well. It suggested that an acceleration in productivity is a powerful disinflationary event.[3] Its disinflationary effect explained why inflation was declining despite robust growth and a declining unemployment rate.

Economic theory tells us that a leap in productivity will raise wages in the long run. But experience tells us that wages are not initially much affected. As a result, in the short term, an increase in productivity tends to lower the cost per unit of output.[4] This, in turn, will generally push prices down.

The disinflationary effect of the productivity acceleration means that, at a given unemployment rate, the rate of inflation would be lower than otherwise would be possible. This, in turn, means that it would be possible to maintain steady inflation at a lower unemployment rate than otherwise. In this case, a productivity acceleration could be interpreted as lowering the NAIRU—lowering the unemployment rate consistent with steady inflation.

We now had an explanation for the puzzling, apparent breakdown of the NAIRU model. According to that model, the economy would overheat if the unemployment rate fell below the NAIRU. But if the NAIRU and the unemployment rate were falling simultaneously, it was possible that inflation could be stable—or even decline—despite the continuing decline in the unemployment rate.

This explanation was reassuring to those of us who championed the NAIRU model. It allowed us to change the model's parameters (the estimate of the NAIRU) without having to abandon the paradigm altogether. In addition, it left room for us to argue that once the unemployment rate fell beneath the revised estimate of the NAIRU, the economy would indeed overheat and inflation would begin to rise.

Furthermore, this analysis implied that the effect of the productivity acceleration on inflation and the NAIRU would only last for a while. Once wages began to rise in response to the productivity acceleration, the productivity acceleration's effect on inflation and the NAIRU would disappear.[5] At this point, if unemployment remained very low, inflation would begin to rise.

The simulation's conclusions were so clear, you would have thought it would have convinced us immediately. Had we only been able to open our eyes, we would have seen that the events predicted by the Chairman were not only possible, but were already well under way. Yet I have to say that we weren't yet convinced. We were still bound to the conventional aggregate data that was pouring in each month, which still showed no signs of an acceleration in productivity. Only when the data finally supported the productivity acceleration did we finally see the light.

Fortunately, this didn't take long. By November 1997, the staff noted an uptick in productivity in the data. That month, they raised their estimate of potential output growth to 2½%, consistent with a 1½% rate of increase in productivity. This was more than ½ percentage point above the estimate they had clung to throughout most of the previous year and a half. Once the staff saw the productivity boost reflected in the data, they moved quickly to revise upward their forecast for productivity, still well ahead of many private forecasters.

—ɯ—

BY THE BEGINNING OF 1998, the Chairman had become the poster boy of the New Economy. To his credit, he *was* the first to see the productivity acceleration. But he never went overboard by suggesting, for instance, that tight labor markets had absolutely no implications for rising inflation (as some New Economy converts were espousing).

But if the Chairman was hailed as the prophet of the new order, I was cast as the party pooper—the policymaker who would prevent the economy from ever continuing to infinity and beyond. The debate over the New Economy, in fact, was often framed with me on one side of the issue and the Chairman on the other.

I didn't see it that way, and I don't think the Chairman did either. To be sure, Greenspan was prepared to tolerate above-trend growth longer and an unemployment rate lower than I felt comfortable with.

But he also recognized that there were still limits (for instance, an ever-tightening labor market would ultimately ignite overheating and higher inflation). My side of the argument wasn't one-dimensional either. Once I came to appreciate the productivity acceleration, and its effect on the NAIRU, I accepted that the economy could linger at a lower unemployment rate, at least for a while, without igniting inflation.

In truth, the difference between the Chairman and me probably did more good, in terms of giving the New Economy a thorough examination, than it did damage. I let people know that the Fed was still traditional and disciplined. The Chairman let them know that the Fed also recognized the possibilities of the new technology and economy. My presence let him sing out with less restraint and more passion about the wonders of the New Economy.

I think this is what Richard W. Stevenson was driving at in a *New York Times* article on September 18, 1997: "An Old School Inflation Fighter: Fed Official Resists Notion of a New Era in Economics."[6] (The *St. Louis Post-Dispatch* ran the same story, with a snappier title, a few days later: "Meyer Sure Old Rules Still Apply: He's the Rain on Greenspan's Parade.")[7]

"Inflation is almost nonexistent despite steady growth and an unemployment rate hovering near a quarter-century low. Companies are chalking up ever-higher profits. Millions of investors are basking in the glow of the longest, strongest bull market in record. Even curmudgeons like Alan Greenspan . . . are increasingly optimistic that the economy is undergoing transformations that should yield more good times ahead. So who would dare rain on the parade? Larry Meyer might, for one.

"Larry Meyer . . . has emerged as one of the most outspoken and influential of those disputing the notion that the economy has entered a new era in which old rules about the interplay among growth, unemployment and inflation are becoming less reliable and less relevant. In doing so, Mr. Meyer is subtly but unmistakably challenging some of the views held by Greenspan. . . . Yet at the same time, Fed officials said, Meyer's role as an intellectual foil for Greenspan has helped invigorate the debate within the central bank over some of the most critical issues of the day. And they said that by articulating the cautious, traditionalist view, Meyer was acting as a powerful anchor at the Fed. That gives Greenspan greater leeway to show Congress and the public that the central bank takes seriously the possibility that the economy's ability to grow faster without inflation has been permanently improved by factors like corporate America's huge investments in technology."

Stevenson then quoted from a speech of mine: "There are limits. They may not be the old limits that disciplined policy in the past. But even if the limits are new, they must be respected. Overheating is a natural product of expansions that overtax these limits. Recessions typically follow overheating. Good policy must therefore balance regularities and possibilities."

The *Times* went on to note, correctly, that the difference in opinion had not resulted in any personal tension between the Chairman and me. "As a sparring match, the intellectual face-off between Mr. Greenspan and Mr. Meyer is not much. There is no animosity between the men, and their statements on the subject are directed at answering the most vexing question to face policymakers in years, rather than at each other."

For my part, I always felt that the Chairman and I were struggling *together* to get to the truth. The real battle was not *between* us, but *within* each of us.

WE ALL HAVE OUR own place for contemplation. The Chairman was famous for doing some of his deep thinking, and even some writing, while submerged in a hot bath. Once, while visiting him in his office, I noticed some hand-scribbled pages on his desk. They were still wrinkled and damp.

I spent much of my time in my office. Sometimes it resembled my office at Washington University, which was filled with the buzz of students and colleagues. The staff and I agreed on many of the key issues—the relevance of the NAIRU model, the lack of evidence of a productivity acceleration under way, and, in broad terms, the forecast itself. Whether or not we fully agreed on the issue at hand, my office was often filled with staffers, brainstorming on issues, assessing the implications of recent data, talking about a draft of a speech, or preparing me for testimony.

This is not to say that my relations with the staff started out easily. Vigorous debates undoubtedly occur among the staff in the bowels of the Federal Reserve. But elsewhere in the buildings, staff members, by tradition, were inclined to speak with one voice. They would certainly not contradict one another during the Board meetings, for instance. I could accept that in those meetings, but not in the privacy of my office. I wanted to hear the staff argue every side of the debate. Now that I was a governor, I wanted them to challenge my ideas (as they had when I was a visitor). That's how I'd shape and refine my points of view.

Right from the beginning, I told the staff that I had to have the luxury of occasionally saying stupid things in my office. But it was their responsibility to shoot down my stupid ideas. If they failed to do so, in fact, and I said something stupid outside the Board, I would blame them. This helped to set the foundation for a constructive relationship—and frequently made my office the noisiest spot on the governors' floor.

But before I lead you to believe that the Fed was the most collegial and communicative of institutions, I have to tell you that, for most of the time, it was a rather lonely place to work. You didn't see the staff walking around the halls by the governors' offices very often, except when they were on their way to see a governor or the Chairman. They rarely dropped in unannounced. I had to make an appointment to see them, and they made appointments to see me.

One staff member, David Small, did flout the tradition, however. He was a former undergraduate student of mine at Washington University who had returned to the school as a visiting faculty member to help me teach a graduate course. He was even astute enough to use my macro textbook when he taught at the University of Wisconsin. Now he was at the Fed, and I was delighted to see him whenever he dropped by my office.

One day my assistant asked me why she hadn't seen David in a while. I joked that he might have become embarrassed: Every time he showed up unannounced, I gave him a hug—a show of gratitude for a spontaneous visit from a member of the staff. It wasn't long, however, before I was finding notes from other staff members on my desk: "Sorry I missed you. I came by for a hug."

—ɷ—

HOWEVER, MY FEELING of isolation remained with respect to the outside world. At my consulting firm, my partners and I were almost continually engaged in discussions with one another, as well as with our clients. But once at the Fed, I was surprised by how few outsiders, even my former clients, sought appointments to see me. Frankly, I was starved for outside opinions. As much as I respected the staff's judgment, I craved other perspectives.

Participation in meetings with outside advisory groups, academic panels, members of the boards of directors of the Reserve Banks, occasional trade associations, and groups of business economists provided some relief. But the agendas for many of these meetings were set in advance, and there were rarely lively discussions between the outsiders and the governors.

I was also surprised by the limited contact I had with my fellow governors. We saw one another at Board committee meetings, as well as at Board and FOMC meetings, of course. But other than that, there was less interaction than I would have expected. We had occasional lunches with one another, and we did socialize from time to time outside the Fed, but that was about it.

To be fair, I didn't take the initiative to visit very often either. I didn't want to be seen as lobbying on behalf of my personal policy preferences. In addition, when I wanted to talk about a particular aspect of the outlook, I preferred to talk with the staff specialists.

The one exception to all this was Janet Yellen. She and I had a lot in common. We were both former academics with a specialty in macroeconomics. Unfortunately, Janet left to become chairman of the President's CEA after we had been on the Fed together for just six months. I had sought out Janet for her views and her conversation. I felt a real loss when she left.

—ɷ—

BY THE END OF 1998, the economy had successfully crossed some boggy ground and had emerged, as strong as ever, on the other side. Those who had warned of slowing growth—and even recession—

were proved wrong. Even the stock market sprang back to life. "The bulls are running again on Wall Street," *BusinessWeek* exclaimed. "Euphoria redux."[8]

Indeed, companies like Yahoo!, eBay, Amazon, and Excite were being snapped up by investors. Anyone who made optical fiber was a star. AOL was seen as the most likely challenger to Microsoft, and *The Roaring 2000s,* which forecast good times for a long period, climbed to the top of the business best-seller lists.[9]

The economy was the proverbial Timex watch: It not only took a licking (again and again) and kept on ticking, it kept perfect time as well. The economy was so good, in fact, that it left us wondering if we had done the right thing back in November 1998, when we made the last ¼-point cut. Should we start thinking about taking back some of that earlier easing?

The surge in profits and equities was not the biggest surprise, however. It was productivity. When it was all talked up, productivity for the fourth quarter of 1998 rose at a rate of 3.7%, beating the 2% rate of the last two years (which itself nearly doubled the productivity rate of the 1970s and 1980s). These numbers convinced me that a productivity acceleration was indeed under way. Yet, how far could the economy go before inflation would begin to rise, and we would have to put a lid on it?

AS WE CONTINUED into the second and third quarter of 1999, the leap in productivity was no longer in dispute. Now, in what was essentially a rewriting of economic history, the government agencies responsible for collecting and publishing the economic statistics, revised upward the data for productivity and real GDP—at the end of October 1999 and again at the end of July 2000. With the revised data, we could see that the productivity acceleration had actually started at the end of 1995. By now, I was using an estimate of 3½% for trend growth in potential output, consistent with 2½% growth in productivity. With these revisions, the apparent disparity between the data and Alan Greenspan's conviction of higher productivity growth was finally put to rest.[10] (Figure 6 in the appendix depicts the level of productivity from 1970 through 2003 and illustrates the productivity acceleration that occurred in the second half of the 1990s.)

As the months passed, the Committee became increasingly optimistic that still further increases in the growth of productivity were possible. In fact, we turned from examining the past data and began to speculate on what further increases in productivity growth might lay ahead.

—∿—

NOW THAT WE HAD definitively identified the productivity acceleration, we wanted to understand why it had occurred. Two economists at the Board, Steve Oliner and Dan Sichel, were among the scholars who took the lead in this.[11]

Economists had long identified the two sources of higher productivity: the amount of capital a worker has to work with and the increase in knowledge about the production process. Economists call the first source of higher productivity "capital deepening" and the second component "total factor productivity," or TFP.

Capital deepening was an important part of the productivity acceleration in the second half of the 1990s. There was an investment boom, after all, which increased the amount of capital available per worker (which led to more output per worker). There were well-established techniques for estimating the amount of productivity gains associated with an increase in the capital stock, so the staff were able to directly estimate the contribution from capital deepening.

Next, they had to determine how advances in the state of knowledge affected how much production was possible from the available amount of capital and labor. Robert Solow, a professor of mine at MIT and a Nobel laureate, had called such technical change "a measure of our ignorance." Indeed, we measure it as a residual—the part of the rate of growth of potential output that we cannot directly attribute to the growth of hours, capital, or the quality of the workforce. What's left is presumably related to advances in technology as appeared to be the case in the second half of the 1990s, especially in the high-tech industries.

I HAVE TO ADMIT THAT, early on, I was too skeptical about the existence of the productivity acceleration. But now I see it as a combination of the permanent bliss and temporary bliss stories. To the extent that the higher productivity growth was permanent—or at least long-lasting—there would be a permanent (or at least long-lasting) increase in the rate of growth of potential output, with more earnings for firms and more wages for workers. This is the permanent bliss part of the story.

But a productivity acceleration also lays a temporary bonus on top of these longer-lasting benefits. First, from the perspective of firms, it boosts the profit share of income for a while because wages respond gradually to a productivity acceleration. This may also temporarily boost equity prices. Second, it has a temporary disinflationary effect, also related to the fact that wages do not begin to rise immediately. This allows the economy to operate, for a while, at a lower unemployment rate without raising inflation.

IN THE END, the Chairman turned out to be right. His call on the productivity acceleration was truly a great one. And it was not just about what was going to happen, but what was happening right then under our feet.

The Chairman invested a lot of energy trying to convince me and others to believe in the productivity acceleration. I appreciate that, but I have one complaint: Never, in my five and a half years on the Board, could I get the Chairman to tell me his estimate of the extent of productivity growth. "Higher," was all he would say.

That frustrated me. I always put my estimates for the NAIRU and productivity growth flat out on the table for everyone to see. I wanted the Chairman to do the same. He never would.

7

IRRATIONAL EXUBERANCE

By the end of 1999, the American economy was just a month short of the longest expansion in U.S. history. By now almost everyone had become a New Economy convert.

Dot-coms were sprouting out of the ground—with improbable names like Boo.com and Fatbrain. High-tech firms, from Lucent to Global Crossing Ltd., saw their valuations skyrocket. "Old Economy" companies, meanwhile, had found their place in the new order in "clicks and bricks," a superblend of old and new. Now you had General Electric's Jack Welch expounding the benefits of the Internet; Ford's Jacques Nasser vowing to remake the company in the image of a dot-com; and Merrill Lynch setting up workplaces where young staffers—between rounds of air hockey—could scribble their thoughts on walls of white-boards.

People were already willing to believe blindly in the New Economy, but in November 1999 they got some solid evidence: The Bureau of Labor Statistics released data showing that nonfarm productivity from 1990 to 1998 had grown at a rate of 2%—not 1.4%, as previously reported—and that from 1995 to 1998, productivity had grown even faster, at a rate of 2.6%, not 1.9%. GDP, meanwhile, grew at 4.2% from 1995 to 1998, not 3.8%. Said *BusinessWeek* columnist Michael J. Mandel, "The new numbers provide dramatic confirmation that the New Economy not only exists, but continues to thrive."[1]

The stock markets couldn't have asked for higher-octane fuel. But with dwindling worries about Y2K, calm markets overseas, rosy prognostications from domestic forecasters, and statistical support from the Bureau of Labor Statistics, they got it. In December 1999, the S&P 500 was up over 20%, and the NASDAQ Composite a blistering 80%, over the last year.

"Irrational exuberance" was upon us. But in truth, it had been building for quite some time.

—~—

ON DECEMBER 6, 1996, in fact, I opened the newspaper and was surprised to find the business pages obsessed with a remark made by Alan Greenspan the previous evening at a dinner at the American Enterprise Institute. In the midst of a long speech, the Chairman had tossed out the term *irrational exuberance* in a way that suggested he was concerned about the degree of speculative excess in the equity markets.

At the time, of course, the Dow Jones Industrial Average had increased by 62% over the last two years, its best two-year performance since 1987. During this period, the Dow had set new highs 113 times, including forty-four times in 1996. And that performance came after the best fifteen years in market history.

The upward dynamism of the equity markets was certainly remarkable. Still, Federal Reserve chairmen have in the past tried to avoid making comments about them, precisely because their comments can send the markets spiraling in one direction or the other. The fact that Greenspan commented then made investors certain that his intentions must have been premeditated. And that made the words *irrational exuberance* very significant.

I have to admit that I had no excuse for my surprise at what has become the single most memorable line from the Chairman. I didn't attend the dinner, but I had received a copy of the Chairman's speech the previous day. He had circulated a copy to all the Board members and even asked for our comments. But I was still a new member of the Board, and did not yet fully understand the principles that determined whether or not the Chairman circulated his speeches beforehand to the Board.

I came to understand, however, that the Chairman would circulate his speeches in advance when they offered an important new opinion about a recent experience or future prospects and, especially, when they provided a hint of some change in the direction of monetary policy. For this reason, it was a good idea to read these speeches. You might even be asked to comment yourself on the issues raised by the Chairman.

It was not that I hadn't read the Chairman's speech in advance. But you have to appreciate the nature of Greenspan's typical speech. He typically sets an issue into a historical perspective. But it's sometimes a challenge to figure out precisely what the issue is.

In this case, the Chairman was using William Jennings Bryan's remarkable quote from the Democratic convention of 1896—"You shall not crucify mankind upon a cross of gold"—to begin a discussion of the role of money and central banking in the United States. I read every word, really, as the Chairman took us on a tour through the Revolutionary War, the views of Alexander Hamilton and Andrew Jackson, the Civil War, the panic of 1907, the creation of the Federal Reserve, the Great Depression, World War II, and the stagflation of the 1970s.

But somewhere along the way, maybe as the story crossed into the 1970s, I must have let my concentration lapse. I don't know why! In any case, on page 6, and seemingly out of the blue, the Chairman dropped a bombshell. It wasn't a statement or a conclusion, but a question. He asked: "But how do we know when irrational exuberance has unduly escalated asset values, which then become subject to unexpected and prolonged contractions as they have in Japan over the past decade? And how do we factor that assessment into monetary policy?"

Alice Rivlin was apparently a more perceptive reader than I was. When she received her copy of the speech from the Chairman, she not only recognized "irrational exuberance" as the key passage, but even went to the Chairman to talk to him about it.

My failure to catch this now famous line shouldn't have caused me too much embarrassment, however. When the Chairman was headed back to his table after the speech, his wife, Andrea Mitchell—always the probing reporter that she is—asked those at the table, including many well-known businesspeople and economists, if they thought there was anything newsworthy in her husband's remarks. No one identified this line as especially newsworthy. It must have been the delivery!

I came to see that reading the Chairman's speeches and testimony was a bit like reading the children's book *Where's Waldo?*[2] In the case of the children's book, a child is confronted with hundreds of faces on the pages and has to learn to find Waldo. In terms of the Chairman's speeches, Waldo is the key "message," often a single sentence, buried somewhere in the speech.

If the Chairman wanted the sentence to get maximum attention, he might place it toward the beginning of the speech. If he wanted it to receive less market reaction, he might place it somewhere in the middle and flash it quickly, rather than drawing attention to it with further elaboration. In this speech, I missed Waldo; but I must be forgiven because I hadn't yet learned the Chairman's ways.

"IRRATIONAL EXUBERANCE," of course, was the Chairman's way of asking whether the stock market had formed a bubble. In other words, had stock prices ballooned from a value consistent with a sober and objective analysis of the fundamentals?[3]

Stock prices, of course, are supposed to be driven by four levelheaded considerations: the level of the dividends; the expected growth of the dividends; the interest rate on "safe assets" (such as government bonds); and the relative riskiness of the equities in relation to the safe assets.[4, 5]

A bubble, on the other hand, occurs when investors lose their heads and commit speculative excesses. They may run around buying Dutch tulip bulbs at exorbitant prices,[6] or, as the Chairman put it, buy high-tech stocks with irrational exuberance.[7] Bubbles are about mass psychology and specifically about the herding instinct: When the bulls start to run, everyone wants to be part of the herd. This is the madness of the crowd.

Bubbles are often driven by new technologies, especially those that happen to have great "stories." There have been railroad stock bubbles, steamship stock bubbles, and electricity stock bubbles—all based on a good story about future earnings. The "story" of our time, of course, was the transformational nature of communications technology, as well as the frothy expectations for the Internet. This story was sweetened with the possibility that we could have strong growth *and* low unemployment *and* meek inflation. All through the magic of accelerated productivity.

So when the Chairman aimed a knitting needle at that story—with the words *irrational exuberance*—it was little wonder that the markets jumped back. On Monday, December 9, *The Wall Street Journal* summarized the reaction of investors. The article began, "Alan Greenspan spoke, and the markets quaked."[8] Indeed, the Dow Jones index had declined 145 points the previous Friday in early trading.

But then a strange thing happened. The markets soon recovered. Instead of a major correction, as some had feared, "the bull spirit triumphed" and the Dow Jones Industrial Average closed the day with just a 55-point decline. Remarkably, the Chairman's question about "irrational exuberance" had only a fleeting effect on the equity markets. It lasted a day. And its effect went down from there: Though resurfacing every time the markets rose dramatically, it eventually became a hollow refrain.

—∾—

WAS THE CHAIRMAN RIGHT? Were equities substantially overvalued in December 1996? At the time, I didn't think they were, and I still don't. The P/E (price-to-earnings) ratio for stocks at the time Greenspan made his comment was about 19. Going back to the mid-1800s, the average P/E ratio for the S&P 500 index of stocks was between 14 and 15. By this standard, equity prices might have been significantly overvalued at that time.

But if you use a somewhat shorter number of years for computing the average P/E ratio, and also take into account the fact that equity values tend to be higher in low inflation periods, a case can be made that the fundamental value of stocks in the second half of the 1990s (and today) would be in the very low 20s.[9] At the end of 1996, when "irrational exuberance" was first suggested, then the case could be made that stocks were still very close to their fundamental values. (Figure 7 in the appendix depicts the P/E ratio for the S&P 500 stock market index in the second half of the 1990s and through the end of 2003.)

But there is another explanation of the equity bubble in the late 1990s: that it was encouraged by the "Greenspan put." A "put" is an option to sell a stock at a specific price on or before a given date. When you buy a put, you pay a premium to, in effect, insure the value of the stock. If the stock declines, the option can be sold for the specified price.

The "Greenspan put" refers to the general feeling in the markets at the time that the Chairman and the FOMC would not raise the federal funds rate to restrain a rise in stocks but would intervene quickly to cushion a sharp decline. The possibility of such one-sided intervention could lead investors to believe they were protected against downside risk. This could encourage them, in effect, to reduce the equity premium, the incremental return on equities relative to government bonds that investors demand as compensation for their higher risk—thus raising the value of equities.

This explanation has some validity. The FOMC eased rates in the midst of the financial turbulence and during the decline in equity prices in the fall of 1998, for example, and again following the bursting of the equity bubble. Yet, the FOMC failed to tighten during the dramatic rise in equity prices from 1996 to mid-1999, save for a single 25-basis-point move in March 1997. At that point, spurred by fears of overheating, the Committee finally decided to take preemptive action.

However, during the financial turbulence in the fall of 1998, we were not concerned so much with the decline in equity prices as with the breakdown in the functioning of the financial markets—an inability to trade. Our decisions to ease rates in 2001, after the bursting of the equity bubble, were driven by the downward revisions in the staff's forecast for growth. In both cases, I would argue that these moves were not made to assuage the equity markets.

Under these extraordinary circumstances, we decided to ease rates to head off a possible sharp decline in growth. On the other hand, when equity prices were rising in the second half of the 1990s, and specifically before and after the global financial turbulence, economic performance was exceptional and inflation was stable to declining. The rise in equity prices, therefore, did not seem to threaten the FOMC's objectives of full employment and price stability.

There was also another important difference between periods of falling and rising equity prices. There is simply more potential for a "free fall"—a discontinuous and sharp break in asset prices—when equity prices are declining than when they are rising.

I was more concerned with protecting jobs than with the interests of equity owners. But I can see that in protecting the market against downside risks, we might have inadvertently lowered the equity premium—the additional return investors require to compensate for the higher perceived risk of holding equities compared with bonds. In this case, the effect would have been to boost equity prices—whether that was our intention or not. Still, it should be appreciated that any effective monetary policy that increased the stability of the economy would have had a similar result.

AROUND THE FOMC TABLE, we occasionally wondered whether equities were overvalued and less frequently asked whether a bubble might be emerging. At my first FOMC meeting, in July 1996, Mike Prell said: "We have a feeling that the market has been defying [gravity] to some extent recently."[10] In a September 1996 FOMC meeting, Larry Lindsey worried out loud that a bubble might be emerging and even suggested that we might move to burst the bubble now, so as to minimize the effects on the economy. Janet Yellen, on several occasions, also voiced concern that the market was overvalued.

The staff focused most of their attention on how soaring equity prices might contribute to the strength of spending by households and businesses. Still, staff members were concerned enough about excessive stock valuations that, in their forecasts from 1996 on, they built in a future correction, often assuming a decline of about 20% over the next year or two. Of course, at just about every forecast round, the staff would find that they had missed the latest run-up in equity prices and would have to "relevel" upward the "jump-off" value for equities. From that point, they would usually, once again, assume a correction over the next several quarters.

But the staff also worried that monetary policy might be too stimulative. In the December 1996 Greenbook, they warned, "The surprisingly high level of the [stock] market may be signaling that monetary policy is more expansionary than we thought . . . and it usually means that short-term interest rates are low relative to the expected returns on stock market investments."

Don Kohn agreed, noting that the "high stock prices meant that real interest rates were too low to contain inflation." But what if interest rates were appropriate for the level of inflation, Kohn asked hypothetically, yet a bubble still existed? Should the Fed deflate it? Kohn had hit the nail on the head. That was precisely the issue we would face in the next few years.

THE CHAIRMAN'S REMARK about "irrational exuberance" in December 1996 was not his last warning. The following February, in his semiannual monetary policy testimony before the Congress, he noted that, "History demonstrates that participants in financial markets are susceptible to waves of optimism, which can in turn foster a general process of asset-price inflation. . . . Excessive optimism sows the seeds of its own reversal in the form of imbalances that tend to grow over time. When unwarranted expectations are ultimately not realized, the unwinding of these financial excesses can act to amplify a downturn in economic activity, much as they can amplify the upswing."

The Chairman referred directly to his previous "irrational exuberance" utterance. "We have not been able, as yet, to provide a satisfying answer to this question," he said, "but there are reasons . . . to keep this question on the table."

In all, the Chairman called attention to soaring equity prices at least ten times from December 1996 until the bursting of the equity bubble in early 2000 (although only occasionally hinting that they might be overvalued).[11] In each of his semiannual testimonies, beginning in February 1997 through July 1999, he made some mention of equity prices. And in 1999 alone, he made four references to equity prices in testimonies and speeches.

While the Chairman raised his concerns frequently, they were with less and less conviction than the original "irrational exuberance" line from December 1996. Greenspan would refer to "soaring prices in the stock market" in a July 1997 testimony, for example, but without at the same time indicating whether or not he thought that the prices reflected speculative excess.

In July 1998, he said, "These rising expectations [of earnings growth] have . . . driven stock prices sharply higher . . . , perhaps . . . to levels that will be difficult to sustain unless the virtuous cycle continues." But the section in which he talked about equity valuations was titled "Economic Fundamentals: The Virtuous Cycle." In this case, the message was mixed—on the one hand, noting the possibility that equities were overvalued, and on the other, praising the extraordinary fundamentals that might justify high valuations.

And in June 1999, he noted, "The 1990s have witnessed one of the great bull stock markets in American history. Whether that means an unstable bubble has developed in its wake is difficult to assess. . . . But bubbles are generally perceptible only after the fact." Again, he raised the question but concluded that it was difficult to tell whether or not there was a bubble.

In retrospect, by the summer of 1999, we all should have seen the bubble in our midst. I'm still embarrassed that I failed to recognize the high probability that this was the case. I *was* accounting for the rise in equity prices in my forecasts for consumer spending and investment, and I *was* alert to any adjustment of monetary policy that might be called for in the event of a sharp equity price correction. But since I wasn't sure I knew what to do if there was a bubble, I think I simply avoided thinking about it. I don't think I was alone inside the Committee, incidentally, in this respect.

BUT WHY DID "irrational exuberance" fade, not only from the Chairman's lips, but also from the agenda of the FOMC?

First, I believe the Chairman became increasingly reluctant to second-guess the judgment of investors. This reluctance grew in proportion to the criticism he received whenever he did challenge the wisdom of the investors. By the time of the August 1999 Jackson Hole conference, in fact, the Chairman gave a speech that was laced with humility about his ability to judge appropriate stock values. After all, he noted, market prices are set by millions of investors, many of whom are highly knowledgeable about the prospects for the companies that make up our broad stock prices indexes.[12]

Second, there were doubts about the effectiveness of cautionary comments on the stock market. The fact that the markets "quaked" the morning after Greenspan's "irrational exuberance" remark—and then bounced back on the very same day—certainly raised doubts that the Chairman's "open-mouth policy" could suppress equity prices.

That observation was later confirmed in research by now governor Don Kohn and Fed staffer Brian Sack.[13] They found that while "central bank talk" about the outlook and monetary policy prospects had a significant effect on interest rates, the Chairman's comments on the stock market had very little effect on stock prices. Investors apparently felt that while the Fed had a clear advantage in forecasting future monetary policy, it had no special claim to understanding the stock market.

Third, if such verbal interjections about a possible equity price bubble were effective, the Fed might find itself in the "wealth destruction" business. It would be as if the Chairman were telling the American people: "Sure I just took a trillion dollars out of your portfolios, but believe me, you will come to appreciate the wisdom of my action."

This is not a path that any policymaker would be comfortable following. Yes, the warning might prevent a bubble from developing in the first place. But more likely, by the time the Fed had identified the equity boom as a bubble, the bubble would have been too big to deflate without great harm.

In this case, Fed intervention could perhaps prevent it from becoming still more dangerous. But by this point, the main issue might already have become the circumstances under which the bubble would burst. In particular, would the bubble burst spontaneously (a market-driven correction), or would the bubble be pricked by an explicit arrow thrown by the policy authorities?

At this point, it would be understandable that policymakers would prefer not to have their fingerprints on the correction. Better to prepare for the downside risks associated with a market-driven correction than to deal with the outcry should the Fed precipitate the correction itself.

—w—

THERE WAS ANOTHER REASON why many people, perhaps even including Greenspan, backed off from concern about "irrational exuberance." As the months and years went by, the New Economy and the roaring stock market looked less and less "irrational." After all, there seemed to be some rational arguments for higher equity values.

First, there was some evidence that the economy had become more stable since the early 1980s. At the August 2002 Jackson Hole symposium, Greenspan specifically noted the "apparent reduction in the volatility of output and in the frequency and amplitude of business cycles. . . ." We were, for example, in the middle of a second unusually long expansion, separated by an unusually mild recession. A more stable economy meant less volatility in earnings and hence in equity prices, and therefore less risk in holding equities relative to bonds, which justified a lower equity premium. A lower equity premium, in turn, warranted higher equity valuations.[14]

Second, the productivity acceleration promised a faster rate of growth in corporate earnings and dividends and, thus, a higher valuation of equities. If the technology had no limits, and the New Economy was just getting started, who could put a ceiling on expectations? This was the "New Economy" story, that of transforming technology that was sending growth and equity values skyward.

Another reason "irrational exuberance" faded from view may have been that the Chairman no longer wanted to discuss it, even at FOMC meetings. Once, at the August 1997 FOMC meeting, Boston Fed president Cathy Minehan asked the Chairman what the Fed's role should be in staving off an equity bubble. "What do we do with monetary policy when there is no inflation, but asset prices are booming?" she asked.

Greenspan, seated a few feet down the table, responded: "That is a question that I raised in a speech just before the sentence in which I expressed concern about how we will know when we encounter irrational exuberance. . . . We have not been able to address that issue because I don't think we know how to handle a problem when we have one instrument and conflicting goals. What do we do? What should the Japanese have done when confronted with a very benign product price environment and rapidly escalating asset prices?"

Minehan pressed the Chairman for more. "Hindsight tells us to prick the bubble sooner," she suggested. "But how does foresight tell us we have a bubble?"

Greenspan snapped back: "That was the context of that speech, and the state of my knowledge, at least, has not gone beyond that," he said. "I do not know what to do." That was the end of the discussion.

—∞—

THE EQUITY BUBBLE raises another frequently asked question: By hyping the productivity acceleration, did Greenspan encourage the belief that we were in a "new era" of higher, sustainable P/E ratios?

While I understand the criticism, I don't believe it is fully justified. First, the Chairman was among the first to recognize the productivity acceleration and tie the exceptional economic performance to the acceleration. He can be forgiven for being passionate about a development of profound importance, and one that most others failed to recognize in a timely manner.

Second, while I think it was regrettable that he became the poster boy for the New Economy, there *was* a technology revolution under way. Furthermore, the Chairman always balanced his enthusiasm for the productivity acceleration with a warning that there were still limits and that if they were crossed, higher inflation would follow.

Third, the Chairman was among the first to note the possibility of an equity bubble in December 1996 and did at least continue to caution about the sustainability of the elevated equity values thereafter, though admittedly with somewhat less zeal.

So I can't criticize the Chairman for not speaking out more forcefully, more consistently, or more frequently about a possible equity bubble. He at least had the possibility on his mind earlier than the rest of us and clearly was more focused on this possibility, even with his New Economy passion, than I was.

—∞—

SOME PEOPLE QUESTION why the Fed didn't confront the possibility of an emerging equity bubble through a sharp and early adjustment of monetary policy.[15]

The answer is that by the time most of us were convinced that the bull market had grown into an equity bubble, we were too late to stop it. A bubble exists when stocks "diverge dramatically from their fundamental value," but how confident could we be in our ability to estimate fundamental value? And how willing should we have been to substitute our judgment for that of millions of investors? Finally, even if we had wanted to respond directly to the soaring equity prices, how could we do so without taking our eye off the objectives that the Congress had set for us, that is, full employment and price stability?

After the correction, Greenspan did finally put forth a simple and virtually indisputable guide to defining an equity bubble: A rise in equity prices constitutes an equity bubble, he said, if equity prices subsequently fall by 40% or more. You may object that this rule does not help to identify an equity bubble before it bursts. But that is precisely the point the Chairman was trying to make.

Another problem in using monetary policy to counter the equity bubble is that the bubble was highly concentrated in a particular segment of the stock market, the technology sector, and especially among Internet stocks. That is clear from the fact that when the bubble burst, technology stocks fell by around 80% and Internet stocks by about 90%, while nontechnology stocks fell by a more modest 30%.[16] The concentration of the bubble in a narrow segment of the market suggests the need for a scalpel, whereas monetary policy affects the entire market, acting more like a hammer. (Figure 8 in the appendix depicts the S&P 500 stock market index and the technology and nontechnology components of that index in the second half of the 1990s and through 2003.)

Rather than a direct response to the surge in equities, we at the Fed, during the 1996–2000 period, felt that we should take an indirect approach. By this I mean that we would respond to rising equity prices only to the extent they began to affect output relative to potential and inflation, the traditional domain of the Fed.[17] For instance, if rising equity values hike aggregate demand, thus boosting the risk of higher inflation, the Fed can step in and raise interest rates to assuage the situation.[18] Normally, that approach should lead to rising interest rates in response to higher equity prices, thereby providing a countervailing force and reducing the prospect of an open-ended rise in equity prices.

This sounds like a good strategy and one that probably would work much of the time. But it didn't work in this case. The problem was that just as growth was charging ahead, with the unemployment rate falling, and stock prices soaring, the productivity acceleration was driving down inflation. This combination caused the Fed to sit back on its heels. As a result, we didn't raise rates (other than a single 25-basis-point move) as stock prices soared, at least until mid-1999.

Second, every time we got close to tightening, an adverse shock of some kind would hit the economy, threatening to slow growth. This put our tightening plans on hold and in 1998, in fact, made us turn full circle and ease rates. In retrospect, we were wrong to assume that the adverse shocks of Asia, Russia, and LTCM would slow the economy. But at the time, under these circumstances, we would have been hard-pressed to raise rates. Paradoxically, the Asian financial crisis, the Russian devaluation and default, and the implosion of LTCM may, therefore, have actually contributed to the emergence and ultimate extent of the equity bubble.

So if neither the direct nor the indirect approach worked, what was left? The leading candidate was the use of margin requirements. Margin requirements limit the amount of funds that can be borrowed directly from the brokerage firm through which the stocks are bought. The "margin" refers specifically to the amount of the purchase that has to be made with cash rather than with borrowed funds. The Federal Reserve, by statute, sets the initial margin.[19] It is currently set at 50% and has not been changed since 1974.

During my time at the Fed, Greenspan was against raising margin requirements. "Some have asserted that the Federal Reserve can deflate a stock price bubble—rather painlessly—by boosting margin requirements," he said in a speech in 2003 that summarized the position he had taken during the time I was on the Board. "The evidence suggests otherwise. First, the amount of margin debt is small, having never amounted to more than about 1¾ percent of the market value of equities. . . . Second, investors need not rely on margin debt to take a leveraged position in equities. They can borrow from other sources to buy stock. . . . Thus, not surprisingly, the preponderance of research suggests that changes in margins are not an effective tool for reducing stock market volatility."

I agreed with this position. But given the damage a bubble can deliver, I now regret that we did not even move to have a formal discussion of this option while I was at the Fed. Even though raising the margin requirement might not have had a direct effect on equity prices, even a discussion about this option might have served to send a message from the Fed to investors, signaling our concern and dropping a note of caution into the equity markets. Of course, it might not have made any difference, just as the Chairman's "irrational exuberance" remark failed to suppress the markets in 1996.

FINALLY, WE SHOULD HAVE more aggressively resisted the view that a decline in the equity premium or a productivity acceleration could lead to a dramatically higher sustainable P/E ratio. While the structural changes in the economy could have justified modestly higher P/E ratios, they did not justify the ratios at the height of the bubble, much less the wildly higher ratios that some pundits were predicting.[20]

In the second half of the 1990s, for instance, the decline in the equity premium raised equity prices, which in turn boosted both consumer spending (through the wealth effect) and investment spending (through a decline in the cost of financing investment through issuing equity). The increase in aggregate demand would ultimately have raised real interest rates, although real rates did not rise immediately. Nevertheless, over the longer run, the net "economic" effect of a decline in the equity premium would have been dramatically less than what would have been the case if the decline in the equity premium did not also affect the real interest rate.[21]

It is not surprising that a higher rate of productivity growth would raise the P/E ratio, at least initially. But accelerated productivity not only raises the expected rate of growth of earnings, it also tends to raise the economy's real interest rate, at least over time. The rise in real interest rates, in turn, would offset at least part of any increase in equity prices associated with a productivity acceleration, and perhaps most of it.

In retrospect, we should have been paying more attention to the lessons of history—that following significant run-ups in P/E ratios, they always return to their normal bounds—rather than giving any credibility to the possibility that structural changes might justify permanent dramatically higher P/E ratios.

I regret that I didn't make this point at the time. If I had been more focused on the emerging equity bubble—and its danger—I would have. But given the circumstance, as well as my reluctance to talk about equity valuations, I never addressed this issue.

—~—

THERE IS A STORY at the Fed about the time Joe Coyne tried to get Paul Volcker, then chairman, to make a comment about the stock market. Volcker was sitting in a barber chair, getting his hair trimmed, and Coyne was trying to persuade him to say something that might calm the market, which was in a tailspin at the time. The barber, incidentally, was Lenny, who had clipped the hair of many a Fed chairman and governor over the years. In any case, Volcker was resisting Coyne's advice and finally asked Lenny for his opinion. Lenny launched off into a remarkably sound argument supporting Volcker's view. When Lenny finished, Volcker turned to Coyne and, with a quizzical expression, asked, "Joe, can you cut hair?" That's as close to a promotion as Lenny ever got.[22]

I agreed with Lenny, so I generally tried to avoid saying anything about the rationality or irrationality of equity prices. If anyone should tackle that issue, I believed, it was the chairman—and even then, as Lenny concluded, he might be better saying nothing.

But I slipped, once. I regret what I said—and when I said it. I was giving a speech in October 1999, very close to the peak of the market, when I answered a question about equity valuations. *The Wall Street Journal* reported that "Laurence Meyer, the Federal Reserve governor, played down suggestions that the stock market is a bubble, saying 'one could argue that structural changes in the economy' could 'justify at least a substantial portion of the rise in equity prices.' "[23]

I wish I had deflected the question. I didn't want to publicly question the sustainability of equity prices. On the other hand, I would have preferred not to be seen as rationalizing the prevailing level and continuing surge in equity values. It was a mistake. I should have listened to Lenny.

8

LANDINGS

By the time of the May 18, 1999, FOMC meeting, Greenspan's view on the productivity acceleration was widely accepted inside the FOMC. The acceleration was clear in the data, staff members were working it into the forecasts, and even the staunchest skeptics had come around.

But ironically, just as we were realizing that the productivity acceleration had allowed the economy to grow beyond expectations, we now recognized that the strength of the expansion had also pushed down the unemployment rate to a twenty-nine-year low (slightly above 4%). With the unemployment rate now so low, there was a growing concern on the Committee that it might very well ignite inflation. So as we left the May 18 meeting, many of us felt that we would soon be moving toward a preemptive tightening of monetary policy.

Some observers have said that in the second half of the 1990s, we were conducting an experiment, in effect, to find the NAIRU. While I don't feel that we were conducting an experiment per se, we *were* searching for the limits to sustainable growth and especially for the new trigger point of the NAIRU. We did this by allowing the economy to grow robustly—and allowing the unemployment rate to fall—until the inflation rate, not the conventional NAIRU estimate, told us that we had reached full employment.

In the weeks after the May meeting, the unemployment rate continued to fall toward 4%, and, by now, even those on the Committee who were skeptical of the conventional NAIRU model seemed to agree that it would now be prudent to tighten rates. We needed to slow the growth to trend—wherever that was—and stabilize the unemployment rate. This would give us the opportunity to assess whether or not the prevailing level of the unemployment rate was compatible with stable inflation. The Chairman never used these exact words, but I interpreted his sentiments as "I don't believe in the NAIRU—but I'm pretty sure it isn't below 4 percent."

I called this incremental strategy the "FOMC two-step." First, you tighten to slow the economy to trend, in order to stabilize the unemployment rate. Then, if you find that inflation is still rising at the prevailing unemployment rate, you tighten rates further.

For those who believed that the prevailing unemployment rate might be sustainable, this solution, in principle, allowed a continuation of that rate. For those who believed the unemployment rate would not be sustainable, this strategy would at least be a start in reducing the threat of overheating. It would also allow an opportunity to build a consensus for further tightening if inflation began to rise.

Many on the Committee still thought a soft landing was in the cards. But as we entered early summer, the staff warned us that we were probably too late: Even if we could stall the unemployment rate at its prevailing level, that rate would prove unsustainable. And once inflation began to rise, as they predicted it would, there would be the likelihood of a more aggressive tightening and the potential of a hard landing. We would be like an airplane that had not slowed sufficiently before touching the runway.

If inflation began to rise, what strategy would be sufficient to contain the rise in inflation—and at the same time avoid a hard landing? The trick would be tighten further—step two—to slow growth to a rate below the growth of potential. This would give potential output the opportunity to catch up to the level of actual output. It would be as if the lead runner (actual output) slowed for a period to allow his lagging buddy (potential output) to catch up. By the time they could shake hands again, the risk of rising inflation would have been contained. I called this a "reverse" soft landing because output converges with potential from an initial position above potential, rather than from below, which is the hallmark of a traditional soft landing.

Of course, a reverse soft landing would not be politically correct. Its goal would be to raise the unemployment rate by slowing the economy. If the Committee wanted to appear more politically correct, it could refer to the strategy as a "closing of the output gap" rather than a rise in the unemployment rate. But that gentler-sounding language wouldn't fool many people for long.

The two-step strategy was useful not only in building a consensus within the Committee for a move, but also in explaining to the outside world why we were tightening rates. It was consistent with the hopes of many Committee members for a soft landing. And it allowed the FOMC to communicate its desire to slow growth to trend (focusing on the first step), rather than emphasize the specter of higher unemployment.

I would have applauded my colleagues if step one had worked—if inflation proved to be stable at the prevailing unemployment rate. That would have disproved my concerns about an overheating economy.

However, I felt that even if inflation began to rise, we might still be able to navigate our way to a reverse soft landing. This would stabilize the unemployment rate at a somewhat higher level than now prevailed, but without a recession. If we could do this quickly, so that inflation did not rise too much during the transition to a sustainable unemployment rate, we would end the second step with an acceptable rate of inflation. That would have been good. But it didn't happen that way.

IN TESTIMONY BEFORE the Joint Economic Committee on June 17, 1999, Greenspan noted that the continuing decline in the pool of available job seekers was an unsustainable trend. This was the Chairman's oblique way of saying that further declines in the unemployment rate might spark a rise in inflation. He went on to clarify his position: "Should the labor markets continue to tighten, significant increases in wages, in excess of productivity growth, will inevitably emerge, absent the unlikely repeal of the law of supply and demand."

In other words, growth needed to be slowed in order to stabilize the labor markets and prevent overheating. The Chairman was still holding out hopes for a soft landing. He was focusing on the first step.

Furthermore, he noted that the Fed needed to move preemptively. "Because monetary policy operates with a significant lag," he said, "we have to make judgments . . . about how the economy is likely to fare a year or more in the future under the current policy stance." Greenspan then explained why the FOMC had moved to a tightening bias a month earlier: "The return of financial markets to greater stability . . . led the Federal Open Market Committee to adopt a policy position at our May meeting that contemplated a possible need for an adjustment in the federal funds rate in the months ahead." That was Greenspan's way of signaling the markets. The markets got the message. Wrote *New York Times* reporter Richard W. Stevenson the next day: "Analysts quickly connected the dots and concluded that Mr. Greenspan was all but guaranteeing a quarter-point increase in rates at the end of the month."[1]

Stevenson was correct. At the June 30, 1999, meeting, the FOMC raised the funds rate by ¼ percentage point. Our statement read, in part: "Last fall the Committee reduced interest rates to counter a significant seizing-up of financial markets in the United States. Since then much of the financial strain has eased, foreign economies have firmed, and economic activity in the United States has moved forward at a brisk pace. Accordingly, the full degree of adjustment is judged no longer necessary."

The move was explained as the withdrawal of an earlier stimulus. "Withdrawal of stimulus," incidentally, is the term generally preferred by the Fed to "tightening" on occasions when the move is a return toward a neutral funds rate, especially for the initial moves in a tightening cycle. The Fed prefers this because, psychologically, it sounds less severe.[2]

There was only one dissenter, Dallas Fed president Bob McTeer, who was still not convinced that the robust growth and declining unemployment rate posed an inflation threat. He believed, rather, that the New Economy permitted the economy to grow faster, and operate with an even lower sustainable unemployment rate, than the rest of us envisioned. In this, he was even more adamant than the Chairman.

The Chairman, on the other hand, voiced a more balanced position. He recognized that there were still limits to the speed with which the economy could grow, and limits to the depths to which the unemployment rate could sink, without triggering higher inflation. Greenspan was prepared to act preemptively to avoid overtaxing those limits.

After the statement had been distributed to the Committee, the Board members excused themselves and retreated to the Chairman's office to discuss approval of pending discount requests by the Reserve Banks.

The Board normally reviewed these requests at its Monday Board meetings but generally accepted them only after the FOMC made a change in the federal funds rate target (at which time they would normally accept all requests that matched the change in the funds rate target). This would maintain a stable spread between the two rates. Reserve Banks that had not made requests that matched the funds rate increase would generally convene by phone after the FOMC meeting with similar requests, which were quickly approved.

Sometimes, however, the first move of the funds rate in a given direction was not accompanied by a discount rate increase. This signaled the tentative nature of the first move. Conversely, when subsequent moves were accompanied by a change in the discount rate, it signaled the markets that these policy adjustments would probably last for some time.[3]

—~—

THROUGH THE END OF 1999, the economy continued to roar ahead. The labor markets tightened further, but inflation was still well contained. Nevertheless, we continued to tap the brakes: The funds rate was raised ¼ percentage point in August, then left unchanged in October, before another ¼-percentage-point rise in November.

But there was another concern as we headed toward the end of 1999: the looming century date change—Y2K. In retrospect, we have almost forgotten how frightening and pervasive that term had become as the millennium approached.

I hadn't thought much about the century date change before becoming a member of the Board. It didn't seem like an issue for either monetary policymakers or bank supervisors. But once I joined the Board, I learned of the concern, inside and outside the Fed, that software used on computers around the world (especially those more than a few years old) might confuse one century with another.

In this case, it was anybody's guess how software would handle the transition from 99 to 00. Would it understand that 00 was one year after 99? Would it think that 00 was 1900? Or would it just be confused? This posed massive risks, especially in the financial sector, where a miscalculation could affect the integrity of bank records and the calculation of interest on deposits and loans.

As Y2K approached, the Fed worked with other banking supervisors to make sure that the banking system had assessed the risks to its computers and software, taken corrective steps as necessary, and were "Y2K compliant," ready to cross smoothly into Y2K. The Fed was also providing additional cash to banks, so that they could meet any increased demand (from customers who worried that Y2K would disrupt the banks and ATMs).[4]

If there were glitches in the payment system related to Y2K, then there would be further and likely much more extreme increases in the demand for cash. The FOMC, therefore, implemented special programs to ensure there would be adequate liquidity and that the prevailing funds rate could be maintained, even in the event of significant glitches related to Y2K. It established a new facility for banks to borrow reserves if they needed, and it even sold options, giving banks the right to borrow at a rate only modestly above the target funds rate, even if the funds rate increased dramatically owing to Y2K-related problems.

In the end, Y2K was a non-event, arguably because of the efforts to mitigate its effects. Considering that some countries did not prepare as well as we did and still survived Y2K, however, did we overreact? Frankly, facing the risks we perceived at the time, I don't think it is fair to second-guess the decisions that we made.

BUT ONE OTHER QUESTION from Y2K still lingers: When the Fed injected money into the financial system in 1999 to meet the Y2K-related increase in demand for liquidity, did it inadvertently pump up the equity bubble?

I don't believe so. The reserve injections merely allowed the Fed to increase its funds rate target gradually over the second half of 1999, and then hold the funds rate steady right around the millennium change. This prevented any increase in the demand for liquidity from driving up interest rates further. These operations clearly were not allowed to push interest rates lower or even to interrupt the steady rise in the funds rate.

Y2K had only one effect on monetary policy: The FOMC decided at the November 1999 meeting to adopt a symmetric directive, signaling its intention not to tighten in December. Of course, the FOMC rarely tightens in December anyhow—a gesture that could be attributed to goodwill but is rather a recognition by the Fed that policy actions in December, a seasonal point of low trading volume, could have relatively large and possibly disruptive effects.

SO WITH Y2K out of the way, the FOMC could refocus on the challenge of achieving a soft landing. But that wasn't going to be easy. As James C. Cooper and Kathleen Madigan noted in their weekly *BusinessWeek* "Business Outlook" column, "There is no sign that the economy is going to settle back on its own to a pace that the Federal Reserve will be comfortable with. That's why 2000 is shaping up to be the trickiest year yet for monetary policy in this remarkable economic expansion."[5]

Indeed, by the beginning of 2000, the unemployment rate had already moved below almost everyone's estimate of the minimum sustainable rate. Yet the economy was still strong enough to drive it lower. If the economy was not yet overheating, I felt it was getting close. And if it was already overheating, it was about to get a lot hotter.

But there were other problems. There was, for example, increased speculation about an equity bubble. At the beginning of 2000, the Dow hit 11,400, up some 25% from the year earlier. The NASDAQ was at about 4,000, up about 80% from a year earlier (that, on top of the NASDAQ's 35% rise in 1998).

Beyond that, we were also worrying that households and businesses, stuffed as they were with debt, might begin to cut back on spending. In 1980, household debt was about 63% of disposable income. By 1999, it had grown to about 90%. Business debt was likewise burgeoning.

In addition, there was the possibility—many thought a certainty—that foreign investors might tire of absorbing an endless flow of U.S. assets at prevailing interest rates and exchange rates—that is, stop financing the U.S. current account deficit. If foreign investors ever became satiated with dollar assets, we realized, the dollar might depreciate sharply, interest rates might rise, and equity prices might fall.

Finally, we were concerned that the U.S. personal saving rate, which had fallen from about 9% in the early 1990s to about 2% by late 1999, was now unsustainably low. Attempts by households to raise the saving rate would reduce consumer spending and weaken aggregate demand, potentially pushing the economy to the brink of recession. Together, these were gloomy thoughts indeed.

We were well aware that long economic expansions often lead to imbalances that increase the chance of a recession.[6] But how do you prevent an overvalued stock market from adversely affecting the economy? By tightening rates to prick the bubble? By not tightening and, thereby, sustaining or perhaps aggravating the imbalance? Monetary policy was simply not designed to address these kinds of problems.

This was most likely on the mind of Martin Wolf, chief economics commentator for the *Financial Times,* when he wrote an open letter to Greenspan in January 2000. "You will have to slow the growth of domestic demand below that of potential output. You must also . . . keep inflation under control," Wolf wrote. "If you are to pull this off, you will need to avoid a destabilizingly large decline in the stock market." He added, "I am delighted that you will be the one attempting to pull this miracle off. If you cannot do so, nobody can. If you can, you do indeed walk on water."[7]

FOR SOME TIME, the Committee had grappled with the concept of transparency, specifically how to make the objectives of monetary policy, the decisions taken at FOMC meetings, and the rationale for our policy actions more accessible to the outside world.

Transparency is important, contributing to both the accountability of monetary policymakers and the effectiveness of monetary policy.

For Congress to effectively oversee the conduct of monetary policy—that is, hold the Fed accountable for its actions—the objectives of monetary policy must be well defined, and the Fed must reveal the policy actions it takes and explain the rationale for those policies.

Monetary policy is also likely to be more effective when market participants can quickly identify when policy actions are taken and especially when they can anticipate the direction of future policy moves. In this case, interest rates and asset prices will reflect not only the current funds rate, but also expectations about changes in the funds rate in the future. This can speed the effect of monetary policy on aggregate demand, making monetary policy more effective.

Until May 1999, the Committee was issuing a statement only when there was a change in the federal funds rate target.[8] At the May 1999 meeting, we thought we had an improvement to offer. From then on, the Committee decided to also occasionally issue statements following meetings in which we felt we had made a "significant" change in the bias. But now, some eight months later, we were not at all satisfied with the success of this decision.

The problem was that in announcing a change in the policy bias only when the Committee deemed the change "significant," we tended to make the markets more sensitive and volatile to the news than they were before. When the FOMC announced an asymmetric policy bias, for instance, the markets perceived a rate hike as a virtual certainty, not merely a possibility. The markets also expected the rate change to take place immediately, not over the course of the next few meetings, as the Committee was hoping to communicate. Rather than being a solution, the new change was now constraining and complicating the making of policy.

To address the issue, the Chairman appointed an FOMC subcommittee, chaired by the Board Vice Chairman, Roger Ferguson, to study how the language should be changed. I served on that subcommittee. In the end, we suggested changing the language from a direct statement about possible future policy action to one that noted the Committee's assessment of the risks to the outlook and, therefore, commented only indirectly on the prospects for policy. The new procedure was announced on January 19, 2000, and was effective beginning with the next meeting.

Said Ferguson, "We are attempting to be clearer that there is . . . a more attenuated link between these statements and the future path of interest rates." The FOMC was trying to have its cake and eat it, too. The Committee would hint at the direction of future policy (the risk assessment), while not talking directly about future policy (as had been the case with the policy bias). This would allow the markets to glean information from the statement about the future course of policy but hopefully make investing less confident that an unbalanced risk assessment implied a virtually certain and immediate policy move.

I felt that the markets were focused on hints about which way the Committee was leaning with respect to policy. Market participants would, therefore, read through the language about risks to the outlook and translate it into something they could deal with directly—and that was a policy bias. In that case, communicating directly in terms of a policy bias would result in less noise in the communication process and perhaps even less volatility in the bond market.

I lost that battle. In the new language, the Committee would say the risks to the outlook were "balanced" (instead of saying there was a symmetric directive, indicating an equal chance of a tightening and an easing). When the risks were "unbalanced," the Committee would say that it saw the risks as weighted either toward "heightened inflation pressures" (instead of saying that it was more likely the Committee would tighten than ease) or toward "economic weakness" (instead of saying that a policy easing was more likely than a policy tightening).

In addition, the Committee decided to refer to the "foreseeable future" rather than to the "intermeeting period" as the period over which the risk assessment applied. The "foreseeable future" was described as an "elastic" concept, a period of time that depended on circumstances.

Finally, the Committee decided that it would announce its risk assessment after every meeting, to avoid amplifying the volatility of the market by announcing changes in the risk assessment only when the change was deemed "significant."

The decision to refer to the foreseeable future (rather than to the intermeeting period) and to announce every change (not just ones the Committee considered "significant") was, in my view, a step in the right direction. While I would have preferred to retain the policy bias, as opposed to move to the risk assessment language, I still viewed the changes as an improvement.

—∞—

AS THE NATION EASED into the first weeks of the new millennium, the markets grew suddenly unsettled. The NASDAQ took a surprising 229-point plunge on January 4, 2000. And the Dow, along with markets worldwide, declined about 7% by the end of the month. Some people began wondering whether the bear market had finally arrived.

For its part, the FOMC didn't see January's stock market gyrations as a bursting of the equity bubble, let alone the prelude to a recession. The staff continued to report that "the expansion would gradually moderate . . . to a rate around or perhaps a little below the growth of the economy's estimated potential." The staff also reported that consumer price inflation had remained moderate. Finally, they predicted that "core price inflation was projected to rise somewhat over the forecast horizon, partly as a result of . . . some firming of gains in nominal labor compensation in persistently tight labor markets that would not fully be offset by productivity growth."

The Committee members were also confident that they would see continued vigorous growth and subdued inflation, but, as always, threw in the caveat that if growth continued to be robust for too long, inflation might be a problem down the road.

The economic news, in fact, seemed to offer something good for both sides of the debate. For those looking for a soft landing, there was a slowing in growth of the Wilshire 5000 Total Market Index. The index, which had climbed 44% from mid-1997 to mid-1999 while personal income rose only 12%, was no longer growing faster than personal income.

For those who were looking for sustained growth, however, there was also evidence that the economy was still rocking along. AOL had just announced its merger with Time Warner, a milestone in merging the New Economy with the old. Further evidence of the New Economy's vitality came during January's Super Bowl, when a stream of dot-com advertisers—Autotrader.com, Computer.com, E*Trade, Hotjobs.com, Kforce.com, and Pets.com, among others—paraded their wares across millions of TV screens. Sure, the Fed had raised rates three times in 1999, the pundits were saying, but that was just payback for the three cuts in 1998. There was lots of gas left in the car.

It was no surprise, then, when the Committee unanimously supported a further ¼-percentage-point tightening in February 2000. It was, we said, "intended to help bring the growth of aggregate demand into better alignment with the expansion of sustainable aggregate supply in an effort to avert rising inflationary pressures." Even with this further tightening, the Committee agreed that the risks remained weighted mainly in the direction of rising inflationary pressures. This was followed at the March meeting by a similar discussion, another ¼-percentage-point tightening, and retention of the unbalanced risk assessment.

WE WERE STILL DETERMINED to slow the economy. But we also realized that if there really was an equity bubble, then in the process of slowing the economy, we might burst it. That would certainly reduce—even preclude—the prospect that we could still achieve a soft landing.

The staff had long assumed that a correction in equity prices would be one of the factors that produced a spontaneous slowing in the expansion. But as the unemployment rate fell toward 4% and the Committee leaned toward a tightening, I urged them not to assume that a sharp correction in the stock market would spontaneously slow the economy. I did not want the assumption of a spontaneous decline in equity prices to take the pressure off us to tighten rates in order to slow the expansion. This was underscored by the fact that the staff had expected spontaneous corrections in the past—and the market had not cooperated.

We all realized that should the bubble burst, we would have to reverse policy fast to soften the blow. But we also worried that we wouldn't be able to slow the economy sufficiently without sending stocks into a downward spiral that would take the economy into a much steeper downturn, even a recession. Monetary policy, in this case, was a blunt instrument for so delicate a task.

So what should we do? Tolerate an economy that was possibly overheating? Or move policy aggressively against it—and risk a sharp downturn?

—w—

BY FEBRUARY 2000, the expansion became the longest on record—107 months—surpassing the boom of 1961–1969. The Bureau of Labor Statistics delivered more evidence of its strength in early February, with a report that cited strong productivity numbers for the second half of 1999 (5% annual growth). In mid-February, more impressive news arrived: In the fourth quarter of 1999, the economy grew at a stunning 5.8%.

To be sure, the stock markets were down overall in the first six weeks of the new year—the Dow was off 6.7%, and the NASDAQ was off 3.8%. But the concern at the Fed was not that the economy was faltering, but that overheating was imminent. As evidence, there was hard data now that inflation was finally creeping up. Dimming the lights might not be enough to slow this party, observers were saying. Had the Fed let this booming market get out of hand?

—w—

IN HIS SEMIANNUAL TESTIMONY to Congress on February 17 and 23, 2000, Greenspan spoke in hawkish tones. He noted that "there is little evidence that the American economy . . . is slowing appreciably," adding that the growth in demand was still outstripping the growth in supply. This, he said, was increasing the risks of overheating and higher inflation.

While applauding the exceptional performance of the economy over the second half of the 1990s—calling it "unprecedented in my half-century of observing the American economy"—the Chairman worried out loud that the persistent robust growth was "engendering a set of imbalances that, unless contained, threaten our continuing prosperity." He seemed to be clearly signaling that further increases in interest rates lay ahead.

Then, on March 6, in a speech that made an even more explicit argument for further tightening, Greenspan said he wanted to see "market forces, assisted by a vigilant Federal Reserve," bring the growth of demand into line with the growth of supply. At the time of his speech, the NASDAQ was just days away from its ultimate peak, and the broader market was only a few weeks from its highest point.

The Chairman's remarks sent shivers through the markets. Would the FOMC boost rates relentlessly until the equity markets began to fall? Indeed, that might slow the economy. But if it poured some water on the sizzling NASDAQ performers, would it also take the Old Economy company stocks into a steep downward spiral?

—w—

ON MARCH 10, 2000, the NASDAQ peaked at 5048, almost four times higher than the level in December 1996, when the Chairman had first raised the question of "irrational exuberance." Although the Dow Jones index had been sliding since the first of the year, the NASDAQ's cumulative gains seemed to confirm the resilience of the New Economy.

It was a bright, shining moment—the apex of the New Economy and the furthest stretch of high-tech's great bull market. Had we only known that, we might have celebrated it. But we went to bed that night not realizing that we had just reached the tipping point.

After the NASDAQ peaked on March 10, it fell during the next three trading days by 141, 200, and then 124 points—a cumulative decline of about 9%. But by the end of the following week, the market had rebounded and closed above 4900.

The "bursting" of the equity bubble would not come as a sharp, concentrated implosion, revealing itself definitively; rather, it would be an extended decline, with some steep dips and occasional reversals, lasting over two and a half years. It would not be clear that the bottom had been reached until some three years after the peak had been attained.

On March 27, 2000, a *Wall Street Journal* article by Greg Ip asked, "How will you know the end is near?" Even by then people were not ready to write a eulogy for the bull market, preferring to see the end sometime in the future. *The Wall Street Journal* article described the difficulty in spotting the pin that would ultimately prick the bubble: Stock market history suggested that "sometimes broad economic factors, such as interest rates, brought down the curtain, sometimes bad news from one of the market's favorite companies, sometimes both." He concluded, "Unfortunately, both bubble and pin are usually apparent only after the fact."[9] How true it was.

Shortly thereafter, the NASDAQ declined sharply again, falling by almost 350 points on April 3, and by April 14 it closed at 3321, by then a cumulative decline of almost 35%.

Interestingly, the Dow Jones Industrial Average had declined by only 12% since its peak in January. In terms of the decline in household wealth, the broader measures of equity values, such as the Dow Jones, were more important than the technology-dominated NASDAQ. To us, then, this looked not like a bursting equity bubble, but like what we might have seen normally in an extended period of rising interest rates.

Ironically, it appeared that the decline in equities was now making overall financial conditions less accommodative, thereby helping us to slow growth. This seemed to contribute to the direction we had wanted the economy to go. But the decline in the broader equity market was not over. Indeed, it had only just begun.

TODAY WE LOOK BACK upon the bursting of the equity bubble as a watershed event, the prelude to the recession the following year and, following that, a subpar expansion and "jobless recovery." Ultimately, the NASDAQ would plummet by almost 80% and the broader market by nearly 50%. But for some time after the peak in March 2000, it was not obvious that such a major correction was at hand.

Indeed, the economy continued to grow robustly through the end of the first half of 2000. From the fourth quarter of 1999 through the second quarter of 2000, the growth rate in real GDP was 4.9%, the highest during the entire second half of the 1990s.

Initially, it's not unusual for the economy to thumb its nose at a tightening. The economy, after all, responded to changes in monetary policy with a lag—a "long and variable" lag—as Milton Friedman had taught us.[10] So, too, in this case: The expansion was still enjoying the stimulus associated with the earlier rise in equity prices, the productivity acceleration, and the long period of moderate interest rates. It would be some time before rising interest rates and declining equity prices would be felt in household and business spending.

—⁂—

AS WE RAISED interest rates from mid-1999 through mid-2000, I was frequently singled out as the chief instigator. A *Dow Jones Newswires* column in May read: "There is a clutch of important U.S. economic indicators due this week and several important figures are scheduled to speak, including Fed Chief Alan Greenspan and the most feared Fed governor, Laurence 'the Rate Hammer' Meyer."[11]

I had been aiming at MVP, not the most feared, but I've always wanted a snappy nickname. A couple of weeks later, Robert Novak, writing in the *Chicago Sun-Times,* put me in charge of the dreaded hikes, with the Chairman sheepishly following along. He wrote that Greenspan had lost out to the "Larry Meyer Hawkish faction" at the May meeting, resulting in a 50-basis-point rate hike. "There is little doubt that Greenspan's personal preference would have been 25 basis points," Novak wrote. "Meyer had the votes Tuesday, and it is doubtful that Greenspan could have overcome him. But he didn't try."[12]

I would love to tell you that Novak got it right—that I took control of the FOMC and the Chairman had to follow. But, frankly, Novak rarely got the Fed right. All along, I knew that when the Chairman felt it was time to raise rates, he would be the one leading the Committee toward tighter policy. I admit I was helping. But the Chairman and I were working together—he leading and I in a supporting role. Frankly, to this day I do not know if I ever actually influenced a FOMC decision in my five and a half years.

—⁂—

AT THE MAY 2000 MEETING, the staff duly noted the drop in the stock market, particularly the NASDAQ. They forecast a slowdown to a rate equal to or slightly below the economy's estimated potential, as before, but they also reported that inflation might already be edging upward. Now they projected that core price inflation would rise "noticeably" over the forecast owing to the further tightening in the labor market. Several of the Committee members also reported statistical and anecdotal evidence that underlying inflation was already beginning to pick up.

The apparent rise in inflation appeared to confirm that the move to tighten policy in mid-1999 was appropriate and, indeed, might have been just in time—or, at least, almost just in time. The twelve-month inflation rate for the core CPI would ultimately rise from about a low near 2% to about 2¾% by late 2000.

Even though the Committee now expected a slowdown to a rate below trend, the clear escalation of concerns about inflation encouraged us to implement a 50-basis-point tightening. We also retained the assessment that risks remained tilted toward rising inflation.

ON MAY 19, a letter drafted by Barney Frank and signed by sixteen House Democrats urged the FOMC not to raise interest rates at the following week's meeting. That was followed by a letter from Senator Paul Sarbanes and a letter from five Republican members of the House Banking Committee with the same message. I am sure the letters had no effect on the June meeting; they certainly didn't affect my judgment or willingness to act. And, I suppose, we should have been grateful that the members of Congress waited until the end of the FOMC's tightening cycle to rail against further rate increases.

Of course, as we headed toward the June FOMC meeting, we didn't know then that the tightening cycle had concluded. At the meeting, the staff reported the first signs that the expansion was moderating from its rapid pace of growth and added that growth would slow to a rate equal to or slightly below the growth of the economy's potential. That suggested we should, at least, pause in our rate increases. On the other hand, the staff reported that core consumer prices continued to climb.

The evidence of a slowdown persuaded the Committee to remain on hold at this meeting. The Committee agreed, however, that the risks remained weighted toward higher inflation. But it appeared at this point that the FOMC might have been successful in slowing growth to near trend—and that this might soon stabilize the rate of inflation.

—∾—

IN THE SECOND HALF of 2000, the economy slowed sharply from the robust pace over the previous four quarters, and indeed from the persistent robust rates from mid-1996 through mid-2000. At last, the slowdown that had been projected so frequently over the last four years had arrived.

The slowdown initially was greeted, not with dismay by those of us at the FOMC, but with relief. Of course, we now wondered whether the slowdown would be a measured one, in line with a soft landing or even a reverse soft landing, or whether we were on the cusp of a hard landing. At this point, there was reason to be optimistic.

At the August meeting, the staff again reported that the expansion had moderated from earlier in the year but now downgraded their forecast for growth to a rate below that of the economy's potential. The annual revisions to the data underlying the measurement of productivity had led the staff again to revise upward their estimate of potential growth.

The new forecast and revised productivity data suggested the possibility that a combination of a slowdown in demand and an acceleration in productivity might soon close the gap between the growth of aggregate demand and potential supply. In addition, the further increase in productivity growth apparently had helped keep labor costs contained, despite the more rapid pace of gains in compensation.

The upward revision to productivity growth, and hence to the rate of increase in potential output, suggested still another form of "landing." Instead of actual output slowing to let potential output catch up (the reverse soft landing), potential output would shift into an even higher gear and race to catch up to actual output. In terms of the airplane analogy, it was as if the runway had taken off to meet the plane, instead of the plane descending to meet the runway!

But the latter scenario was too optimistic for almost anyone to buy into. Instead, the Committee was concerned that the exceptionally tight labor markets would keep upward pressure on labor compensation. The Committee opted again to remain on hold but indicated that the risks were still weighted toward higher inflation.

—⁓—

BY THE NOVEMBER MEETING, growth appeared to be definitely below the rate of increase in potential. Core inflation had edged upward, meanwhile, but it was projected to rise just a bit further over the forecast horizon.

The Committee continued to be concerned that the risks were still tilted to a gradual and modest increase in inflation. But it was apparent that the risks had now become decidedly less tilted to the upside. Maintaining an asymmetric directive was becoming a closer call. Now, the Committee wrestled with whether the time had come to shift back to a balanced risk assessment. It seemed that the time was close at hand.

With growth so clearly slowing to a rate below trend, and inflation edging higher, the Committee finally realized that the graceful soft landing many had hoped for was not going to be. Instead, the Committee resigned itself to achieving the most benign outcome available, the challenging reverse soft landing.

As the December 2000 meeting approached, the staff seemed cautiously optimistic. They noted that although growth had slowed appreciably, and would probably grow beneath the estimated rate of the economy's potential, it would gradually regain strength over the next two years. Core inflation was now seen as rising only slightly over the forecast period. Overall, the forecast painted a pretty sanguine picture.

But the discussion at the meeting, specifically the stories the Reserve Bank presidents brought from conversations in their regions, was dominated by anecdotal evidence pointing to a sharper slowing in growth, indicating an appreciable erosion in business and consumer confidence. From those reports, it appeared that the balance of risks had shifted rapidly to the downside.

This change was so quick that the Committee, in a rare move, swung its assessment from "unbalanced risks toward higher inflation" to "unbalanced risks toward economic weakness" in a single meeting. The Committee was clearly readying itself for action.

The reverse soft landing, we were beginning to realize, was in danger of becoming a hard landing.

WHAT HAPPENED TO THE NEW ECONOMY?

As the economy entered 2001, the darker anecdotal reports that had been aired at the December 2000 meeting were quickly confirmed. Consumer confidence began to sag, and the Purchasing Managers Index[1] arrived with numbers suggesting that the manufacturing sector was in recession or close to it.

Following the December 19, 2000, meeting, I sensed that an intermeeting move was quite likely. I assumed the move would come on Friday, January 5, following the release of the employment report, which generally set the tone for the rest of the month's economic news.

I was a bit surprised, then, when the Chairman convened the Committee on Wednesday,[2] two days ahead of the unemployment figures, and asked the Committee to vote on his recommendation of a 50-basis-point cut in the federal funds rate target. Obviously, he had decided that the Fed should be seen making a deliberate anticipatory move—one that would not be viewed as a late response to a rapidly deteriorating situation. The fact that he called for a vote, when he could have made an intermeeting policy adjustment without one, suggested he also wanted the Committee to be seen to be in complete accord with his proposal. In fact, we were all for it: Many of us were regretting the December decision not to cut rates.

The markets cheered the news. The NASDAQ composite soared by 325 points on Thursday, a record 14%. The Dow Jones jumped almost 300 points. General Electric CEO Jack Welch reported that he and several other corporate chiefs, meeting with President Bush at the moment the rate cut was announced, "raised a glass of water" to Mr. Greenspan in an impromptu toast.[3] Unexpected moves, and especially unexpected intermeeting moves, can sharply reshape attitudes. This was certainly the case in January 2001.

BUT DESPITE THE MOMENTARY CELEBRATIONS, there was no doubt that the fundamentals of the economy were changing, and not for the better. This was attributable to a number of things.

First, the stock market decline had significantly reduced household wealth, undermining consumer spending. The "wealth effect" that had powered the rise in consumer spending during the period of soaring equity prices was, in effect, working in reverse. Second, companies were reassessing the profitability of further investments in high technology. The high-tech boom had been one of the hallmarks of the second half of the 1990s. Now companies were slashing their high-tech spending, and no one knew how far it would go.

Meanwhile, companies were struggling with their balance sheets. Many of them had taken on considerable debt to finance their surge in capital spending. This didn't seem particularly onerous at the time, especially since the companies' stocks were in most cases soaring. But once the stocks came back to earth, the debt that had once looked relatively manageable began to look unsustainable, especially to the financial markets and the banks. So fixing their balance sheets was another reason to slash spending.

While the economy had decelerated more sharply than we had expected, we still thought we were navigating our way to a reverse soft landing. The reverse soft landing might be a little less graceful than what we had hoped for—with a sharper slowdown than we would have preferred. But it would be a soft landing, we hoped, nevertheless.

Those hopes were further put into question on the morning of January 30, however, when the Commerce Department reported some bad news: Growth in the fourth quarter of 2000 had slowed to a feeble 1.4%, the worst for any quarter since the spring of 1995 (when the FOMC's tightenings of 1994 and early that year finally took effect).

At our regular meeting the next day, we voted to cut rates another 50 basis points and also announced that the risks were unbalanced toward economic weakness. While we stressed that the slowdown was not unexpected, especially "in light of the previously unsustainable rate of increase in output," we conceded that "the speed and extent of the slowdown were much more pronounced than we had anticipated."

The staff forecast, nevertheless, remained relatively optimistic. It characterized the economy as being in a "pause," after which it was expected to strengthen (over the next two years) and gradually return to a rate of growth near potential. In between, said the staff, we could anticipate a period of subpar activity, one that would "foster an appreciable slackening of resource utilization and some moderation in core price inflation." In other words, this slump would raise the unemployment rate, which was actually good at this point, since it would moderate any upward pressure on inflation.

WHILE THE FED REMAINED CALM, the markets were shaken by the abruptness of the slowdown. Few of the pundits were using the R word—recession—at this time. But many were conceding that the New Economy was indeed crossing some rough ground.

This was the view that the Chairman was arguing, in fact, and he was not alone in radiating relative optimism. On February 5, 2001, Federal Reserve Bank of New York president William McDonough told reporters that "the U.S. economy will be back to rather robust growth in the second half."[4]

I, too, was optimistic—too optimistic, as it turned out. First, I saw the recent developments as being consistent with a reverse soft landing, which I felt was necessary. Second, I thought that the cumulative effect of the recent easings—reinforced by expected declines in the dollar and in energy prices, plus the effects of likely fiscal stimulus—would be sufficient to cushion the slowdown and prevent it from becoming excessive.

So while I enthusiastically supported the January 31 easing, I cautioned at the meeting that we shouldn't raise hopes for further easings—because they might prove to be unnecessary.

—⁂—

AS THE MARCH 20, 2001, meeting approached, we began to realize how severe this slowdown might be. Despite having cut interest rates by 100 basis points in January, layoffs were increasing, inventories were up, and consumer confidence had fallen to its lowest level in more than four years. In a February 28 testimony before the House of Representatives, the Chairman noted that the slowdown in demand "has yet to run its full course." That, *BusinessWeek* noted, "sounded slightly more downbeat than he had sounded just two weeks earlier."[5]

By now, the markets were in turmoil. In March 2001, the NASDAQ was down about 58% from a year earlier. The Wilshire 5000 Total Market Index was down about 23%. The markets believed the FOMC would be especially bold. They hoped we would cut the funds rate by 75 basis points at the upcoming meeting. They were counting on it, in fact.

But that was not to be. On March 20, we cut rates by only 50 basis points. The markets didn't waste any time in registering their disappointment: The Dow closed 238 points lower that day, or down 2.4%, and the NASDAQ plummeted 93 points, a whopping 4.8%.

The staff had warned us how the markets would likely respond to the move (as they did before every policy move), so we were prepared for the fact that they would probably react badly. But in the final analysis, we also knew that we couldn't let the markets make the decision for us. We had to do what we believed was appropriate given the circumstances. And we felt that the 50-point cut was the right move.

We, nevertheless, threw a lifeline to the markets. We told them in our statement that under "these circumstances, when the economic situation could be evolving rapidly, the Federal Reserve will need to monitor developments closely." We had used this language once before, at the December 2000 meeting, and in that case it had foreshadowed an intermeeting move. For that reason, I was pretty certain, and so were the markets, that the FOMC would be convening before the next scheduled meeting.

—~—

AND SO IT WAS. On April 18, 2001, at another unscheduled meeting, we cut rates by another 50 basis points. This time the effect of the intermeeting, as well as the depth of the cut itself, cheered the financial markets. The Dow jumped 399 points, and the NASDAQ rose by 156 points.

"Alan Greenspan's Surprise Move," *The New York Times* reported the next day, describing the action as "signaling that [the Fed] will act aggressively to stave off a recession."[6] Indeed, the FOMC had now cut rates cumulatively by 2 full percentage points in the last four months—including two cuts at unscheduled meetings—a remarkable pace of easing. The *Financial Times* called it "unprecedented," and indeed, they were right.[7]

But at the same time that we were being hailed as heroes, another tone was seeping into the media—growing skepticism about the conduct of our monetary policy. "Suddenly, Critics Are Taking Aim at Greenspan," exclaimed a *New York Times* article at the beginning of April. "He raised interest rates too much last year, a sudden chorus of critics is saying, and he has not cut them enough this year."[8] That would not be the last time those charges were leveled.

The media were not the only source of critical comments, however. The mail began to turn ugly as well. Governors do not get much mail from the public, but I will never forget a piece I received at about this time. It was a postcard, with barely readable pink scribbling. It began: "Dear Spawn of Satan."

I quickly established that this was not "fan" mail. It went on to complain—in surprisingly well-reasoned terms—about the trauma of the bursting of the equity bubble and the Fed's role in inflicting this trauma. My first reaction was that this postcard must be for the Chairman. After all, his disproportionate power with respect to monetary policy also carries with it the disproportionate burden of accepting criticism when economic performance disappoints. But I decided instead to file the postcard—so it could have a place in my scrapbook, a reminder of my term at the Fed.

—∾—

OF COURSE, THE CRITICS were partly right. There is a tendency for policymakers to move so aggressively in one direction or the other that they stimulate or restrain the economy beyond expectation. In response, they have to throw policy into reverse gear. That's what we were doing in early 2001.

The reason for this is that there is a lag between the time of a policy action and its effect on the economy. When the FOMC tightens rates, for example, aggregate demand generally doesn't respond fully for a couple of years. That's fine if the FOMC can wait for the effect to build. But if the FOMC needs a quick slowdown, it has to move aggressively to overcome the time delay.

It's not difficult to figure out what happens next. The more aggressive action slows the economy effectively in the first year, but in the second, the economy "overshoots" the desired mark, slowing more than desired. Now the Fed has to reverse policy quickly.[9]

In the economy of early 2001, though, this attempt by the FOMC to reverse direction and avoid overshooting was made more complicated by several factors. First, companies were reassessing their purchases of high-tech equipment, while investors were reassessing their investment in the companies that made the equipment. This backlash to the bubble and its underlying causes made it difficult for the FOMC to produce the measured slowdown it had hoped for.

Second, the easings that we had announced were having less effect on consumers and businesses than might normally have been the case. Consumers and businesses don't borrow at the federal funds rate. The power of monetary policy, therefore, comes from the degree to which the changes in the federal funds rate affect mortgage rates, bank loan rates, home equity loans, corporate bond rates, and even the value of equities and the real exchange rate.

In this case, the easings were being accompanied by further declines in stock prices—a bear market—more stringent financing terms for many business borrowers, and a stronger dollar, all of which were restraining domestic spending and production.

Since the higher perceived increased risk of lending to businesses was leading to more stringent borrowing terms for businesses, the interest rates paid by private borrowers declined much less aggressively than the rates on government bonds.

Why was the dollar continuing to appreciate, despite the fact that the economy was sinking and the stock market had plummeted? Frankly, we had expected the dollar to depreciate, and we didn't really understand why it had appreciated. We surmised that the dollar's appreciation was due to the fact that the rest of the world was taking a longer view than investors in America—and they still saw the United States as the best place to invest—but we didn't know for sure.

BY OUR MAY 15, 2001, meeting, the Committee was beginning to think that the cumulative easing might be sufficient to return the economy to health. Indeed, when first-quarter economic data was released on April 27, it showed that GDP had grown by 2% in the first three months of 2001. Housing was strong, and so was consumer spending. Whatever this slowdown was, we felt, this was no recession.

Furthermore, although inflation had drifted up somewhat, the Committee was convinced that the slowdown would unwind the tight labor markets and prevent an excessive rise in inflation. Things were looking better.

On May 25, *The New York Times* reported that the Chairman, in a speech, seemed to signal that the rate cuts of 2001 were having their intended effect and that "the most aggressive phase of the Fed's efforts to ward off a recession might be over."[10] This was viewed by the markets as a sign that the FOMC's next rate cut might be only 25 basis points, after a series of 50-basis-point moves.

The article, incidentally, noted that I had delivered the same optimistic message to the public in one of my speeches, in what seemed to be "a coordinated effort" between the Chairman and me. True, we both agreed that the speed of easings could be slowed, but our speeches were definitely not "coordinated."

In fact, to my knowledge, speeches by FOMC members are never orchestrated. The Chairman, in particular, did not preview the speeches of other governors during my term. And no one in Public Affairs ever told me what to say—or when to say it. They knew better. The speeches sometimes *seemed* to be coordinated, but only because they tended to reflect the prevailing consensus within the Committee.

—∞—

THE ECONOMY BEGAN to look better and we began to feel better, so at the June 27, 2001, meeting, we eased rates by only 25 basis points. After five "rapid and forceful" interest rate cuts in 2001, this was a notable pullback. In the discussion at the meeting, we agreed that the end of the easing cycle might be near.

In July, everyone was waiting for a nice second-half recovery. But when the Committee met in August, it expressed disappointment that "the anticipated strengthening in the economic expansion had not yet occurred and, indeed, that the . . . near-term economic prospects appeared to have deteriorated marginally further in the period since the previous meeting." Frustrated, we eased rates again by 25 basis points.

By late summer, as the stock markets continued to sink, capital investment declined further, and the profits of most of the high-tech highfliers evaporated, our hopes for a speedy recovery vanished. So did the shine from the so-called transformational, paradigm-shattering economy. Now the question was, What happened to the New Economy?

—∞—

IN MY SEARCH for an answer, I found myself looking for precedents in the history books. I soon came to realize that the New Economy's rise and fall had happened many times before, though in slightly different forms.[11]

In the 1910s and 1920s, for instance, investment in motor vehicle production surged. Share prices soared. General Motors's (GM) share price, for example, increased 5,500% between 1914 and 1920. By the early 1920s, the industry had become overcrowded, and investors, questioning the future profits of the companies in relation to their overblown stock prices, began to run for the doors. Share prices plummeted. GM, for one, lost two-thirds of its value.

The same thing happened in radio. It took some time for the radio companies to adopt a business model in which advertisers paid for programming (which is analogous to the Internet's struggle for a viable business model in the 1990s). In the meantime, many of them failed. Of the forty-eight stations that were the first in their states, twenty-seven were out of business by 1924. Later in the decade, the industry grew and stock prices surged, with RCA jumping nearly twentyfold from 1923 to 1929. Share prices fell during the Great Depression, but unlike stock prices in many other industries, RCA's share price did not return to its pre-Depression level for about three decades, suggesting that the earlier price represented a bubble.

The airline industry followed the same pattern. After Charles Lindbergh's 1927 transatlantic flight, airline stocks soared, and many companies rushed into the business. Stock in a company called Seaboard Air Lines took off—even though it was just a railway company (a phenomenon analogous to that of adding a dot-com suffix to a company name in the late 1990s). In the end, though, the airline stocks fell, burning many overeager investors.

To get more insight, I asked Dan Sichel, a Board staff economist, to produce a historic record of productivity over the last hundred years. The series he produced revealed that from 1889 to 2000 there were intervening periods—of about twenty to twenty-five years—of higher productivity growth and then lower productivity growth. The periods of lower productivity growth average about 1½% for productivity growth and the periods of higher productivity growth average about 3%. (Figure 9 in the appendix depicts the intervening periods of higher and lower productivity growth from 1889 through 2000.)

From this historic perspective, it appeared that each wave of innovation brought with it an acceleration in productivity, while pauses in the pace of innovation were reflected in low productivity growth. What was especially interesting was that productivity accelerations were typically accompanied by a frenzy of investment and an equity bubble in the innovating industries. The eventual correction always involved both a bursting of the equity bubble and a retrenchment of investment in those industries.

In the late 1990s, we saw a similar pattern. There was an acceleration in productivity from about 1½% over the preceding twenty-five years to about 3%, precipitating faster growth in the earnings of firms and incomes of households, soaring equity prices, especially for high-tech firms, and a subsequent boom in consumption spending and business investment. This time the innovations were in information and communications technology—and this was where we saw equity valuations hit hardest in the correction. Peak to trough, for example, the high-tech-dominated NASDAQ declined by 77%. Internet stocks declined peak to trough by more than 90%, compared with less than 50% for the broader market. An index of the nontechnology component of the S&P 500 declined by a more modest 28%, failing the Greenspan test (a 40% decline) for a bubble!

So the New Economy fell victim to the inevitable corrections of the equity bubble and capital overhang (the excessive capital equipment that firms had earlier accumulated). The corrections came when companies became more levelheaded about their investments in high-tech and when investors became more discriminating in the companies they helped finance.

The Fed's attempt to slow growth certainly affected the timing of the bursting of the equity bubble. But the bubble's bursting was due to the fact that there was a bubble in the first place—and that was simply due to the excesses of the New Economy.

And what do I think now of the New Economy? If by that you mean the ability to grow faster thanks to new information and communications technology, then we are still in the New Economy. More precisely, we are in a New Economy *again*. But if you mean the ability to suspend the laws of supply and demand, then there never was a New Economy and probably never will be one.

—ꟽ—

SOME PEOPLE, HOWEVER, feel that it was the Fed, not history, that destroyed the New Economy. That is, the Fed's tightening was an unnecessary preemptive attack on inflation, and the resulting slowdown caused the retrenchment in investment and the collapse in equity prices.

My answer is that the Fed's rate hikes likely contributed to the *timing* of the bursting of the equity bubble. But regardless of the rate hikes, the equity bubble and the "capital overhang" existed. It was the "irrational exuberance" of the New Economy, in effect, that finally did the New Economy in. Would it have been possible for monetary policy to have moderated that enthusiasm and prevented the exuberance from becoming irrational? I doubt it—at least not without having significantly compromised the record of strong growth and well-contained inflation during the period. But I'm sure that that debate will continue for some time.

That's not to say that I don't wish we had done some things differently. Looking back, I wish we had begun to ease in December 2000. But, of course, this would have given us only a few more days than what we got from our first easing. In retrospect, the earlier move would have done more for our reputation than for the economy.

The more important question, in my view, is whether or not we should have tightened earlier and more aggressively in the boom period. Would an earlier and more aggressive tightening have lessened the imbalances enough to have permitted a softer landing? I have to admit that even today I don't know the answer.

I thought at the time, and still do, that a further 25 or 50 basis points of tightening could have been implemented after the 25-basis-point move in March 1997. Another opportunity seemed to present itself at the end of 1997, while the economy was still hot. But that move was forestalled by the Asian financial crisis, the Russian default and devaluation, and finally the collapse of LTCM. In the end, as a result of escalating global financial turbulence, we eased rates rather than tightened them.

But I believe the biggest question about the conduct of monetary policy during this period concerns our delay in taking back the easings once the global financial turmoil had receded. With the benefit of hindsight, I think we should have begun the pullback earlier. Still, the delay following the end of the global turmoil was only about six months. The few months in question certainly did not cause the bubble.

NOW THAT WE'VE LIVED through an equity bubble, I believe the mere suspicion of one should send a signal to policymakers: "Warning. Your current monetary policy may be more accommodative than you believe and, therefore, inappropriate in terms of your traditional objectives. Please reassess your current policy posture."

I think we were too accommodative during much of the period in the second half of the 1990s. At least from mid-1996 through the fall of 1998, the nominal funds rate was relatively constant. The real funds rate was edging slightly higher as a result of the gradual disinflation, but the rise in equity prices was more than offsetting the restraining effect of the rise in the real funds rate. Financial conditions were, as a result, becoming increasingly accommodative during this period, in fact reinforcing the robust growth and ever-tightening labor markets rather than restraining them.

A second reason why monetary policy may have been too accommodative is that we may have allowed a large gap to open up between the funds rate and its neutral value. The Taylor rule begins with the presumption that there is some neutral level of the real federal funds rate—a level that neither stimulates nor restrains aggregate demand and is, therefore, appropriate when the economy is operating at full employment and price stability.

It is often assumed that the neutral real rate is constant. This is precisely what Taylor assumed. But economic theory suggests that the neutral real rate may vary over time. One important determinant is the underlying rate of productivity growth. Specifically, an increase in productivity growth that increases the profitability associated with new purchases of capital equipment tends to raise the neutral real interest rate. Research at the Board suggests that the neutral real rate rises approximately percentage point for percentage point with increases in underlying productivity growth.[12]

If the productivity acceleration resulted in a higher neutral real rate, while the FOMC maintained a largely unchanged real interest rate, monetary policy, in effect, would have unintentionally become more accommodative during this period. To avoid that outcome, the federal funds rate would have had to increase over time in line with any increases in the neutral real rate.[13] If the funds rate had risen in this fashion, it would have acted as a countervailing force on equity valuations, reducing the prospect of an open-ended rise in equity valuation that might have turned into a bubble. The rise in the funds rate would not have been implemented to target a particular level of equity prices, but simply to keep the funds rate in line with its neutral value.

By the way, when we did begin to tighten in mid-1999, one of the reasons given was to close any gap that might have opened up between the funds rate and its neutral value as a result of the productivity acceleration. The logic was good, but the same logic might have suggested an earlier rise in the funds rate—not to "tighten," but to avoid the passive easing that otherwise might have accompanied the productivity acceleration.

HISTORY HAD PRECEDENTS for the collapse of the New Economy, but none for the events of September 11, 2001. It is still difficult to deal with.

But from the narrower perspective of the Federal Reserve itself, 9/11 demonstrated the resilience of our financial institutions, our markets, and the American spirit. It also demonstrated the Fed's effectiveness in responding to threats to the nation's financial stability and, in this case, to the possibility of a sharp and extended downturn.

When the attacks came, Vice Chairman Ferguson was the only governor who happened to be in Washington, D.C. at the time. He moved swiftly to have the Board issue a statement. It assured the nation that the Fed was ready to supply liquidity as needed. "The Federal Reserve is open and operating. The discount window is available to meet liquidity needs," it read—short and to the point.

The Fed then used every existing vehicle it had to inject liquidity into the economy. It even invented a new one—the use of large swap lines with foreign central banks to inject dollar liquidity into foreign banks operating in the United States. Discount window loans soared instantly, from around $200 million on a normal day to $45 billion on September 12. Later, as markets began to function better, Federal Reserve open market operations soared from $25 billion to nearly $100 billion.

The Fed also used monetary policy to counter what we expected would be a sharp adverse shock to demand. Before the stock markets reopened on Monday, September 17, 2001, we held another of our unscheduled meetings and this time cut the funds rate a further 50 basis points. No one doubted that further easings would be forthcoming, if necessary. The Fed and its sister banking agencies also asked the nation's banks to work with their customers to meet their legitimate credit needs.

The Fed, of course, had its own operational responsibilities—it had to ensure that the payment system was working smoothly, including its own operations for electronic transfers and check clearing. Finally, with its sister banking agencies, the Fed worked with market players to resolve the clearance and settlement disruptions that were caused by damage to telephone and other communications equipment.

—ɯ—

THE FINANCIAL SYSTEM held together following 9/11, and to our great relief, the markets returned to relatively normal operations more rapidly than we could have imagined. The economy also proved itself remarkably resilient.

Consumer confidence did move sharply lower in September 2001, and we worried that consumer spending might follow. But, remarkably, by October, consumer sentiment and the economy seemed to be rebounding. The Business Cycle Dating Committee of the National Bureau of Economic Research would later date the end of the recession as November 2001. This was earlier than I was expecting, even before September 11. In the fourth quarter of 2001, the economy actually advanced at a surprisingly healthy 2.7% rate. And by December, the indicators suggested the economy was soaring.

As the economy headed into 2002, and I prepared to leave the Board, it seemed that the recession might be over. I might be leaving the Board at a time when the economy was on the mend and a recovery at hand. That felt good.

But I did not anticipate, in the months ahead, the great challenges that my former colleagues would face.

10

NEW CHALLENGES

At the beginning of January 2002, I announced that I would resign from the Board at the end of my term, January 31, and return to the private sector. I had been serving a "remainder term," which is the unused portion of a previous governor's term. Under the Federal Reserve Act, I could have been renominated for a full fourteen-year term at this point, though such a renomination was at the discretion of the President and subject to confirmation by the Senate.

When I had accepted President Clinton's nomination in 1996, my wife and I had decided that I would serve the five and a half years of that term and then return to the private sector. I loved the job, but the arithmetic was clear enough: If you ran down your wealth year after year, as we were doing, you wouldn't be able to retire well. In any case, with a Republican president in power now, the prospects of my being renominated were slim.

Before leaving the Board, I had agreed to join the Center for Strategic and International Studies (CSIS), a Washington, D.C. think tank, as a visiting distinguished scholar. I was eager to take up my new responsibilities. But before doing so, I had one stop to make: the White House.

My former colleague on the Federal Reserve Board, Larry Lindsey, who was now chairman of President Bush's National Economic Council, arranged for me to have a brief visit with the President. When appointees of his own party leave their government positions, the President often greets and thanks them for their public service. So it was somewhat unusual for a Republican president to thank a Democratic appointee for his public service. But former governors look out for one another. I was grateful for the opportunity, and the picture.

—ʊʊ—

GOVERNORS CANNOT ATTEND their last FOMC meeting: It's tradition at the Fed. So as the FOMC meeting of January 2002 got under way, I was sitting, rather lonely, in my office. I suppose I could describe how I packed my boxes and took my pictures off the walls. But I think you'd be more interested in what was happening in the boardroom down the hall.

It's the story I will tell as an outsider now—but with the insight of someone who knows some of the secrets of the temple.

—ʊʊ—

AS THE FOMC GATHERED around the table, the staff reported that the economy seemed to have steadied in the fourth quarter, following a sizable decline in economic activity that summer. The economy would expand in 2002, gathering strength gradually, the staff added, and then push forward appreciably in the second half. Although the forecast predicted two more quarters of slow growth, the rest of the picture was more positive than most of the Committee had expected. The economy appeared to be bottoming out, and the Committee noted that "recovery might already be under way."

I imagine the Committee members were relieved by the staff's forecast. There seemed to be some light ahead. Still, there were concerns about whether the postbubble hangover was truly behind us. This concern was magnified by the experience in Japan: The country had suffered a long period of stagnation and ultimately slipped into deflation, a period of decline in the overall price level. The Bank of Japan (BOJ), Japan's central bank, was forced to lower its policy interest rate all the way down to zero. Once they hit zero, the BOJ couldn't cut their policy rate any further, so they were left trapped in a postbubble economic hangover, wondering what else they could do to stimulate their stagnant economy.

In the United States in January 2002, overall prices were still rising—in fact, the rate of inflation measured by the core CPI was at about 2½% over the last year. But given the slack in the economy, following the recession, inflation was likely to decline for at least the next year or two. If the economy remained weak, mired in a postbubble hangover, the result could be a slide toward deflation. The United States had had very little experience with deflation in the twentieth century, but the Japanese experience suggested it was not a place we wanted to go.

Deflation raises unique fears. First, we know how to end inflation: Raise interest rates. There's no limit to how high they can go, so there's no doubt that at some point you can end inflation. But how do you end deflation, especially if your policy rate hits zero and you have exhausted the ability to further stimulate the economy by conventional means (further cuts in the policy)? This is exactly what happened in Japan. Then what?

Second, deflation has a nasty habit of becoming a death spiral of declining demand and a faster and faster decline in prices. One source of such a deflationary spiral is escalating "balance sheet stress." Deflation puts an especially great burden on households and firms that accumulated large amounts of debt before the deflation. Even if they can refinance that debt at lower interest rates as deflation takes hold, they are still forced to pay back the principal in dollars of increasing real value. The result can be what economist Irving Fisher called a "debt deflation spiral": Falling prices create balance sheet stress, which undermines aggregate demand, which intensifies the deflation, which causes more balance sheet stress.[1]

In addition, falling prices encourage households and firms to postpone spending. After all, prices will be lower in the future. Such postponement undermines aggregate demand, intensifies the deflation, and reinforces the incentive to postpone purchases—again resulting in a self-reinforcing deflationary spiral.

—⁂—

AS THE FOMC MEMBERS SAT around the table at the January 2002 FOMC meeting, these were the critical issues before them. The staff had been studying the experience of Japan and were ready to share the lessons they had learned.[2]

The first lesson, the staff said, was that the Bank of Japan had been too optimistic in its forecast for a fast recovery and was, therefore, slow in easing rates after the bursting of the bubble. The lesson for policymakers, then, was that following the bursting of a bubble, they should appreciate the difficulty of returning to a self-sustaining expansion and avoid being overly optimistic. Rather, they should move quickly in the face of continued economic weakness and, in effect, "err on the side of ease."

Erring on the side of ease means taking out "insurance" against the asymmetric downside risks associated with deflation. This can be done by implementing a more stimulative monetary policy than might otherwise be justified. If the downside risks are not realized, the insurance can be withdrawn. In other words, it is easier to reduce inflation later than to dig out of a deflationary spiral caused by inaction.

The second lesson was the importance of a positive inflation target—what I call "price stability plus a cushion." If the central bank aims for true price stability, and achieves it, any adverse shock would leave the economy with deflation. On the other hand, if the central bank sets a positive inflation target, the cushion—the amount above zero inflation—would provide protection both against the policy interest rate being driven to zero and against the economy slipping into deflation.[3] Of course, a positive inflation target protects against deflation only if the target is understood as being symmetric. That is, you have to pay as much attention to it when you are below the target as you do when you are above it.

The third lesson was that policymakers should move more aggressively to raise inflation when inflation is *below* the target than they would move to lower inflation when it is *above* the target. Simply put, that's because deflation is riskier than inflation. When inflation is already low, and the economy stumbles, policymakers must be particularly quick and bold.

When there's not much room to lower rates, you would think policymakers should "save their ammunition" and "keep their powder dry," just in case they need it in the event of an unexpected adverse shock. But simulation studies at the Board reached just the opposite conclusion: When rates are low and the economy weakens, policymakers should not only cut rates, but do so especially quickly and in larger increments than otherwise. As former governor Lyle Gramley said of the 50-basis-point rate cut in November 2002, "When you don't have much ammunition, shoot to kill!"

A fourth lesson was that fiscal policy needs to be part of the stimulus package in a postbubble economy confronted with the risk of deflation. To be sure, there are well-appreciated political constraints on how fast fiscal policy decisions can be made and implemented. Tax cuts, for instance, typically take a year or more to move through the Congress, while recessions generally last less than a year.

Still, it is difficult for monetary policy alone to succeed in preventing a postbubble economy from slipping into deflation—or escaping from one.[4] If the central bank is asked to go it alone, there will be a greater risk that it will find itself forced to drop its policy interest rate to zero. In times of stress, then, fiscal policymakers have to be prepared to shoulder more of the stabilization burden than they would otherwise. That will be a great challenge. But fiscal authorities must try to overcome the normal delays in the political process—and monetary policymakers should welcome their efforts to do so.[5]

The last lesson from the Japanese experience was the importance of contingency planning, just in case the policy rate is driven to zero. When that happens, you need some "unconventional" policy options that have been fully explored and are already on the shelf. The Japanese didn't have this and spent valuable time debating what to do next.

The staff presentation concluded. The minutes duly noted: "The members agreed that the potential for such an economic and policy scenario seemed highly remote, but it could not be dismissed altogether."

Indeed, they shouldn't have. Deflation was about to become a far greater concern.

IN THE FIRST YEAR of the expansion, through the third quarter of 2002, the economy grew at a rate of about 3%. That wasn't bad, considering what it had gone through in the last two years. But toward the end of the year, the economy weakened. The postbubble hangover was still there, and new corporate scandals were now pushing into the headlines amid growing concerns over Iraq. Recovery was not at hand, as some had predicted.

Now, growth was slowing, inflation was falling, and the funds rate was already low. Fortunately, the Fed was ready. Its playbook, primed by the staff presentation on Japan in January 2002, instructed that if the economy stumbles in the aftermath of the bursting equity market, cut rates—quickly and boldly. That's what the FOMC did: a 50-basis-point cut to 1¼% in November 2002, a larger decline than what the markets expected.

The easing was welcomed, yet it raised dark concerns: Would the FOMC, like Japan's central bank, be forced to drive its policy rate to zero? Then what?

The answer wasn't long in coming. On November 13, 2002, in testimony before the Joint Economic Committee, Greenspan was asked the tough question. He replied that if it got to that point, the Fed would buy a wide range of assets—including longer-term government securities—and in the process would lower long-term rates relative to the zero federal funds rate.

Greenspan noted a historical precedence for such a move. "We, in the past, have engaged in purchasing assets all along the maturity spectrum of the yield curve. And, indeed, during World War II and until the accord with Treasury in 1951, the Federal Reserve essentially pegged the Treasury market," he said. By doing so, the Fed had effectively set a ceiling for long-term Treasury securities at 2½% for about ten years during and after World War II. Now that possibility was in the air again.[6]

AS THE ECONOMY LIMPED through the second half of 2002, the Fed's options, should the funds rate fall to zero, were frequently discussed. Governor Ben Bernanke provided the most comprehensive discussion of policy options and suggested two basic strategies.[7]

The first was for the Fed to commit to holding the funds rate at zero for some specified period. To the extent that this lowered market expectations for future short-term interest rates, this strategy would also lower long-term interest rates today. A second approach, more direct and the one Bernanke preferred, was to announce explicit ceilings for longer-term Treasury securities, enforced by a willingness to buy such securities as necessary to ensure that outcome. This essentially replicated the Fed strategy during and immediately after World War II.

Bernanke's message was that a central bank never runs out of ammunition as long as it has access to the printing press. The FOMC could expand the money supply by buying a wide range of assets, starting with longer-term Treasury securities. If that proved insufficient, there were other assets to buy, including foreign government securities and private sector securities.[8]

It sounded so easy—such a sure thing. But the staff didn't share the confidence of either Bernanke or Greenspan on this issue. They had already written a paper (in November 2000) analyzing virtually all the options that the Chairman and Governor were now suggesting. Each of these had "limitations," said the staff, noting that there was "considerable uncertainty regarding their likely effectiveness."[9]

Long-term interest rates, the staff study noted, depend on current and expected future short-term rates, as well as a term premium (the added interest that investors typically demand for holding longer-term as opposed to shorter-term assets). There was little evidence that monetary policy could affect this term premium, the staff argued. In that case, the only way to lower long-term rates would be to encourage the markets to expect that short-term rates would be lower for longer.

The staff was not alone in their criticism of the Greenspan and Bernanke plan. Another critic was Michael Woodford, a professor at Princeton. Woodford presented a seminar at the Board in March 2003, arguing that the strategy the Chairman had talked about and that Bernanke had laid out in his paper—flattening the yield curve by purchasing a wider range of assets—was doomed to failure, as the staff had earlier suggested.[10] The only way to lower long-term rates, Woodford argued, was to convince market participants that the Fed would hold short-term rates lower for longer than now expected. But how could they accomplish this?

Woodford had an answer: Monetary policy had to focus on making a credible precommitment to holding rates lower for longer than expected by the markets.[11] The expectations of lower short-term rates for longer would immediately translate into lower long-term rates today, stimulating the economy.

While this idea had been discussed by the staff for some time, and Bernanke had mentioned this option in his paper, Woodford's seminar gave the idea renewed attention and added traction.

—∞—

IN NOVEMBER 2002, I organized a conference at the Center for Strategic and International Studies on the economic consequences of an attack on Iraq.[12] By now I was working with my former consulting partners at Macroeconomic Advisers in addition to serving as a distinguished scholar at CSIS. For the conference, Macroeconomic Advisers used the scenarios developed by a panel of experts on political strategy, oil markets, and financial markets to simulate the economic effects of an attack on Iraq. The "benign" scenario—involving a quick and decisive end to the combat phase of the war—became the basis for our forecast for 2003 and 2004.

According to that forecast, we expected that the geopolitical uncertainties related to the Iraq war would depress the economy through the first half of 2003, but that a quick and decisive victory in the war would cause the economy to snap back in the second half of the year. We also expected the recovery to be supported by improving fundamentals (reflecting our judgment that the imbalances inherited from the boom period were now largely corrected), by improving financial conditions (led by a rebound in equity prices), and by the combination of aggressive monetary and fiscal policies.[13]

Our forecast called for a rebound to 4½%–5% in the second half of 2003 and solid growth thereafter. It was a tough sell. Few were buying such a strong turnaround in the economy. Pessimism was in vogue.

—∞—

ABOUT FOUR MONTHS LATER, on March 19, the war began. Equity prices were climbing and oil prices were declining even before the start of the hostilities. The quick and decisive victory in the combat phase led to a further rise in equity prices and a rebound in consumer confidence. But the postwar euphoria was short-lived. By its

May meeting, the FOMC was finding its incoming reports from the regions disappointing. It kept the funds rate unchanged but was clearly leaning toward an easing at the next meeting unless there were definitive signs of improvement.

The Committee did surprise the markets with its statement at the end of the meeting. It decided to change its risk assessment language, offering separate risk assessments for growth and price stability. It indicated that it viewed the risks to growth as balanced. But it said that the probability of a further fall in inflation, from its already low level, exceeded that of a pickup in inflation.

This was interpreted as an attempt by the Committee to signal its growing concern about further disinflation and to encourage the view that the funds rate would remain low—longer than the markets had previously anticipated. The Fed, it seemed, was putting into practice a form of Woodford's "precommitment" strategy. The markets interpreted it as such, and long-term interest rates fell. If this was a precommitment strategy, it seemed to be working.

NOW THE MARKETS were not only expecting the funds rate to remain low longer, they were also beginning to speculate about a further easing. Those expectations were reinforced on June 3, 2003, in extraordinary remarks by the Chairman. Up to this point, FOMC members had referred to deflation as only a remote risk. But now, in remarks during a panel discussion at a monetary conference in Berlin, the Chairman shocked the markets by referring explicitly to deflation, again and again—at least eleven times in all—suggesting that the Committee was now seriously concerned about deflation and ready to take further steps to avoid it.[14]

Greenspan explained that the policymakers understood inflation and knew how to deal with it but had much greater uncertainty about the effects of deflation. It was a more difficult challenge—especially if the policy rate was driven to zero. As a result, he said, we needed a wider "firebreak" to contain deflationary forces.

The first reaction of market participants was to scramble for a dictionary: What was a firebreak—and what did this have to do with monetary policy? But they got the point. The Chairman was more worried about deflation than everyone had realized. That signaled that the Fed would at least hold rates lower for longer and might even ease further.

The speculation was now building, in fact, for a 50-basis-point easing at the June meeting. And there was also speculation that the use of the nonconventional policies might be imminent as well, perhaps the next step after the June 2003 meeting.[15]

AS WE APPROACHED the June 2003 meeting, I told my clients to expect only a 25-basis-point cut. Our forecast was more optimistic. We already saw signs that the economy was beginning to turn the corner. This was not the time to become more aggressive in easing policy, we believed, regardless of the lessons from the Japanese experience.

Then I saw an article by John M. Berry in *The Washington Post.* Berry said to expect a 50-basis-point cut.[16] Ouch, I thought. Could the Chairman have tipped him off to that during Berry's last talk with him? The next day, however, Greg Ip of *The Wall Street Journal* reported something different—that a 25-basis-point cut was still on the table.[17] They couldn't both be right.

When the FOMC statement finally appeared, I sat at my computer and wrote my own headline: "Ip 1, Berry 0." The cut was 25 basis points—for the reasons I had anticipated.

Once the decision was announced and the statement absorbed, the markets were demoralized. They had been sure the cut in the funds rate would be 50 basis points. After all, the Chairman had led them in that direction in his June 3 remarks. Market participants weren't just unhappy; some of them were much poorer for the outcome, and they were angry at the Fed for misleading them. Did the Fed mislead the markets? The Chairman's June 3 remarks, in particular, were over the top, in my view. It was too alarmist. It contributed to the misunderstanding.

But in truth, the biggest source of confusion came from the fact that the economy finally began to stage a recovery after the May 6 statement and particularly after the Chairman's June 3 remarks. That rebound left an enormous gulf between how the economy looked to the Committee at the time of the May FOMC meeting (and to the

Chairman in early June) and how it looked at the time of the June FOMC meeting.

The improvement was not decisive enough for the Committee to pull back from the easing for which it had worked so hard to prepare the market. But it was enough to discourage a bolder 50-basis-point move in June.

—~—

THE MARKETS ALSO SIMPLY missed the evolution in the views inside the FOMC about the efficacy of nonconventional policies and its willingness to move in this direction. The first sign of a change appeared in a paper presented by Governor Bernanke in Japan in May 2003, one that offered recommendations for the Bank of Japan.[18] These recommendations didn't look at all like the policy he had suggested for the United States. Instead, Bernanke emphasized Woodford's precommitment policy.

Where was the recommendation to run the printing press and buy a wider range of assets? Gone. It turned out the earlier staff skepticism about the efficacy of those policies had finally become the prevailing view of the Committee. Purchasing a wider range of assets would be effective, in this view, only if it complemented a strategy aimed to alter expectations about the future course of monetary policy. The precommitment strategy was really the only strategy.

There was also some skepticism about the effectiveness of what seemed to be a vague form of a precommitment policy. The role of the FOMC, after all, was not to manipulate the bond market using its policy statements and other communication as tools to lower long-term rates. Its role should be limited to giving the markets the opportunity to see the economy through the Committee's eyes—appreciating, to be sure, that the FOMC's perception of the outlook would affect private sector and market forecasts—and allow the markets to understand the strategy the Committee believed was appropriate under the circumstances. If the effect was to convince markets that the funds rate would be lower for longer than previously expected, and long rates declined, that would be an excellent outcome. But it was not assured.

—~—

AS THE COMMITTEE became less confident in the efficacy of nonconventional policies, it came to realize that it would have to continue to rely on conventional policy.[19] Even if there were some concerns about the side effects of lowering the funds rate to zero, in other words, lowering the rate remained the most reliable tool the Fed had—and it would use it if necessary.[20]

In his July 15, 2003, semiannual monetary policy testimony, the Chairman noted that the FOMC "stands prepared to maintain a highly accommodative stance of policy for as long as needed to promote satisfactory performance." He added, "policy accommodation can be . . . maintained for a considerable period without ultimately stoking inflationary pressures." The Chairman was signaling the markets to expect policy to remain on hold for a relatively long time. This was followed, at the August meeting, by the inclusion of the same sentiment in the Committee's statement: that, given the concern about further disinflation, "the Committee believes that policy accommodation can remain for a considerable period." This seemed like another attempt at a vague precommitment strategy.

IN THE COMING MONTHS, the Committee gradually evolved its "considerable period" story.[21] This had two components. First, there was "resource slack" in the economy. This referred to the fact that output was below its potential level (and the unemployment rate was above the NAIRU). This gap was expected to close slowly. Thus the FOMC would not be pressured to tighten rates for some time. Second, the combination of the resource slack and elevated productivity growth was likely to keep inflation quite low for a considerable period, lengthening the period that monetary policy could remain on hold.

Governor Bernanke had been especially effective in telling this story.[22] His message was that a return to robust growth did not necessarily mean that monetary policymakers should immediately begin to tighten rates. Monetary policy, after all, is not driven by growth per se. It is driven by what happens to the "resource slack" (the output gap or unemployment rate) and what happens to inflation (specifically to core consumer price inflation). If you want to understand the prospects for monetary policy, he was saying, keep your eyes on the latter.

Growth can be robust, yet slack in the labor market can be absorbed quite gradually. This would be the case, for example, if the higher production is achieved by higher productivity rather than by higher employment. Persistent slack, in turn, would reinforce the disinflationary effect of an apparent further acceleration in productivity, keeping inflation low, and perhaps even causing it to decline.

AFTER THE AUGUST 2003 MEETING, the economy showed further signs of turning the corner. The stock market, led by the mercurial NASDAQ, began charging ahead. Growth surged in the second half of 2003—advancing at an impressive 6% rate. The FOMC was projecting growth of 3¾%–4¾% in 2004.

The recovery quickly created problems for the FOMC's "considerable period" language.[23] From the beginning, the use of this phrase was controversial within the Committee. Now, with the strength of the recovery, the Committee was even more uncomfortable with this language.

Many in the markets interpreted the "considerable period" language as a "time-based commitment," a commitment of the FOMC to keep policy on hold for an unspecified but considerable period of time. This would have been a very bold precommitment. Clearly, the Committee did not think of it that way.[24] They viewed it as an "event-based commitment," tied to their concerns about disinflation and their belief that disinflation was likely to remain the concern for a considerable period of time. The Committee recognized that a central bank should not be making time-based commitments, given the uncertainty of future outcomes, and soon regretted that the phrase was being interpreted in this way.

Second, the "considerable period" sentiment—even interpreted as an event-based commitment—was becoming the victim of the recovery, one that they believed was so robust that the "resource slack" was likely to decline appreciably over the next few quarters, notwithstanding the still elevated productivity growth. In December, the Committee clarified the meaning of the phrase, making explicit that it was an event-based commitment. Then, in January 2004, it dropped the language altogether, substituting "With inflation quite low and resource use slack, the Committee believes that it can be patient in removing its policy accommodation." What is the difference between "maintaining accommodation for a considerable period" and being "patient in removing accommodation"? As usual, the Committee left the markets to figure out the subtlety of this distinction.

The distinction, in my view, was the distinction between "maintaining accommodation" and "removing accommodation." The Committee was most of all moving to a position of greater flexibility, focusing the markets on the timing of the beginning of the tightening cycle rather than on how long policy would remain on hold. They were buying flexibility to tighten earlier, perhaps by the middle of 2004, if the incoming data and forecast suggested that this was appropriate. They did not know for sure whether such an early move would be necessary, but they wanted to position themselves to be able to pursue this course of action if appropriate—without concern that they had misled the markets.

The Committee moved in this direction as a result of what I call the "two gaps" story. The two gaps that monetary policymakers were focusing on were the gap between the unemployment rate and the NAIRU (or between actual and potential output) and the gap between the prevailing funds rate and its neutral value. We were miles away from a neutral rate, but the unemployment rate, at 5.7% at the time, was not that far from the NAIRU (which I believe the staff was estimating to be near 5%).

Under these circumstances, the Committee had to worry about remaining on hold too long and possibly getting to or beyond the NAIRU before even starting toward the neutral rate. Otherwise, inflation could begin to rise so quickly that it might blow by their implicit inflation target, at least without an extremely aggressive and therefore disruptive pace of increase in the funds rate.

Once again the Committee was scrambling to keep up with another turn in the economy. This time, at least, the signs were pointing toward a robust recovery.

11

LOOKING FORWARD

When I see my former colleagues these days, I sometimes joke: "I really envy you. You seem to be repeating the experience of the second half of the 1990s. Maybe you'll get it right this time!"

In fact, the present economy mirrors the economy of the second half of the 1990s in several ways. First, we are experiencing another remarkable surge in productivity—an average rate of growth of about 5% in 2002 and 2003. This is the highest two-year period of growth in productivity in almost forty years—and double the average rate of productivity growth in the second half of the 1990s (when we also celebrated a remarkable acceleration in productivity).

What makes the more recent productivity surge even more stunning is the fact that it has not come at a time of exceptional economic performance.[1] Instead, productivity climbed through the recession of 2001 (instead of declining, as is typical during recessions) and then soared during the first year and a half of the expansion (despite the fact that the expansion was less vigorous than expansions in the past). Like the productivity acceleration of the 1990s, this one is being accompanied by a decline in the rate of inflation.

It's déjà vu all over again: As in the late 1990s, we have faster-than-expected growth and lower-than-expected inflation. This brings around a familiar debate: Will such rapid growth and declining unemployment rates trigger an early tightening of rates? Or will the lower-than-expected rate of inflation, due to the powerful disinflationary effect of the productivity acceleration, convince the FOMC to delay a tightening? Finally, will this acceleration, because of its effect on the neutral real interest rate, eventually demand a greater cumulative amount of tightening? You can be sure the FOMC is discussing these issues.

Equity prices are also surging again, and that's another similarity between now and the second half of the 1990s. In 2003, the Dow rose almost 25% and the NASDAQ by over 50%. Growth is robust. Profits are soaring. "Animal spirits"—the willingness to take risks—are returning. Sound familiar?

It's premature to call this an emerging equity bubble. But another sharp rise in equity prices in 2004 would raise concerns. Will equities become overvalued and be subject either to a correction (as the staff predicted in the second half of the 1990s) or to "irrational exuberance" redux? There is at least a possibility that policymakers may face these questions once again, particularly in terms of the timing of a move to tighten policy. Those decisions will be as tough as ever.

—∞—

WHILE THE ECONOMY resembles the late 1990s in many ways, it's also different. And that muddles the picture considerably. In the second half of the 1990s, for instance, the productivity acceleration stimulated the demand side of the economy. Firms were driven to buy the capital goods that embodied the new technology, and consumers contributed to the spending boom as well. As a result, demand increased even more rapidly than supply and the labor market improved steadily.

Today, the productivity acceleration is driven by competitive pressures and a desire to cut costs. This has translated into a restraint on both hiring and investment. Thus, while demand and production are on a steeper trajectory than they were a year ago, this trajectory has not created more than a moderate increase in employment. Economists believe that higher productivity is a blessing—an opportunity to boost living standards. But the present productivity acceleration appears, for the moment, to be standing in the way of a more vigorous improvement in the labor markets.

If the rate of productivity slows from the extraordinary pace of recent quarters, as it is likely to, we should see an improvement in employment growth. In any case, for policymakers, this dynamic relationship among the productivity acceleration, aggregate demand, and employment will significantly affect the timing of a possible tightening.[2]

There's another significant difference between now and the late 1990s. Then, the Committee believed that the federal funds rate was already a bit above its neutral value. Thus, policy was already positioned to slow the economy to trend and avoid a possible overheating. Today, the funds rate is dramatically below the neutral value. Thus—as the economy returns to full employment and inflation stabilizes and begins to rise—the FOMC must remove the stimulus that was appropriate in a weaker economy and when inflation was falling.

A third difference is that in the second half of the 1990s, inflation was above the FOMC's implicit target. The FOMC, therefore, had to be prepared to tighten preemptively to avoid a further increase in inflation. Today, inflation is well below the FOMC's implicit target and, as of this writing, appears to be stabilizing. As a result, the FOMC can be patient. It can wait longer for improvements in labor conditions before beginning to tighten.

But perhaps the biggest difference between today and the boom-and-bust period is that inflation today is very, very low, leaving less of a cushion to protect the economy against the possibility of deflation. In the late 1990s, we also had declining inflation. But the disinflation was mild. Core inflation (measured by the twelve-month inflation rate for the core CPI) declined from 2½% in mid-1996 to about 2% in late 2002. This was still at or above the FOMC's implicit target. But today, core CPI inflation is just a shade above 1%—well below the implicit target.

While the economy is closer to deflation today than previously, the Committee, interestingly, has begun to signal that it is no longer as concerned about deflation. This reflects two considerations.

First, it reflects the Committee's confidence in the strength of the recovery. This has reduced the risk that the economy may slip into deflation. Second, the Committee apparently no longer fears deflation as much as it had earlier indicated, when, for example, it worried that the U.S. economy might slip into the kind of deflation recently suffered by Japan.

The Committee now recognizes that while some deflationary periods are damaging, others, historically, have been marked by favorable performance. During the period between 1873 and 1890, for instance, labor productivity rose by more than 2.5% a year, considerably higher than the average rate over the previous hundred years. The gains in productivity came from a surge of investment in a range of new technologies, from the development of railroads to better methods of making steel.[3] There was even the invention of the telegraph, the Internet of its time. This period was marked by deflation—falling prices but, in general, a healthy economy.

From 1917 to about 1927, there was another spurt of productivity (an annual growth of about 3¾%), attributable to the automobile and overall gains in manufacturing. With this came another period of deflation, although, once again, the falling prices did not impair overall economic performance. For the most part, in fact, these earlier deflationary periods featured impressive economic gains.

The difference between good and bad deflationary periods generally turns on whether the source of the deflation is a positive supply shock or a negative demand shock. If the source is a negative demand shock—such as the collapse of the stock market and the fall in consumer and business confidence during the Great Depression—then the deflation is likely to be accompanied by weak growth and a possible spiral of deepening debt. If the source of the deflation is a positive supply shock—such as the technology and capital-infusion-driven productivity gains of the late 1880s and of the 1920s—then the deflation is likely to be accompanied by good economic performance.

Given the robust growth in our current economy, and the improving labor market, I believe the chances of deflation in the next few years are relatively low. But if we did slip into deflation, would economic performance be more like that of Japan, with a long period of stagnation, or more like the deflationary periods of the late 1800s and 1920s in the United States, which were accompanied by quite favorable economic performance?

This is still an open question. In today's economy, we have both the legacy of a negative demand shock (the slack in the labor market and very low inflation and interest rates caused by the bursting of our equity bubble) and a positive supply shock (the further productivity acceleration). With both forces in play, predicting how a period of deflation might affect the economy is difficult.

Of course, no central bank would want to risk deflation, even in its most benign form: Even if a positive productivity shock was driving the deflation, the federal funds rate could still end up at zero. In that case, monetary policymakers would not be able to respond, at least with conventional policy, should an adverse demand shock suddenly arise. Such a situation could rapidly turn a benign deflation into a pernicious one.

IN ADDITION TO the possible issues of deflation, the Fed will be dealing with the issue of its own transparency. In fact, I used my last statement as a member of the FOMC to set out a series of improvements in transparency that I hoped the Committee would consider.

The two most important steps, in my view, are a more timely release of the FOMC's minutes and the adoption of an explicit, numerical inflation target.

The minutes provide a frank and revealing account of the discussions within the FOMC. They help the public understand how the Committee views recent economic developments and where it is leaning, in terms of changes in monetary policy. Today, there is about a six-week delay. The information is stale and of limited use by then. If the release time could be shortened to two weeks, the markets would benefit from this timely insight into the Committee's thinking.[4]

Second, the FOMC should adopt an inflation target, an explicit numerical objective for inflation. This would allow the Fed to be clearer in communicating its objectives—and more accountable for its actions.[5] Furthermore, it would also "institutionalize" the Chairman's commitment to price stability, ensuring the continuation of a disciplined monetary policy after Greenspan.[6] Inflation targets are a well-tested idea: The central banks of New Zealand, the United Kingdom, Canada, Sweden, and many other nations use them.[7]

At the July 1996 FOMC meeting, a majority of the Committee

agreed that a 2% inflation rate was consistent with its "price stability" mandate. But the Committee did not agree to set policy based on a 2% inflation target. Nor was there any discussion about the possibility of announcing the 2% inflation rate as the FOMC's official numerical target. One reason the Committee did not go further in this direction, at that time, was the Chairman's opposition to the idea.[8]

What is my view on inflation targets? On the one hand, you could say that we have already achieved price stability in the United States, even without an explicit numerical target. On the other hand, I believe that adopting an explicit numerical inflation objective would increase the transparency and accountability of U.S. monetary policy. It would, therefore, be a step toward a "best practice" in central banking.

But this issue is more complex than that. Where "inflation targeting" is practiced around the world, it is generally within what is called a "hierarchical mandate." The hierarchical mandate makes price stability a priority. Other objectives, such as full employment, can generally be pursued only after price stability has been achieved.[9]

A hierarchical mandate is very different—in spirit and in practice—from the Fed's mandate.[10] The Fed has a "dual mandate," set by Congress, to address inflation and full employment equally. The Congress has not ranked one objective (employment or inflation) over the other. So the Fed is left to balance the two, resolving any short-run conflicts.

While there is a strong case for adopting a numerical inflation target, I'm quite sure the Congress would not accept a down weighting of the Fed's present commitment to full employment implicit in a hierarchical mandate. Nor should it. The Fed has had great success in managing the economy under the dual mandate regime, including success in achieving price stability. This is the role the Fed should play—by keeping both objectives in mind.

That said, let me suggest a middle ground—an intermediate regime that would blend the best of the U.S. regime and that of the typical "inflation targeting" regime. Under this intermediate regime, an explicit numerical inflation target would be announced—but executed under the Fed's commitment to a dual mandate.[11] This would increase the transparency of monetary policy in the United States while retaining the traditional objectives and maintaining continuity in the basic approach of American monetary policy.

If the objective is continuity, not change, the question becomes, Why bother? First, adopting an explicit numerical inflation target would increase both the transparency of monetary policy and the accountability of monetary policymakers in the United States. Second, it would, at the margin, likely enhance the ability of the Fed to anchor inflation expectations.[12] Third, it would improve the coherence of internal decision making at the FOMC—because the members of the Committee would now be shooting at the same target.

An inflation target is already being discussed and debated inside the Fed (as well as outside it).[13] Bernanke is the leading proponent on the FOMC of an explicit numerical objective for inflation.[14] For his part, the Chairman has made clear his opposition. Don Kohn has provided the most coherent set of arguments opposing an inflation target.[15] Merely by identifying an explicit inflation target, he warns, the Committee might alter the way it balances the full employment and price stability objectives. This could tilt the Committee's concerns more toward inflation and, thereby, in practice, lower its commitment to full employment.

Because of Greenspan's opposition to an inflation target, there will probably never be one while he is chairman. But when he departs, the issue is likely to be further discussed and debated. Perhaps, as I have suggested, the middle ground may provide the best answer.

—~—

WHEN WILL THE FOMC begin to tighten rates? Could the next move be an easing? I always give the same answer to questions like these: It depends! The answer depends on how the economy evolves in the coming months—how robust economic growth turns out to be, how well the growth in GDP translates into labor market improvements, and how inflation fares—whether it stabilizes, and at what rate, or moves upward, meekly or aggressively. Even the presidential election plays a part—making the beginning of the tightening cycle less likely immediately before or possibly immediately after the election.

It appears that growth is quite robust. The FOMC's latest forecast shows a "central tendency" for GDP growth in 2004 of 4½%–5%. Consumer spending seems resilient, investment spending is rebounding strongly, and a cyclical rebound in inventory investment appears under way.

How quickly will the robust pace of growth in real GDP translate into a more rapid pace of improvement in the labor market?[16] When will inflation begin to stabilize and turn upward? The answers depend on the balance between the growth in GDP and the underlying pace of productivity growth. The higher the growth in GDP (relative to the growth in productivity), the stronger the improvement in labor conditions. The stronger the improvement in labor conditions, in turn, the more quickly inflation will stabilize and begin to edge upward.

—w—

I BELIEVE THE ECONOMY has weathered the worst of the storm. We are putting the postbubble hangover behind us. But the legacy of the postbubble hangover—the very low and perhaps still declining inflation rate—remains with us. And we cannot forget the very low federal funds rate. This creates a continuing challenge for monetary policy.

Before the FOMC begins to tighten, the recovery must be strong enough to yield improvements in the labor market (which ultimately defines how healthy an expansion is) and inflation must at least stabilize. If, on the other hand, the economy slipped into deflation, the Fed should not tolerate it—even if the deflation was accompanied by favorable economic performance. The reason for this is that we don't want to risk the funds rate falling to the zero nominal bound. For all these reasons, the FOMC is likely to wait for some time before it begins to tighten.

But lingering too long at today's low interest rates—in an environment of improved profitability and an increased willingness to take risks—could begin to inflate equity prices. This could leave the Committee to grapple with another period of speculative excess. Overstaying the current policy posture could also force the FOMC to hike rates sharply, once it begins to tighten, to subdue inflation.

The election could also influence the timing of the first tightening move, discouraging the FOMC from changing rates in September, the meeting immediately preceding the election.

But other than the timing of the election, the first and subsequent tightenings will be determined by the pace of improvement in labor market conditions and the trend in core inflation.

Once the tightening cycle is under way, it is possible that the economy will get back to "normal"—if we can remember what that was. The talk of deflation, the zero nominal bound, and nonconventional policy will fade, the economy will adjust to the apparent further acceleration in productivity, and the tension between the strength in production and the weakness in employment will disappear. In this case, making monetary policy will become less exciting than it was during my term at the Fed.

But I wouldn't bet on it. The experience of the last decade suggests that we live in a rapidly changing economic environment, one with unpredictable shocks and challenges. If there's anything my former Fed colleagues won't have to worry about, it's boredom.

12

ALAN, I HARDLY KNEW YOU

Toward the end of my term, I was having lunch with Arthur Levitt, chairman of the Securities and Exchange Commission (SEC). As chair of the Board's banking committee, I often interacted with Levitt on regulatory issues that were of mutual interest to the Board and the SEC, and we got along very well. We had a wide-ranging discussion over lunch, partly about personal matters (families and so forth) and partly about our regulatory responsibilities. Toward the end of the lunch, Levitt asked me, "Larry, what's the Chairman really like?"

The question surprised me. After all, Levitt and the Chairman played golf together; I assumed they'd invited each other home for dinner. They undoubtedly had seen each other at the A-list parties that mere governors like me don't get to attend.

I responded, "Arthur, I've been here five years and I have never had a conversation like this with the Chairman." I knew I would be leaving the Board soon and that people would be asking me the same question for the rest of my life. But I wasn't sure I could tell Levitt anything that he didn't already know, because the fact was, on a personal level, I hardly knew the Chairman at all.

MY LIMITED KNOWLEDGE of Alan Greenspan the person reflects both the character of the Chairman and the nature of the Federal Reserve. And it reflects my personal decisions while at the Board as well.

The Federal Reserve Board is a pretty formal place. Governors see one another most often at Board and FOMC meetings, committee meetings, and meetings with advisory groups. These are highly structured events, for the most part, particularly the Board and FOMC meetings. Participants are introduced there as Governor, Mr. Chairman, or Mr. President. Discussions then circle the table in go-arounds, with little opportunity for casual exchanges.

Other than those meetings, the Chairman is not very visible. He doesn't take part in the committee meetings, in which the conversations are less formal, nor does he frequently seek out the governors for casual conversations. To be sure, early in my term, Greenspan did drop by my office (and that of the other governors) a week before the FOMC meetings to preview his recommendation for the upcoming FOMC meeting. In addition, I was asked over to his office on one occasion to talk about the economic outlook, and on several occasions I either visited him in his office or he visited me in mine—sometimes at his initiative and sometimes at mine—to talk about bank supervisory and regulatory topics. But he never sought me out for an informal chat.

This is not to say that Greenspan was unavailable or unwilling to talk. Whenever I took the initiative to see him, he never made me wait or feel that I shouldn't be occupying his time. He always greeted me warmly. And I always came away from our conversations admiring his insight and judgment. Still, something about the Chairman made me very efficient in the amount of his time that I expended. I rarely arrived with an issue that couldn't be explained in a few sentences—and answered in a matter of minutes.

I wouldn't call the Chairman a chatty person. He is a private person, someone who seems uncomfortable in a large group (particularly when the formal structure of the Board or FOMC meeting is missing). The irony is that Alan Greenspan is a very interesting person and a warm, wonderful conversationalist—who simply doesn't seem to like to have conversations. Once I realized this, I didn't take his manner as arrogance or an absence of appreciation for others. It was simply his way.

I also began to realize that a certain space between myself and the

Chairman was probably beneficial. If we were to disagree on policy, as we sometimes did, better to vent ourselves before the full Board and the FOMC than to defuse our differences in private.

—∞—

OVER TIME, I have watched Greenspan evolve his distinctive approach to monetary policy. It begins with a commitment to lowering inflation to the point of price stability. This accomplishes a prime objective of his policymaking—anchoring long-term expectations about inflation. Greenspan believes that inflation expectations can best be achored by a history of having achieved price stability rather than by a mere promise to do so.

Once inflation expectations are anchored, the job of monetary policymaking is much easier. Should the economy suffer an adverse shock that threatens to increase inflation, for instance, the Fed's established commitment to low inflation would reassure businesspeople, consumers, and investors. This would reduce the chances for a self-reinforcing spiral of ever-rising inflation and inflation expectations, and give the Fed the opportunity to contain the damage and regain control.

Greenspan also believes in using monetary policy to counter adverse shocks that may pull the economy away from full employment. This position is not apparent to most observers—perhaps not even to Greenspan himself. The Chairman, after all, frequently waxes eloquent on the importance of price stability—and almost never on the role of monetary policy in encouraging full employment. Still, the Greenspan FOMC has always positioned itself to respond quickly to shocks that might threaten full employment. During my term, we saw the Greenspan FOMC respond in this way during the Asian crisis, Russia's devaluation, and the collapse of LTCM. Greenspan's emphasis on restoring full employment was also evident after the slowdown and recession that followed the bursting of the equity bubble.

The first two principles—anchoring inflation expectations and responding aggressively to departures from full employment—may appear to be somewhat contradictory. Policymakers who emphasize price stability, for example, may be reluctant to push the economy aggressively back to full employment, fearing a rise in inflation if they overshoot full employment. Conversely, policymakers who emphasize full employment may not make lowering inflation a priority, particularly if the attempt to lower inflation would require pushing the economy below full employment for a while.

The Chairman, however, sees full employment and price stability as being mutually reinforcing, not contradictory. Maintaining price stability, for example, reduces the risk of an overheated economy, which could lead to higher inflation, sharply tighter monetary policy, and the possibility of a recession. If policymakers start from price stability, on the other hand, they have the freedom to react aggressively should the economy weaken and unemployment begin to rise. Having anchored inflation expectations, they don't have to worry that their aggressive stimulus might dislodge those expectations.

In effect, the Chairman has created the best of all possible worlds for himself: He appears to be a hawk in terms of inflation (by building credibility for his commitment to price stability and anchoring inflation expectations). But when facing adverse shocks to aggregate demand and employment, he acts like a dove.

FLEXIBILITY AND PRAGMATISM are additional components of Greenspan's vision. As a forecaster and a policymaker, he has learned that the economy's behavior is often both unpredictable and inexplicable. In the latter half of the 1990s, this was certainly the case: Greenspan felt that something unusual was under way, and he identified it as an acceleration in productivity. From there, he crafted a monetary policy that addressed both the uncertainties surrounding the definition of full employment and the relationship between the unemployment rate and inflation.

Greenspan calls this his "risk management" approach to monetary policy.[1] Under this approach, he has urged policymakers to expand their horizons to the full "probability distribution" of outcomes rather than limiting their focus to the outcome that seems most likely. This approach was evident in the FOMC's response to 9/11 as well as in the Committee's reaction to the dramatic decline in inflation in 2002 and 2003.

In the case of 9/11, the FOMC eased more aggressively than justified by the baseline forecast. This reflected the view that the downside risks were so large that it was prudent to take out some "insurance" against them. If the insurance proved unnecessary—if the downside risks did not materialize—it could always be withdrawn, given the flexibility of monetary policy and its ability to change direction quickly.

In the case of the disinflation of 2002 and 2003, the lessons of the Japanese struggle with deflation (following the bursting of their equity bubble) suggested that the United States itself faced an asymmetric risk of slipping into a self-reinforcing deflationary spiral. In this case, even if the chance of a decline in inflation was about equal to the chance of a rise in inflation, the damage caused by a further decline could be so great that policymakers would be wise to take out some protective insurance. Once again, it was the asymmetric risks—rather than the most likely outcome—that determined policy. For this reason, the FOMC cut rates by more than what the baseline forecast suggested.

So while the Chairman's vision for monetary policy—anchoring inflation expectations and responding aggressively to departures from full employment—is fully consistent with the Taylor rule, his risk management approach emphasizes that fixed formulas must sometimes make way for more flexible approaches. As a result, while the Chairman is willing to play by the rules in normal times, he does not hesitate to depart from them in unusual circumstances.

A FINAL COMPONENT of the Greenspan playbook is not endorsed by most economists, nor, I expect, is it accepted by most of the members of the Committee—or by me. Unlike most of us, Greenspan believes that monetary policy has a significant influence on long-term economic performance. He believes there is a strong link between price stability and higher productivity growth—so much so that the achievement of price stability would also raise the economy's maximum sustainable growth. According to this conviction, the only way that companies can increase their profit margins (when they do not have pricing power) is by lowering costs. To do so, the firms would most likely have to innovate and invest in new technology.

The more widely held view is that long-term economic growth, at least in periods of modest inflation, is determined by population growth, the pace of innovation, and other factors beyond the control of the Fed.[2] For example, I do not believe that the Fed's effort to reduce inflation was somehow responsible for the wave of innovation that propelled the acceleration of productivity in the second half of the 1990s.

YOU MIGHT NOT EXPECT to find the words *Greenspan* and *transparency* in the same sentence. The Chairman has certainly earned a reputation for his oblique public pronouncements. I believe he is not only well aware of this reputation, but actually enjoys cultivating it. One Congressman, receiving a typically convoluted answer from Greenspan during congressional testimony, thanked the Chairman for his answer and said he believed he now understood the Chairman's position. Greenspan quickly replied, "If that's the case, then I must have misspoken."

Still, there has been a remarkable increase in the transparency of monetary policy during the Greenspan years. Just consider how obscure the FOMC was before Greenspan, when the FOMC didn't even admit it had a target for the federal funds rate and did not publicly announce any changes in its target.

Recall that the policy directives, even when I arrived at the FOMC, described policy decisions in terms of maintaining the existing degree of reserve restraint (for an unchanged funds rate) or increasing the degree of reserve restraint (for an increase in the funds rate target). In addition, before Greenspan, there were no statements immediately following the meetings that identified the changes in the federal funds target, much less explaining the reasoning behind those decisions.

Today, the public is informed immediately about any change in the FOMC's target for the federal funds rate. Furthermore, the FOMC provides a statement after each meeting that offers at least a brief rationale for its decision. The statements today also include the Committee's assessment of the balance of risks relative to the outlook, which provide a signal as to whether or not the Committee is leaning in the direction of a near-term policy move or not.

—∞—

DESPITE MY ADMIRATION for the Chairman, I've had a few bones to pick with him as well. One deep disagreement (and continuing source of frustration) is Greenspan's propensity to speak out on issues that are beyond the authority of the Federal Reserve, including those that are politically contentious. This is especially true with respect to fiscal policy.

I see several problems in that. First, I believe the Chairman shouldn't insert himself and the Fed into political debates over the direction of fiscal policy. The Fed cherishes its independence. That means the Fed should expect the administration and Congress to leave monetary policy to the FOMC. Both the Clinton and the Bush administrations have disciplined themselves not to discuss monetary policy. While Congress does, on occasion, share its views on monetary policy with the Fed—and members of Congress sometimes write strongly worded letters urging the Fed either to ease or to refrain from tightening—Congress never infringed on the FOMC's decision-making authority during my term.

I think there should be a quid pro quo—if the administration keeps its nose out of the Fed's business, the Fed will keep its nose out of the administration's business. But I always feared that by inserting himself into the political debate about fiscal policy, the Chairman might encourage others in government to reciprocate by meddling in monetary policy. Fortunately, that never happened.

Second, I feel that the Chairman's willingness to participate in the fiscal policy debate sometimes left the public confused. Was the Chairman speaking for himself, or was he speaking for the FOMC? This was particularly the case when the Chairman presented to Congress his semiannual testimony on monetary policy. That testimony is supposed to convey the FOMC's views about the outlook, its rationale for recent policy decisions, and considerations that will influence the Committee's conduct of policy in the months ahead.

The Chairman is certainly free to offer his personal perspectives along the way, but he should be speaking for the FOMC at these hearings, not for himself. Many times, the Chairman did explicitly say, as he turned to fiscal policy issues, that he was now speaking for himself and not for the Committee. But I always felt that there was still some public confusion as to whether the Chairman was speaking for himself or for all of us.

Third, I felt that the Chairman's willingness—indeed, eagerness—to discuss contentious political issues encouraged many Congressmen on the monetary policy oversight committees to try to get him to say something, anything, that might support their views on fiscal policy (or on any other contentious political issue unrelated to the conduct of monetary policy). Sometimes I felt that the Chairman and the committee members were co-conspirators in using the hearings for purposes other than the discussion of monetary policy.

In my opinion, the Chairman should restrict his testimony before the monetary policy oversight committees to issues relating to the economic outlook and monetary policy. If Congress wants the Chairman's personal views on fiscal policy, then the appropriate committees should call on him to testify, but not on behalf of the FOMC.

The Chairman's handling of FOMC meetings is another concern. When I joined the Board, the two-day meetings always included the opportunity to discuss longer-term policy issues. In July 1996 and July 1997, for example, we had two interesting discussions on the topic of price stability.

By my third year, however, these special topics had disappeared from the agenda. I can only surmise that the Chairman didn't want them on the agenda anymore, perhaps because he saw them tilting the Committee in the direction of an explicit inflation target. Toward the end of my term, a number of Reserve Bank presidents finally asked Greenspan to renew these discussions, and he obliged. But I felt that the absence of these discussions during the greater part of my term was a lost opportunity. We could have used these discussions to focus the Committee's energies on longer-run strategy issues, perhaps contributing to further enhancements in the transparency of monetary policy and further improvements in the conduct of monetary policy.

To be truthful, I was also frustrated by the disproportionate power the Chairman wielded over the FOMC. While I respected his judgment and leadership, I had envisioned a greater opportunity to make a difference than I believe I had. I'm not suggesting that I was ignored or that the rich discussions inside the Committee room of which I was part did not influence policy. But the Chairman exercised such disproportionate power that unless you could sway him over to your point of view, your view was not going to prevail.

—~—

THIS IS A GOOD TIME for you to ask, perhaps, whether I ever wanted to become Chairman and ever thought I had a shot at it. The answer is simple: Yes and no. As a lifelong student of monetary policy, as an award-winning forecaster, and as a member of the FOMC, I think I could be excused if, yes, I dreamed occasionally, even continuously, of becoming Chairman of the Federal Reserve System.

For someone of my experience, it is without question the best job in the world—even better than playing second base for the Dodgers. So I have to admit to those dreams. But I also realized, from the time I joined the Fed, that the timing of Greenspan's term and my own effectively shut me out of the game.

My first opportunity could have been in 2000, when Greenspan's term was up. But I was quite certain that President Clinton would prefer Greenspan to me, and I probably would have made the same pick. But even if Clinton had wanted to replace Greenspan, I was certain that I would not be his choice. For one, Clinton knew I believed in hiking interest rates to keep the economy from overheating. The President didn't (this was evident in his interest in nominating Felix Rohatyn). For another, I would have had less than two years remaining on my term at the end of Greenspan's term. Even if Clinton chose to replace Greenspan, I was sure he would select someone who could serve a full four-year term as Chairman.

This realization was actually liberating. I didn't have to worry about whether or not the administration or Congress liked my speeches or my votes. I could do the best job possible and, when I returned to the private sector, look back at what had been a wonderful experience.

I think the staff recognized the freedom I had secured. They particularly appreciated my style in testifying, which was to pull no punches. Toward the end of the term, for instance, the Chairman asked me to represent the Board at a hearing about the wealth effect. Greenspan had been asked to testify but was also afforded the opportunity to delegate the task to another member of the Board.

It seemed clear that the testimony was really an opportunity to grill the Chairman about prebubble and postbubble monetary policy. In fact, the chairman of the subcommittee had a reputation for being very critical and, indeed, hostile toward Greenspan.

So when the staff showed up to discuss what my testimony would be, they asked me why Greenspan had tapped me. I joked that it was either because of his respect for me as an economist and monetary policymaker—or because he didn't like me and was, therefore, sending me to testify at what was going to be an unpleasant hearing. The staff suggested another motive: Perhaps Greenspan didn't like the subcommittee chairman and was sending the ultimate weapon. They smiled momentarily, imagining my sharp response to the subcommittee chairman's attacks. Then, regaining their composure, they suggested how I might deal with a hostile situation. In the end, however, they concluded that if their strategy didn't work, "just let Larry be Larry."

MY DECISION NOT TO SEEK reappointment had nothing to do with Greenspan. I would have happily served longer under Greenspan. But it was my time to go.

When governors leave the Fed they get a party, and mine was a memorable one. There were plenty of jokes about me and my well-known shortcomings, but they were offered with a warmth that I often felt was lacking in the formalities of the Board. The Chairman offered me many kind words.

Governors always receive a number of departing gifts, some more humorous than others. The Steuben eagle now sits on my living room mantel, a reminder of my service on the Board and the FOMC. The flag of the Federal Reserve System (yes, we have a flag, but I promise there are no parades) stands tall in my office at CSIS. The chair from the boardroom (with my name, of course, on a plaque on the back) adorns my office at home.[3] A framed set of dollar bills—one from each district, signed by the president of the respective Federal Reserve Bank—hangs on the wall above the desk in my home office.

But my favorite gift is from the staff: a bound five-volume set of all the speeches I gave while on the Board. It came in a bookcase, with the title "LONG Meyer Speeches."[4] I have to admit, I had a tendency to write very long speeches that took the staff a lot of time to review and edit. We all had a good laugh about this gift. Today it sits on my bookshelf in my office at CSIS—reminding me both of the challenges I confronted and the extraordinary efforts of the staff to support my efforts during my term at the Fed.

The day before my term was up, I scheduled a meeting with the Chairman. I kidded his secretary that I needed Greenspan to give me my PMP (performance evaluation procedure), a review that is actually required of everyone but the governors. The Chairman was waiting for me in his office just down the hall from mine. As I went in, I noticed that Greenspan's desk was cluttered, as though reflecting the intensity of his work. It reminded me a little of my desk, although his did not quite match my standards for office chaos.

It was a quiet, reflective conversation. I sat on the couch and the Chairman in a nearby chair. Greenspan made it clear how much he respected me for what I had brought to the Board. I told him how much I had enjoyed being a member of the Board and working with him. One regret, I said, was that we hadn't had as much time together—like this—as I would have liked. Greenspan smiled and nodded sympathetically, but I think he actually savored his distance from the rest of us.

We talked about some of the challenges we had faced together—the bull market, the bubble, the crises overseas, and the sobering collapse of the markets. We laughed about our differences in style—how he preferred to communicate with the staff through memos, while I enjoyed convening them in my office for a high-volume debate; how his testimonies could soothe the wildest soul, while mine tended to pour fuel on the fire. Greenspan was warm and relaxed, a charming conversationalist. It was exactly the kind of personal conversation that I had expected when I had joined the Board.

We had a photograph taken of the two of us that afternoon, standing in his office. It's up on my office wall at home now. It's one of many memories that I have of my term at the Fed.

APPENDIX

Figure 1:
POTENTIAL GDP AND ACTUAL GDP

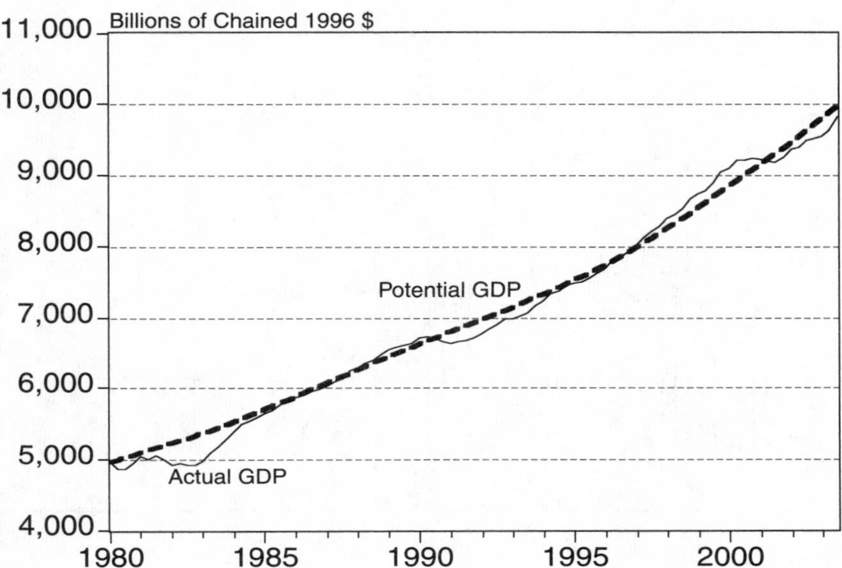

Potential Gross Domestic Product (GDP) is a measure of the economy's maximum sustainable output, the maximum output that can be sustained without rising inflation. Potential output rises over time at a rate that reflects the growth of hours worked (and hence the growth in population and specifically the labor force) and the growth in labor productivity. The slope of the potential output line steepens after the mid-1990s, a reflection of the implications of the productivity acceleration for the rate of growth of potential output.

A soft landing occurs when output, beginning from a position below potential, moves up to and then grows just at the rate of potential, as occurred in 1995 and 1996.

When output grows faster than potential, as in the second half of the 1990s, the level of output rises relative to potential, and in this case it rose above the potential level. That indicates a situation of excess demand, likely to result in overheating and higher inflation. After the slowdown and recession, the level of output slipped below potential in 2001. As growth picked up again in the second half of 2003, the economy has been gradually closing the gap between actual and potential output.

Source: Bureau of Economic Analysis and Congressional Budget Office

Figure 2:
GROWTH RATE OF REAL GDP

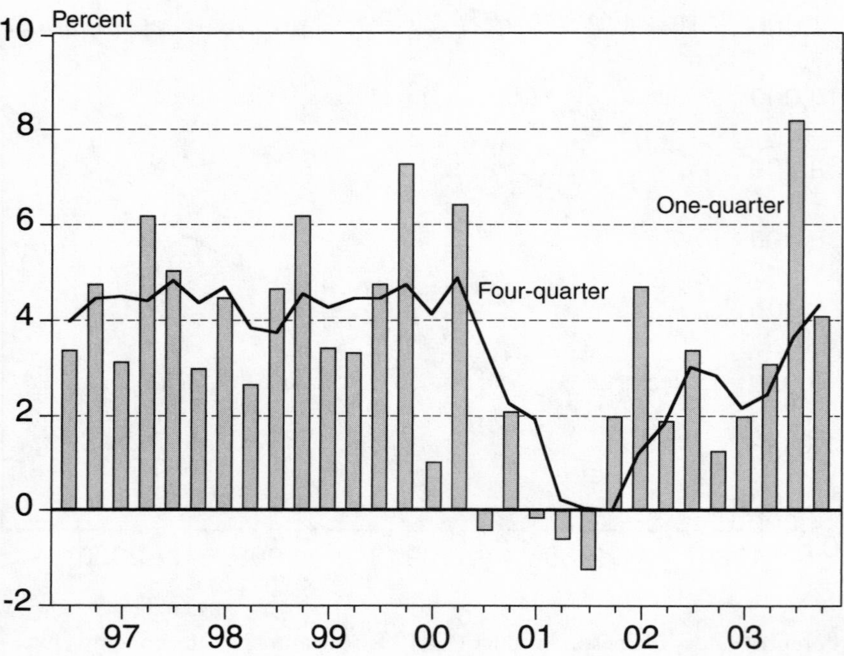

The growth of GDP was in the 4%–5% range for most of the second half of the 1990s. This robust rate of growth reflected the faster rate of growth of productivity and, hence, potential output growth. But actual output consistently grew more rapidly than potential, resulting in the steady decline in the unemployment rate to a low of 3.8% in April 2000. After the bursting of the equity bubble, real GDP growth slowed sharply in the second half of 2000, and the economy slipped into recession in 2001 and grew at a subpar rate during the first couple of years of the expansion. Growth finally rebounded strongly in the second half of 2003.

Source: Bureau of Economic Analysis

Figure 3:
CORE CPI INFLATION

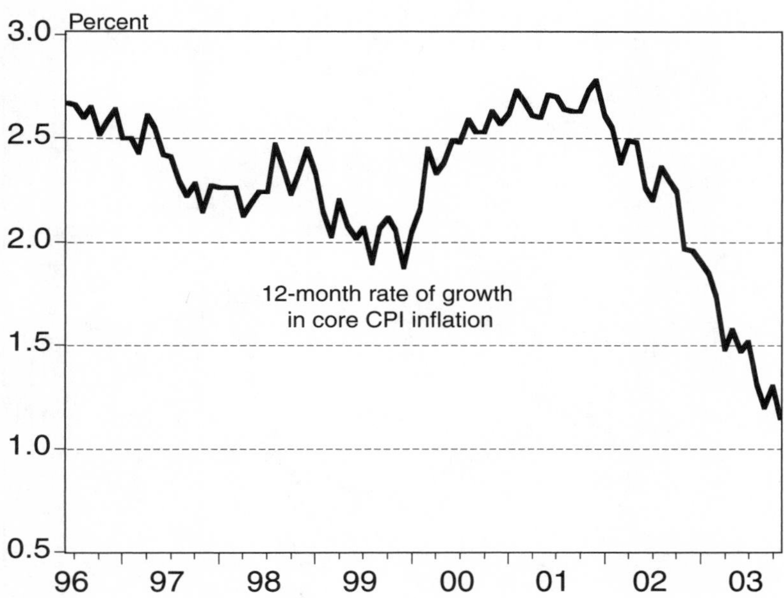

This chart depicts the 12-month inflation rate for the core measure of the Consumer Price Index (CPI). When I arrived at the board, core CPI inflation was running a bit above the level the Committee associated with price stability. Despite robust growth and a decline in the unemployment rate, core inflation fell steadily through the end of 1999, reaching about 2%. Thereafter, core CPI inflation rose to about 2¾% in 2001. This rise appeared to justify the concerns about an overheated economy when the FOMC began to tighten in mid-1999. The slowdown, recession, and long period of disappointing growth after the bursting of the asset bubble, combined with surprisingly strong productivity growth, resulted in a dramatic decline in core inflation, to near 1% at the end of 2003.

Source: Bureau of Labor Statistics

Figure 4:
THE UNEMPLOYMENT RATE AND THE NAIRU

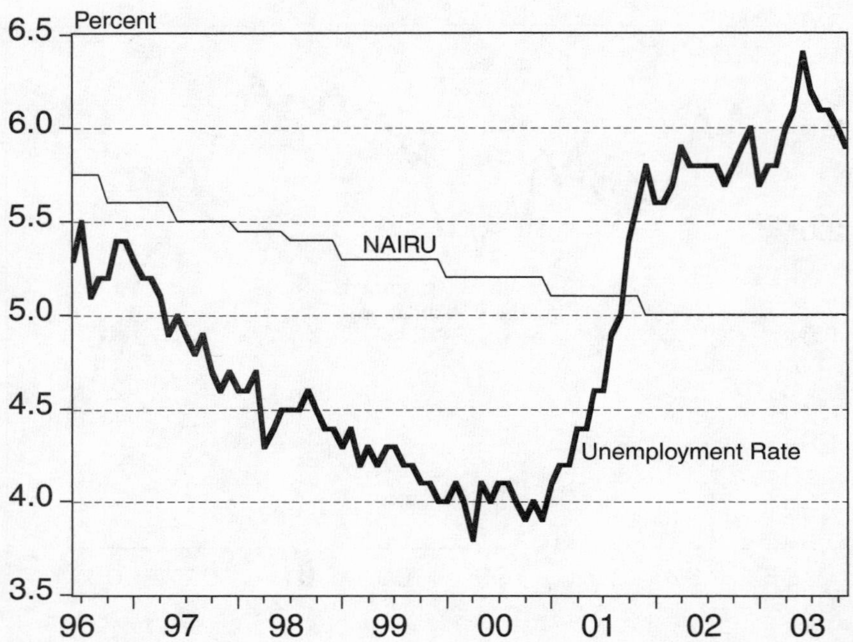

I use an estimate of the NAIRU of 5¾% in mid-1996, the estimate the staff was using when I arrived at the Board. I assume that the NAIRU then gradually declined to 5%. The unemployment rate fell from 5½% when I arrived at the Board and FOMC to a low of 3.8% and remained at about a 4% rate from late 1999 through early 2000. One of the puzzles of the period was the failure of inflation to rise despite a decline in the unemployment rate to a level below prevailing estimates of the NAIRU. The most likely explanation is a temporary decline in the short-run or effective NAIRU (relative to its longer-run average plotted here) as a result of the disinflationary effect of the productivity acceleration.

Source: Bureau of Labor Statistics and my estimate of the NAIRU

Figure 5:
THE FEDERAL FUNDS RATE TARGET

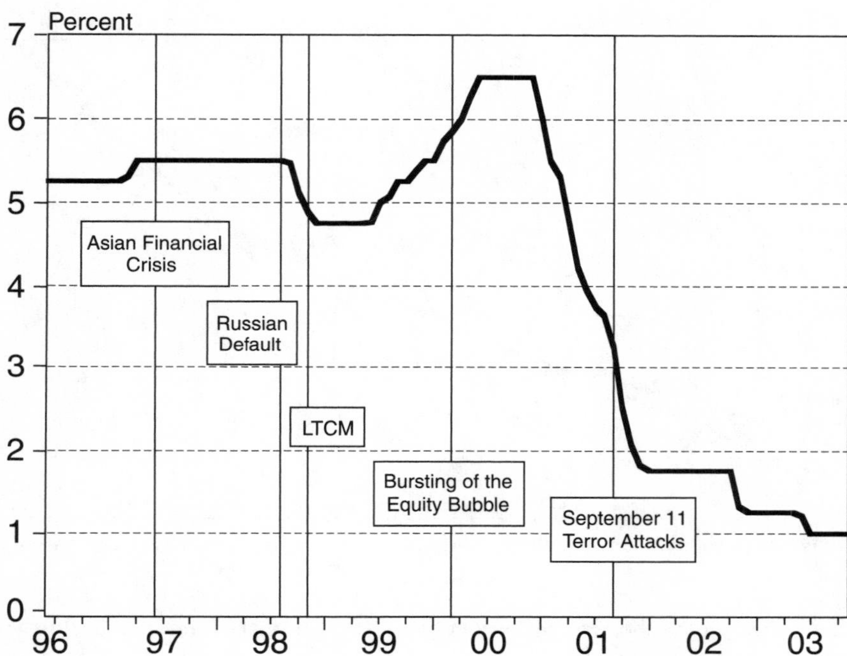

The FOMC raised the funds rate ¼ percentage point in March 1997, the only move from mid-1996 until the fall of 1998, when the FOMC began its three-step 75-basis-point cut in response to global financial turbulence related to the Russian default and devaluation and the implosion of LTCM. The FOMC raised the funds rate 175 basis points from June 1998 through May 2000, in a pre-emptive effort to stave off an overheated economy. The FOMC then began to cut rates on January 2001, as the economy was sliding toward recession, and ended up cutting rates thirteen times, by a cumulative 550 basis points, to 1% by June 2003.

Source: Federal Reserve Board

Figure 6:
IT'S PRODUCTIVITY, STUPID!

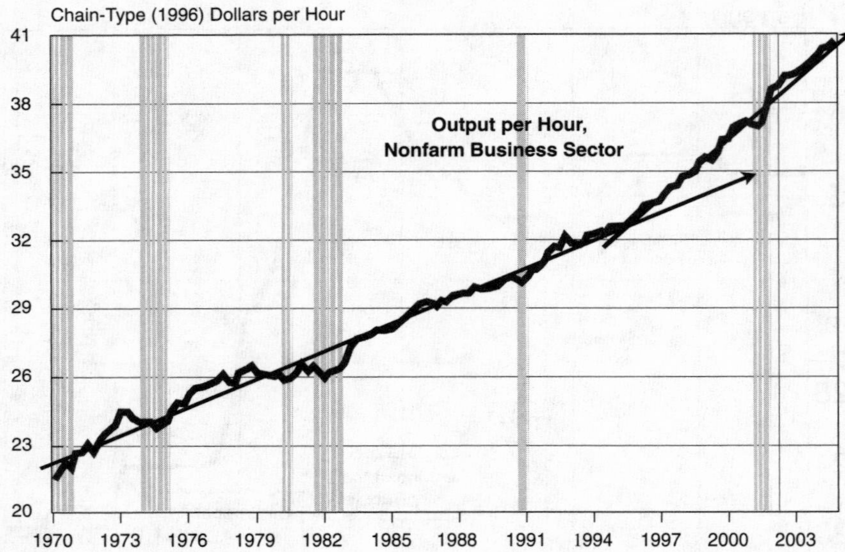

This chart shows the level of "productivity" (nonfarm labor productivity) from 1970 to 2003 and identifies the "productivity acceleration" in the second half of the 1990s. The slope of the two lines shows the average rate of growth in productivity before and after the acceleration—the steeper line after the mid-1990s shows the higher rate of productivity growth in the second half of the 1990s (and beyond), compared with the earlier period.

Source: Bureau of Labor Statistics

Figure 7:
THE P/E RATIO FOR THE S&P 500

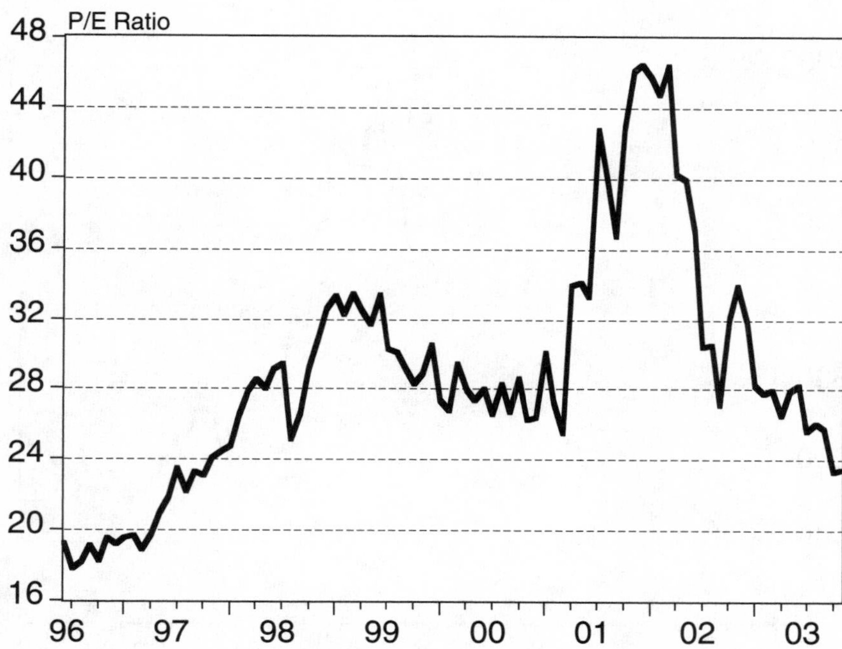

The Price-Earnings (P/E) Ratio was initially around 18 when I arrived at the Board and when the Chairman made his "irrational exuberance" remark in December 1996. That is above the 14–15 level that is the long-term historical average for the P/E, but below the low 20s level that many today believe is a better measure of long-term fair value for equities. The P/E ratio rose in 1997 and then through 1999, reaching a peak of over 32—dramatically above any reasonable estimate of long-term value. It then declined to a low of about 25 by mid-2001. The rise immediately, thereafter, reflects a common pattern of rises in the P/E ratio during cyclical downturns as earnings fall very sharply relative to the value of equities. By late 2003, as profits were recovering, the P/E ratio declined to below 24, still a bit rich by historical comparisons.

Source: Standard and Poor's

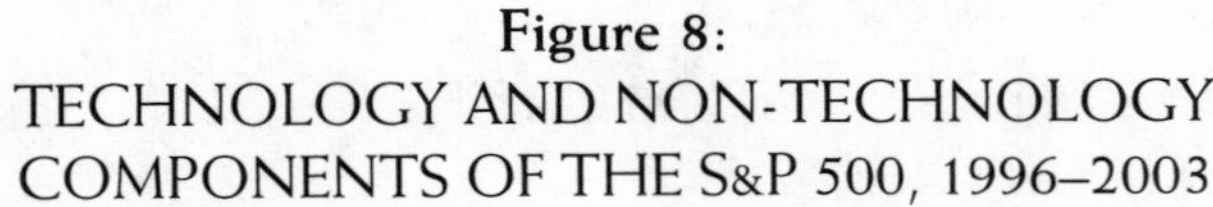

Figure 8:
TECHNOLOGY AND NON-TECHNOLOGY COMPONENTS OF THE S&P 500, 1996–2003

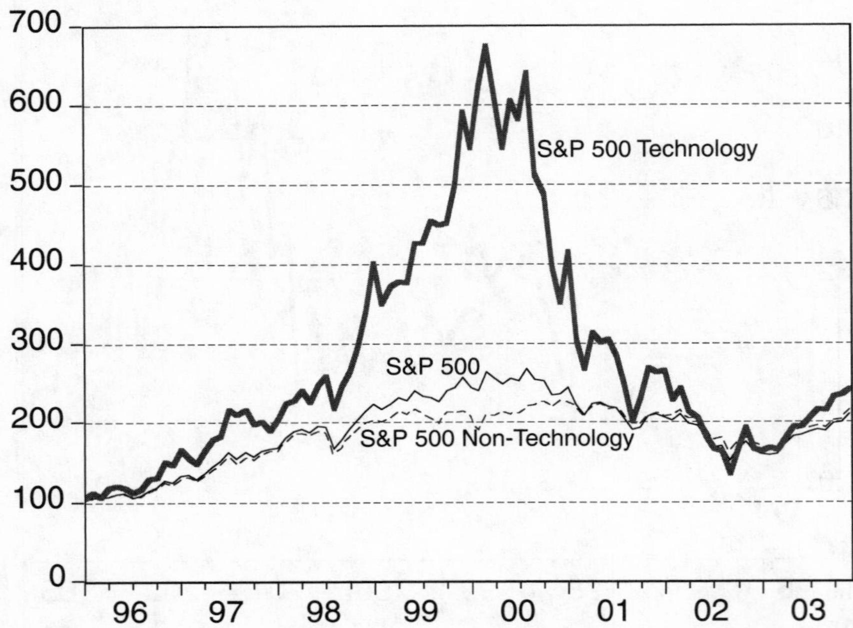

There was an equity bubble, but it was concentrated in the technology sector. The chart shows a broad index for equity prices (based on the S&P 500) and decomposes that index into its technology and non-technology components. From the end of 1995, the overall market and the non-technology component increased 167% and 127%, respectively, to their peaks. The technology component, in contrast, rose 574% during the same period. The overall and non-technology component declined peak to trough by 44% and 29%, respectively, while the technology component declined by 80%. Thus, the technology component met the Greenspan test for a bubble—falling by more than 40%—but the non-technology sector did not.

Source: Standard and Poor's for S&P 500 and Jeremy Seigel for decomposition components

Figure 9:
PRODUCTIVITY GROWTH: THE LONG VIEW

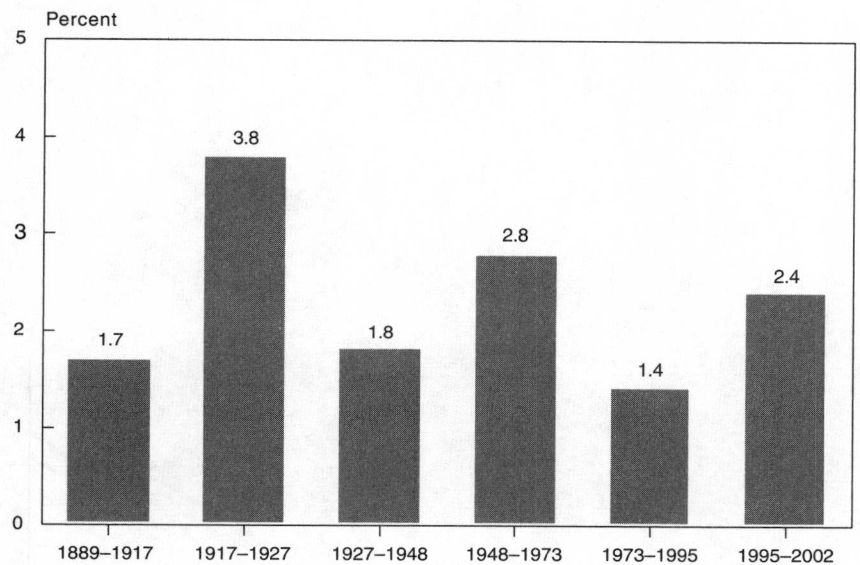

The chart shows intervening periods of slower and then faster productivity growth. The periods tend to be about twenty to twenty-five years on average. High-growth periods feature about 3% productivity growth and low-growth periods about 1½%. I interpret the second half of the 1990s as just another high-productivity period.

Source: Through 1947, the data are from Kendrick (1961). From 1947 forward, the data are from the Bureau of Labor Statistics.[1]

NOTES

PREFACE

1. Laurence H. Meyer, "Come with Me to the FOMC," Federal Reserve Board, April 2, 1998. I borrowed the title of this paper from a pamphlet written by Edward A. Wayne, a former president of the Federal Reserve Bank of Richmond, in 1951.
2. In addition, no two governors can be drawn from the same Federal Reserve district.
3. Irving Fisher wrote a simple identity to get the point across: MV = PQ, where M is the money supply, V is "velocity," P is the price level, and Q is the level of output. Velocity is the ratio of the money supply to nominal income (output measured at current prices). In the long run, this is determined by institutional features of the economy and tends to be constant or to increase at a relatively stable rate. Let's treat it as a constant. The level of output is independent of the money supply in the long run, determined by the growth of population and increases in our knowledge about production. In this case, P will be proportional to M, and the rate of inflation will be equal to the rate of money growth. See Irving Fisher, *Elementary Principles of Economics* (New York: MacMillan Company, 1912).
4. For a brief period from 1979 to 1982, the Committee did focus more directly on money growth, but it soon became apparent that the relationship between money growth and inflation had become much less stable, making control of the monetary aggregates less useful as a way of conducting monetary policy. The FOMC therefore returned to its earlier practice of setting policy in terms of a target for the federal funds rate.

5. The Committee was required to report the ranges to Congress twice a year, at the time of the Chairman's semiannual monetary policy testimonies. The Committee would therefore review the ranges and decide on whether or not to adjust them at the two-day meetings that preceded these testimonies.
6. I believe that money growth, despite being less reliable as a guide to the effect of monetary policy on the economy than earlier, nevertheless can play a useful secondary role in the conduct of monetary policy, providing, at times, a warning that policy may be too stimulative or restrictive. For example, rapid money growth can, on occasion, provide a warning to reassess whether the current stance of monetary policy might be too stimulative. I discussed this view in "Does Money Matter," Federal Reserve Board, March 28, 2001.
7. There is also an administrative governor, a couple of Federal Reserve System–wide committees, including representation by a few Reserve Bank presidents along with some governors, and a number of other assignments, typically involving serving on committees with other regulators or representing the Board at various international forums.
8. The Taylor rule is named after John Taylor, a professor at Stanford when he introduced this rule and now Under Secretary of the Treasury for International Finance. See John B. Taylor, "Discretion vs. Policy Rules in Practice," *Carnegie-Rochester Conference Series on Public Policy,* 1993, pp. 195–214. Taylor initially specified the rule in an effort to summarize the policy responses that were effective in promoting the Fed's objectives of full employment and price stability. He later showed that the rule also does an excellent job of describing how the FOMC actually conducted policy.

INTRODUCTION

1. The data reported here correspond to what was available at the time, not the data that have been revised on many occasions since that time. For the most part, I try to use the data that were available at the time to understand the basis on which the FOMC was making its decisions.

1: GETTING THERE

1. John Cassidy, "Fleeing the Fed," *The New Yorker,* February 19, 1996.
2. John Berry, "At the Fed, a Power Struggle over Information," *The Washington Post,* July 8, 1996.
3. In addition to the qualitative discussion of the paths in the Greenbook, the Deputy Secretary of the FOMC, Norm Bernard, visited each member of the Board in advance of FOMC meetings to discuss the agenda, and he also provided a qualitative discussion of the paths of the funds rate, long-term bonds, and equity prices.

2: COME WITH ME TO THE FOMC

1. The Federal Reserve Act specifies the FOMC's objectives as price stability and maximum employment. "Price stability" is typically interpreted as a low, stable rate of inflation. "Maximum employment" has typically been interpreted by the FOMC as maximum "sustainable" employment, meaning the maximum level of employment sustainable without rising inflation. This is usually referred to as "full employment." With this definition, price stability and full employment can, in principle, be achieved simultaneously.
2. I am alluding of course, to the phrase William Greider used in his prize-winning history of the Fed, *Secrets of the Temple* (New York: Simon & Schuster, 1987).
3. The other presidents served as voting members of the Committee on a rotating basis for one-year periods every two or three years.
4. Monetary policy is implemented through open market operations, purchases and sales of government securities from the Fed's portfolio. When the Fed purchases bonds from the private sector, it injects reserves into the banking system. When it sells bonds, it withdraws reserves. The FOMC does not directly control the federal funds rate, but through open market operations it can generally keep the funds rate very close to its target. The manager of the system's portfolio, an officer at the Federal Reserve Bank of New York, oversees the conduct of open market operations.
5. Potential output is the economy's maximum sustainable level of output, the maximum level of output sustainable without upward pressure on inflation.
6. By full employment, we mean the maximum sustainable level of employment—that is, the maximum level of employment sustainable without rising inflation. This is equivalent to the minimum sustainable level of the unemployment rate, or the NAIRU.
7. Both energy and food prices are particularly vulnerable to sharp but transitory increases and decreases, so core inflation generally provides a better measure of the underlying momentum in inflation going forward.
8. English engineer A. W. Phillips developed this relationship between the inflation rate and the unemployment rate, based on his observations of unemployment rates and wage change in the United Kingdom between 1862 and 1957. A. W. Phillips, "The Relationship Between Unemployment and the Rate of Change in Money Wage Rates in the United Kingdom, 1862–1957," *Economica* 25 (November 1958). The relationship became known as the "Phillips curve." Economist Milton Friedman significantly refined the theory in 1968, when he noted that there was "a natural rate of unemployment," a level consistent with steady inflation. Milton Friedman, "The Role of Monetary Policy," *American Economic Review* 58 (March 1968). The natural rate of unemployment today is generally referred to as the NAIRU. For a thorough discussion of the relationship between inflation and

the unemployment rate, see Laurence H. Meyer, *Macroeconomics: A Model Building Approach* (Cincinnati: South-Western Publishing Co., 1980), chapter 18.

9. Some disparage the usefulness of such anecdotal reports, viewing them as unreliable "gossip." I always think of a quote I once heard, attributed to George Stigler, an economics professor at the University of Chicago for most of his career: "Data is just the plural of anecdote."
10. Such anecdotal information likely plays a more important role for the Fed than for other forecasters, in part because Reserve Bank presidents specialize in collecting such information and can be expected, over time, to learn to sort through the comments they receive and identify early signs of changes in the outlook. In addition, they might have access to higher-quality anecdotes than others, because firms will more candidly share information on their spending and hiring plans with the Fed than with others.
11. I am told that the presentations used to be more spontaneous and interactive. But this changed once the decision was taken to release the transcripts after five years. Committee members apparently want to make sure that their remarks, when read five years later, will be coherent and graceful. So most would write them down and read them. I quickly fell into the practice of doing the same.
12. This was one of the two two-day FOMC meetings each year. These preceded the Chairman's semiannual testimony on monetary policy before the Congress. It was typical at the two-day meetings to reserve a portion of the time to discuss a broader topic of monetary policy strategy, one not necessarily immediately related to the policy decision to be taken at that meeting.
13. The effect of changes in the federal funds rate on household and business spending occurs through the effect of these changes on the "real" federal funds rate. The real funds rate is the nominal funds rate less the expected rate of inflation. The expected rate of inflation is often proxied by the actual rate over the last year. If there is zero inflation, and expected inflation is zero, the lower limit for both the nominal and real federal funds rate is zero. If there is a 2% inflation rate, on the other hand, and expected inflation is 2%, the FOMC can drive the real federal funds rate to -2% if it lowers the nominal rate to its lower limit of zero.
14. When inflation is low, the average rate of increase in (nominal) wages will also be relatively low, leaving little room for adjustment in relative wages without some wages falling. However, the average rate of increase in wages also depends on the rate of increase in productivity. If productivity growth was relatively high, therefore, it would be less necessary to "grease the wheels" of the labor market with a higher inflation rate.
15. There was, however, an important area of ambiguity about the 2% inflation rate—precisely what measure of inflation did it apply to. Most members of the Committee appeared to be talking about the Consumer Price Index

(CPI), specifically the core measure of the CPI, which was running at about a 2½% rate at the time. The Chairman argued that the price index for Personal Consumption Expenditures (PCE) was the better measure of consumer prices. The core rate for this measure was running at about 2% at the time. My interpretation is that the consensus was for a 2% inflation rate for the core CPI and that, given the average differentials between these measures over the last few years, this would be consistent with a 1½% rate for the core measure of the PCE price index.

16. Before each meeting, the staff sent Committee members a chart showing the path of the funds rate consistent with the Taylor rule. This was a useful point of departure for some members in thinking about possible adjustments to the federal funds rate target. However, there was little explicit discussion about the Taylor rule in general and few references to the Taylor rule prescriptions for the funds rate during FOMC meetings.
17. Technically, the policy bias applied to the intermeeting period. Most members of the Committee, however, interpreted the bias as applying over the near term, perhaps over the course of the next couple of meetings.
18. Later in my term, the FOMC's "authorization of domestic open market operations" was amended to attach some conditions to intermeeting moves. It now reads: "Any such adjustment shall be made in the context of the Committee's discussion and decision at its most recent meeting and the Committee's long-run objectives for price stability and sustainable economic growth, and shall be based on economic, financial, and monetary developments during the intermeeting period. Consistent with Committee practice, the Chairman, if feasible, will consult with the Committee before making any adjustment." These guidelines were followed scrupulously by the Chairman during my term, including during the period before this language was explicitly introduced into the authorization.
19. This reflects the conventional understanding of the relationship between short-term and longer-term interest rates, often referred to as "the expectations theory" of long-term interest rates. This theory holds that long-term rates depend on current and expected future short-term rates. As expected, when future short-term rates change, the current long rate is immediately affected. Thus, by affecting expectations about future federal funds rates (future short-term interest rates), the FOMC can affect current long-term rates.
20. The staff forecast, in general, avoids any assumption about a change in the funds rate over the forecast horizon. That is, the staff forecast is generally based upon an assumption of a constant funds rate over the forecast period. In this way, the staff avoid appearing to recommend a policy direction to the Committee.
21. On those occasions where it appears clear that a constant funds rate would be greatly at variance with the Committee's objectives, the staff will generally incorporate into the forecast some judgment about the change in the

funds rate over the forecast horizon, though they will generally not assume that a policy change is made at the current meeting.

22. The neutral rate is usually expressed in terms of the real federal funds rate. A typical estimate of the neutral real federal funds rate is 3%. If inflation was 2% at the time, that would translate into a neutral value for the nominal funds rate of 5%.
23. The proposal is called a directive because it provides instructions to the manager of the system's portfolio about how he or she should conduct open market operations during the intermeeting period—specifically, to hit the target for the federal funds rate set by the Committee.
24. Today the language is clearer. The reference to reserve pressures has been replaced by an explicit statement about the federal funds rate target.
25. The woulds and mights have also become history, replaced by language about the way the Committee views the balance of risks to the forecast.
26. Each Monday, the Board reviews the requests by Reserve Banks for changes in the discount rate. Under the Federal Reserve Act, discount rate requests originate with the Federal Reserve Banks but have to be approved by the Board before they become effective.
27. This has a remarkable implication: The probability that a given member will dissent depends on his or her name! If your name begins with a low letter in the alphabet, like Broaddus, you are more likely to be the one to get to the red chair first, compared with, for example, Santomero—because other than the Chairman and the Vice Chairman, everyone else votes in alphabetical order.

3: HAWKS AND DOVES

1. James C. Cooper and Kathleen Madigan, "With Jobs Strong, Consumers Are Feeling Frisky," *BusinessWeek*, September 9, 1996, p. 31.
2. Isabelle Clary, "Rate Hike Request Reported: Eight of 12 District Banks Are Said to Have Appealed to the Fed to Raise the Discount Rate," *Philadelphia Inquirer*, September 18, 1996, p. C1 (Reuters byline).
3. Dean Foust, "Political Hardball Inside the Fed," *BusinessWeek*. September 30, 1996, p. 38.
4. Ibid., p. 31.
5. Usually, a decision to move the funds rate, particularly after there had been no moves for a while, would evolve over at least two meetings. The first meeting would begin to build the consensus, lean the Committee toward the policy action, perhaps with a move to an asymmetric directive, and give the Chairman and the Committee an opportunity to signal markets.
6. Matthew C. Quinn, "Dow Overcomes Jitters," *Atlanta Journal-Constitution*, January 17, 1997, p. 1E.
7. David Wessel, "When Fed Governor Talks, People Listen: But Do They

Hear?—How Hard Mr. Meyer Tries Not to Move Markets; Why He Failed Yesterday," *The Wall Street Journal,* April 25, 1997, p. A1.

8. At this point, statements were issued only when there was a change in the federal funds rate target. Today, statements are issued after every meeting.

4: TEMPORARY BLISS OR PERMANENT BLISS

1. "The Question Now: What's the Fed's Next Move?," *BusinessWeek,* April 7, 1997, p. 31.
2. This was often referred to as the "worker insecurity hypothesis" and was an explanation for the restrained rate of wage gains that the Chairman often relied upon. In addition to globalization, worker insecurity could be aggravated by an uptick in underlying productivity growth that allowed firms to produce the same output with fewer workers and hence, in the short term, might also threaten workers.
3. Lawrence Katz and Alan Krueger, "The High-Pressure U.S. Labor Market of the 1990s," *Brookings Papers on Economic Activity* 1 (1999): 1–87.
4. Katz and Krueger argued that a disproportionate number of those in prison would otherwise have been either out of the labor force or unemployed. The rise in the prison population was estimated to have reduced the NAIRU by one- to three-tenths.
5. An increase in the proportion of temporary workers in the labor force allows firms to avoid bottlenecks when demand increases and to pay a smaller number of workers (temporary workers) higher wages when they quickly need additional workers, rather than raising the wage rates for all their "permanent" employees. Katz and Krueger estimate that this trend could have reduced the NAIRU up to four-tenths.
6. While independence is most easily preserved when there are presidents who respect it, central bank independence is also facilitated by formal institutional arrangements typically incorporated in the legislation creating and defining the central bank. The most important requirement for independence is that the central bank be the final authority on monetary policy. Independence is also protected if other institutions of government are not represented on the monetary policy committee. Independence is further facilitated by long, overlapping terms for members of the monetary policy committee; by limited opportunities for reappointment; and by committee members not being subject to removal except for cause—where "cause" refers to fraud or other personal misconduct but explicitly excludes differences in judgment about policy.
7. I was serving a "remainder term," the unfinished portion of a term begun by a previous governor. In this case, I could in principle be nominated to serve for a full term, though that would be at the discretion of the President and subject to confirmation by the Senate.

8. *Congressional Record,* "Proceedings and Debates of the 105th Congress, First Session," vol. 143, no. 53, April 29, 1997.
9. *Conduct of Monetary Policy,* Hearing Before the Committee on Banking and Financial Services, House of Representatives, 105th Congress, First Session (Washington, D.C.: U.S. Government Printing Office, July 24, 1997).

5: GLOBAL FINANCIAL TURBULENCE

1. Beth Belton, "In Wyoming, an Economic Powwow: Policymakers Pursue Stability in Foreign Markets," *USA Today,* September 2, 1997, p. 9a.
2. Ibid.
3. In a single day, October 1, Indonesia's rupiah fell 6.5%, the Malaysian ringgit fell 4.5%, the Philippine peso fell 2.2%.
4. Hong Kong has a Currency Board, a device for maintaining a fixed exchange rate, so it was not subjected to any decline in its exchange rate. But it nevertheless felt the pressure on its stock market and its real economy.
5. Sandra Sugawara, *The Washington Post,* October 24, 1997, p. A1.
6. As a result of the staff confidence, they included a 75-basis-point increase in the funds rate by the middle of next year. It was unusual for the staff to introduce a change in monetary policy into their forecasts, and the sizable rise in the funds rate they assumed in this case underlined their belief that the economy would not be materially affected by the Asian financial crises.
7. That endorsement of the strength of our economy would turn out to be true. It would have been a very good forecast—if the staff (and the Committee) had only stuck with it!
8. The Six Markets Group included Finance Ministry and central bank officials from Australia, China, Hong Kong, Japan, Singapore, and the United States.
9. APEC began as an informal dialogue among regional economies in 1989 and now includes twenty-one regional economies.
10. When I went over to Treasury in advance of the Manila meeting, I learned one secret of the Treasury. Although the meeting was still two weeks away, Treasury officials had already written, and were even passing around, the communiqué that was to be handed out at the end of the meeting, summarizing its conclusions. I was astounded, but I guess this proves that Treasury doesn't leave much to chance. Apparently, the outcomes of meetings are negotiated in advance. And, as I would come to appreciate, the Treasury was also extraordinarily skilled at attaining the outcomes that they preferred. In this case, however, the communiqué would have to be rewritten on the spot in Manila.
11. This was the inaugural meeting of this group, comprising a fourteen-country subset of APEC members and set up to strengthen surveillance in the region—that is, the monitoring of developments that could pose a threat to regional stability—as well as to focus on reforms and policy directions intended to reduce the vulnerability to crises in the future.

12. Robert J. Samuelson, "A Gathering Economic Storm?" *The Washington Post,* November 19, 1997, p. A21.
13. Paul Blustein, *The Chastening* (New York: Public Affairs Books, 2001), p. 195.
14. Robert J. Samuelson, "The Asian Connection: It May Be More Threatening to Our Economy Than We Complacent Americans Like to Think," *The Washington Post,* December 10, 1997, p. A25.
15. At the Fed, we could also gauge this amount of stress by the growing preference of investors for the most recent and therefore most actively traded government security issues (called "on the run") rather than the less actively traded and therefore less liquid older issues (called "off the run"). In other words, there was a growing demand for liquidity.
16. Roger Lowenstein, *When Genius Failed: The Rise and Fall of Long-Term Capital Management* (New York: Random House, 2000), p. 181.
17. When you sell an asset you don't own, you are said to be "short" in the asset. If the price of the asset you shorted falls, you can buy it back later at a lower price and, after paying back the loan, earn a profit. A "derivative" is a financial instrument whose payoff depends on changes in the value of some underlying asset over time.
18. Merton was a professor at Harvard and arguably the leading scholar in finance—a genius to many in his field. Scholes was a coauthor of the so-called Black-Scholes formula for deriving the price of an option, and he was known to nearly everyone, at least by reputation, on Wall Street.
19. Lowenstein, op. cit., pp. 61 and 78.
20. Ibid., p. 194.
21. Ibid., p. 195.
22. David Wessel, "Credit Record: How the Fed Fumbled, and Then Recovered, in Making Policy Shift—Greenspan, on Second Try, Found Right Formula to Convey His Message—Criticism from a Desk Clerk," November 17, 1998, p. A1.
23. Gerard Baker, "Losing Moral Authority: Man in the News Alan Greenspan," *Financial Times,* October 3, 1998, p. 11.

6: IT'S PRODUCTIVITY, STUPID!

1. Paul David, "The Dynamo and the Computer: An Historical Perspective on the Modern Productivity Paradox," *American Economic Review* 80 (May 1990): 355–61.
2. There were even some hints in the macrodata of an acceleration in productivity. There are two measures of GDP, one based on adding up spending on newly produced goods (the product side) and the other based on adding up the income generated by that production (the income side). The two sides do not perfectly match, so there is a statistical discrepancy that ensures that, in the national income accounts, the two sides will match. The official productivity data are derived from the product side of the account. These

were the data that initially failed to signal any acceleration in productivity. The income-side data, on the other hand, did suggest that productivity was growing more rapidly. This divergence allowed both sides to focus on the data that were consistent with their respective view. The staff and I focused more on the product-side data and concluded there was no acceleration. The Chairman kept pointing at the income-side data to support his conviction that a productivity acceleration was already under way.

3. Interestingly, this result was not a surprise to the staff because it followed from work they had earlier done to explore the implications of a deceleration in productivity growth in the early 1970s. This work was summarized in a paper written by Steve Braun, then a staff member at the Board and now a senior economist at the Council of Economic Advisers. Steven Braun, "Productivity and the NIIRU (and other Phillips Curve Issues)," National Income Section, Working Paper 34, Board of Governors of the Federal Reserve System, June 1984. Braun wanted to explain the sources of the dramatic increase in inflation in the early 1970s. Many had focused on the implications of the quadrupling in oil prices at about this time. But Braun showed that the productivity deceleration was also likely an important contributor to the higher inflation. The same process now seemed to be playing out, in reverse, driven by a productivity acceleration.
4. If the wages paid to workers remain the same, but the amount of output they produce increases (as a result of an increase in productivity), the cost of per unit for the goods will decline.
5. Over time, as wages increase, the costs will increase by the same percentage as output, so the cost per unit will not be lowered by a productivity acceleration.
6. Richard W. Stevenson, "An Old School Inflation Fighter: Fed Official Resists Notion of a New Era in Economics," *The New York Times,* September 18, 1997, p. 1D.
7. "Meyer Sure Old Rules Still Apply: He's the Rain on Greenspan's Parade," *St. Louis Post-Dispatch,* New York News Service, September 21, 1997.
8. "From Panic to Euphoria," *BusinessWeek,* November 16, 1998.
9. Harry S. Dent, *The Roaring 2000s: Building the Wealth and Life Style You Desire in the Greatest Boom in History* (New York: Free Press, October 1999).
10. Later, further revisions in the productivity data would reveal that the acceleration was not quite as sharp as it appeared at this time. There was still a significant acceleration in productivity in the second half of the 1990s, though based on subsequent revisions, it turned out not quite as sharp as it appeared in 1999 and 2000.
11. Stephen D. Oliner and Daniel E. Sichel, "The Resurgence of Growth in the Late 1990s: Is Information Technology the Story?," *Journal of Economic Perspectives* (Fall 2000). An earlier version of the paper was published as a staff working paper at the Federal Reserve Board in March 2000.

7: IRRATIONAL EXUBERANCE

1. Michael J. Mandel, "New Productivity Data Raise Speed Limit on Growth," *BusinessWeek*, November 29, 1999, p. 40.
2. Martin Hardford, *Where's Waldo?* (Cambridge, Mass.: Candlewich Press, 2nd U.S. ed., 1997).
3. Burton Malkiel, in *A Random Walk Down Wall Street*, an insightful and thoroughly entertaining analysis of equity markets, explains the role of both fundamentals and the psychological considerations that dominate in the case of bubbles. My discussion draws upon Malkiel's analysis. Burton G. Malkiel, *A Random Walk Down Wall Street* (New York: W. W. Norton & Company, 2003).
4. Government bonds are usually viewed as the safe asset in models of equity valuations. Equities are subject to the risk of default by the firm; in addition, they have a return that varies depending on the performance of the firm that, in turn, depends on the performance of the overall economy. Government bonds are not subject to the same risk of default (the government can always raise taxes to pay the interest on the debt); in addition, they pay owners a fixed amount per period, independent of the overall performance of the economy. As a result, the returns to equities will be more volatile than the returns for government bonds, especially over shorter periods, and the price of equities will also be more variable than the price of government bonds. That is, investors will view equities as more risky, subject to higher variability in the price, than government bonds.
5. Wealth owners are believed to be "risk averse." That means they don't like risk. As a result, they have to be bribed into holding a riskier asset. The bribe takes the form of a higher average or expected rate of return on the riskier asset. The more risky equities are perceived to be relative to bonds, the lower the price investors will be willing to pay for equities, for given level and expected rate of growth in dividends and the interest rate on bonds.
6. Perhaps the classic example of a bubble, chronicled in Malkiel, is the tulip bulb craze in Holland in the late 1500s and early 1600s. A botany professor in the late 1500s brought back to Holland some exotic plants that originated in Turkey. Many of the flowers subsequently developed a nonfatal infection known as mosaic. It caused the petals to develop contrasting stripes, called "bizarres." The more bizarre the bizarres, the higher the value of the flowers. "Tulipmania" set in, and the prices rose dramatically, with a twentyfold increase in 1637, near the end of the bubble, and an even larger decline followed the next year. Interestingly, Malkiel says that comparing the Internet bubble to tulipmania is "unfair to flowers."
7. Malkiel calls this the "greater fool" theory of equity prices. The justification

for why someone buys equities at what might seem to be an excessive valuation in terms of fundamentals is that the buyer expects to sell the equity at a still higher price to a "greater fool" than he is.

8. Suzanne McGee, "Bulls Start Buying as Greenspan Spurs Big Drop," *The Wall Street Journal,* December 9, 1996, p. C1.
9. Jeremy J. Siegel concludes that the long-term historic average of 14 to 15 is not a good measure of what he calls a justifiable P/E ratio today, in light of the more favorable tax treatment of equities, lower transactions costs, and the effect of low inflation in raising P/E ratios. He believes that a P/E ratio in the low 20s today (and in the second half of the 1990s) is a better measure of long-term fundamental value. See Jeremy J. Siegel, *Stocks for the Long Run,* 3rd ed., (New York: McGraw-Hill, 2002).
10. The concern about equity valuations prompted Mike Prell to convene an academic panel focused on the question of whether or not there was an equity bubble in December 1996, shortly before the Chairman's use of the term *irrational exuberance.* Some thought this panel had convinced the Chairman that there was a bubble and was therefore the incubator of the "irrational exuberance" remark. But the speech had already been written, including the reference to irrational exuberance. Perhaps the panel was an attempt by Prell to focus the rest of the Board on the possibility that there was an emerging equity bubble. Robert J. Shiller participated in that seminar and later wrote a fascinating book about the stock market boom of the second half of the 1990s. Robert J. Shiller, *Irrational Exuberance* (Princeton, N.J.: Princeton University Press, 2000).
11. The occasions of the Chairman's comments on equity prices and the market response is documented in Donald L. Kohn and Brian P. Sack, "Central Bank Talk: Does It Matter and Why?," Board of Governors of the Federal Reserve System, May 23, 2003.
12. Alan Greenspan, "Opening Remarks," in *Rethinking Stabilization Policy: A Symposium Sponsored by the Federal Reserve Bank of Kansas City, Jackson Hole, Wyoming,* August 29–31, 2002.
13. Kohn and Sack, op. cit.
14. Extrapolating on this theme to its illogical conclusion, James K. Glassman and Kevin A. Hassett, in *Dow 36,000,* argued that equities are in fact not more risky than bonds, so that the equity premium should be zero. James K. Glassman and Kevin A. Hassett, *Dow 36,000: The New Strategy for Profiting from the Coming Rise in the Stock Market* (New York: Times Books, 1999). The memory of the crash of the Great Depression had left a residue in the form of a higher perceived riskiness for equities; hence investors, for a long time, demanded a relatively large equity premium. But there had, in fact, long been some mystery as to why the equity premium was as high as it appeared to be. This was referred to, in the literature, as the equity premium "puzzle." Glassman and Hassett speculated that as wealth owners were finally coming to appreciate that equities were not, in fact, more risky than bonds, and as

this process continued, the equity premium would decline and perhaps disappear. In this case, equity values would continue to soar.

15. For a defense of the direct approach, see Stephen G. Cecchetti, Hans Greenberg, John Lipsky, and Sushil Wadhwani, *Asset Prices and Central Bank Policy,* International Center for Monetary and Banking Studies, Geneva, 2000.
16. The calculation of the decline in technology and nontechnology stocks is based on data provided by Jeremy J. Siegel, based on a decomposition of the S&P 500 stock index into technology and nontechnology components.
17. The Taylor rule, for example, a simple summary of monetary policy strategy, instructs policymakers to adjust the real interest rate only in response to movements in output and inflation relative to their respective targets. There is no direct role in this summary of monetary policy strategy for a response of monetary policy to changes in equity prices in general or to a suspicion of an equity bubble in particular.
18. At the August 1999 Jackson Hole conference, Ben Bernanke, later to become a governor, and Mark Gertler presented a paper that supported the indirect approach and explained how the indirect approach still disciplined the equity market and mitigated against the emergence of equity bubbles. Ben Bernanke and Mark Gertler, "Monetary Policy and Asset Price Volatility," in *New Challenges for Monetary Policy: A Symposium Sponsored by the Federal Reserve Bank of Kansas City, Jackson Hole, Wyoming,* August 26–28, 1999, pp. 77–128.
19. The various stock exchanges also had a role in setting margin requirements. They set what are referred to as "maintenance" as opposed to "initial" margin requirements, the amount of cash that must back outstanding equities on a continuing basis after the initial purchase. If equity prices fall after the initial purchase, so that the percent of outstanding value increases, the maintenance margin could become binding. Some of the exchanges explicitly took account of the volatility of stocks in setting maintenance margins and, therefore, raised the margins for Internet stocks that were subject to an especially high degree of volatility.
20. I am referring here specifically to the P/E ratio implicit in Glassman and Hassett's prediction of a Dow Jones at 36,000.
21. I asked the Board staff to run precisely that experiment, and they concluded that there would be a rise in equity values if the equity premium declined to zero, but the rise in equity values would be quite modest and a shadow of the *Dow 36,000* result in Glassman and Hassett. A Board staff working paper also set out the evidence on the link between productivity growth and the equilibrium real rate. See Thomas Laubach and John C. Williams, "Measuring the Natural Rate of Interest," Board of Governors of the Federal System, October 2002.
22. Lenny is not technically a member of the Board staff. He rents space in the basement.

23. "Fed Governor Meyer Counters Suggestions of a Market Bubble," *The Wall Street Journal,* October 13, 1999, p. A17.

8: LANDINGS

1. Richard W. Stevenson, "Greenspan All but Announces That an Interest Rate Rise Is Ahead," June 18, 1999, *The New York Times,* p. C1.
2. There is, in addition, some logic in referring to the early tightening moves as a withdrawal from stimulus. When the funds rate is below its neutral value, it is providing stimulus to the economy. Moving the funds rate back to its neutral value, therefore, can legitimately be interpreted as removing that stimulus. When the funds rate is moved above its neutral value, on the other hand, policy should be described as outright restrictive.
3. Because not all funds rate changes are matched by discount rate changes, some have made a distinction between two types of changes in the funds rate—those that are accompanied by changes in the discount rate and those that are not. In the first case, former governor John LaWare once noted that it was as if the FOMC banged a "gong" to visibly demonstrate the importance they attached to the move in the funds rate, signaling the confidence that the change was going to last for some time.
4. By setting policy in terms of a target for the federal funds rate, the Fed was automatically positioned to meet the demand for additional liquidity without making a specific policy adjustment. If deposits are converted to cash and the resulting decline in bank reserves encouraged banks to sell securities to replenish their reserves or borrow reserves from other banks, the federal funds rate would be driven higher. In this case, the Fed would automatically supply additional reserves to maintain the federal funds rate at the target set at the last FOMC meeting. In this way, an increase in the demand for reserves automatically brought forth a corresponding increase in supply. But the Fed needed, in these special circumstances, to be prepared to act quickly and boldly in the event of an extraordinarily sharp increase in the demand for cash to prevent any even momentary disruptions in the financial markets.
5. James C. Cooper and Kathleen Madigan, "Consumers Keep Stoking the Economy's Fire," *BusinessWeek,* January 10, 2000, p. 39.
6. This was a recurring theme in the work of Hyman P. Minsky, who had been a colleague of mine at Washington University. While I was an academic at Washington University, I was not as moved by Minsky's insights as I was when I turned my attention to forecasting and then to making policy as a member of the FOMC. See Hyman P. Minsky, "The Financial Instability Hypothesis: Capitalist Processes and the Behavior of the Economy," in Charles P. Kindleberger and Jean-Pierre Laffargue, *Financial Crises: Theory History and Policy,* Cambridge University Press, 1982, pp. 13–38.
7. Martin Wolf, "Walking on Troubled Waters: Alan Greenspan Will Need to

Achieve Wonders to Secure a Smooth Slowdown of Demand in the Overheated U.S. Economy," *Financial Times*, January 12, 2000, p. 21.

8. The Committee first made a statement announcing a change in the funds rate target at the conclusion of their February 4, 1994, meeting. They continued to issue a statement each time they raised the funds rate over the following year and officially made this their practice at the February 2, 1995, meeting.
9. Greg Ip, "Pins and Needles: What Catalysts Can Deflate Stocks?—It's Tough to Spot Culprit Before Shares Start Tumbling Down," *The Wall Street Journal*, March 27, 2000, p. C1.
10. Milton Friedman, "The Lag in Effect of Monetary Policy," *Journal of Political Economy* 69, no. 5 (October 1961): 447–66.
11. James Murphy, "Mark to Market: Getting Comfortable with the Incredible," *Dow Jones Newswires*, May 1, 2000.
12. Robert Novak, "For Greenspan, Politics Beat Sound Policy," *Chicago Sun-Times*, May 18, 2000, Editorial.

9: WHAT HAPPENED TO THE NEW ECONOMY?

1. The Purchasing Managers Index, now called the ISM index, is based on a monthly survey of purchasing managers and is one of the first pieces of information available for a given month. Greenspan always considered this a timely and valuable cyclical indicator.
2. As is the case for such "unscheduled" meetings, the governors join the Chairman in the boardroom and the presidents participate via secure phone lines.
3. David E. Sanger, "The Rate Cut: The Reaction; Bush Cheers Fed's Action and Tax Cut," *The New York Times*, January 4, 2001, p. C1.
4. Michael S. Derby and Steven Vames, "Treasuries Are Mixed as the 30-Year Bond Rises on Expectation It Won't Be Sold After This Year," *The Wall Street Journal*, February 6, 2001, p. C18.
5. James C. Cooper and Kathleen Madigan, "The Fed's New Worry: Irrational Pessimism," *BusinessWeek*, March 12, 2001, p. 33.
6. "Alan Greenspan's Surprise Move," *The New York Times*, April 19, 2001, p. A24.
7. Christopher Adams, Gerard Baker, Peronet Despeignes, and Christopher Swann, "Fed's Rate Cut Stuns Markets: Half-Point Move Aimed at Boosting Capital Spending," *Financial Times*, April 19, 2001, p. 1.
8. Richard W. Stevenson, "Suddenly, Critics Are Taking Aim at Greenspan," *The New York Times*, April 2, 2001, p. A1.
9. This problem is sometimes referred to as "instrument instability." If policymakers want to always reach their objective within a year, while policy takes longer than a year to have its full effect, policy will have to move sharply in one direction and then sharply in the opposite direction, in ever

larger amounts. In this case, the economy is stabilized, but the policy instrument becomes very unstable. The alternative is for policymakers to be more patient and be satisfied with returning to their objectives, for example, in two years instead of in one year.

10. Richard W. Stevenson, "Rate Cuts Are Paying Off, Greenspan Says," *The New York Times,* May 25, 2001, p. A1.
11. These historical examples draw heavily from Frank and Browning (2001), Wessel (2001), and White (1990). Stephen E. Frank and E. S. Browning, "A Year After the Peak: Bursting of the Tech Bubble Has a Familiar 'Pop' to It," *The Wall Street Journal,* March 2, 2001, p. C1. David Wessel, "E-Progress Depends on E-Profits," *The Wall Street Journal,* January 11, 2001, p. A1. Eugene N. White, "The Stock Market Boom and Crash of 1929 Revisited," *Journal of Economic Perspectives* 4 (Spring 1990): 67–83.
12. Thomas Laubach and John C. Williams, "Measuring the Natural Rate," Federal Reserve Board, November 2001.
13. The distinction between the prevailing real rate and the equilibrium real rate was emphasized by Knut Wicksell, a Swedish monetary theorist in the 1800s. Knut Wicksell, *Interest and Prices* (New York: Augustus M. Kelley, 1965; originally published 1936). Wicksell labeled the key interest rates the "market rate" (the prevailing rate) and the "natural rate" (the equilibrium real rate). He warned that an increase in the natural rate that opened a gap with the market rate would imply a high degree of stimulus that would ultimately threaten higher inflation and economic instability.

10: NEW CHALLENGES

1. Irving Fisher, "The Debt-Deflation Theory of the Great Depression," *Econometrica* (October 1933).
2. The staff study on which this presentation was based was later published as a working paper. Alan Ahearne, Joseph Gagnon, Jane Haltmaier, and Steve Kamin, "Preventing Deflation: Lessons from Japan's Experience in the 1990s," International Finance Discussion Paper, Federal Reserve Board, June 2002.
3. A higher average inflation rate (consistent with a positive inflation target) would automatically be accompanied by a higher average nominal interest rate. The FOMC would, therefore, have more room to cut rates in the face of an adverse shock under these circumstances. And the inflation cushion would also ensure that there would be time, in the event of an adverse shock, for the Fed to ease and stabilize inflation before inflation declined first to zero and then turned negative.
4. One reason it is difficult for monetary policy alone to get the job done is that the link between the funds rate and broader financial conditions becomes attenuated after the bursting of an equity bubble. In the recent experience, for example, the Fed aggressively cut the funds rate, but financial

conditions continued to deteriorate for much of the two years following the bursting of the equity bubble, as equity prices continued to slide, the dollar appreciated, and risk spreads in the capital markets widened.

5. There is an important difference, as Greenspan loved to point out to Congress, between how monetary and fiscal authorities should approach taking out insurance against downside risks. Monetary policymakers can take back the insurance if it is not needed. It will be far more difficult for fiscal policymakers to reverse any tax cuts implemented to spur the economy during a postbubble period, once the economy has turned the corner. For this reason, Greenspan opposed the last round of tax cuts (implemented in mid-2003 and retroactive to January of that year) recommended by the Bush administration and passed by Congress.
6. Testimony of Chairman Alan Greenspan, "The Economic Outlook," Joint Economic Committee, U.S. Congress, November 13, 2002.
7. Ben S. Bernanke, "Deflation: Making Sure 'It' Doesn't Happen Here," Federal Reserve Board, November 21, 2002.
8. Buying foreign government securities is a form of foreign exchange intervention—since we have to in effect buy the foreign currency to purchase the foreign government bond. The result might be to encourage a depreciation of the dollar, which would in turn stimulate net exports and, hence, aggregate demand in the United States. Buying private U.S. securities would directly lower the interest rates on such securities, reducing the cost of borrowing for U.S. firms and consumers. The Fed has the authority to purchase foreign sovereign debt but would have to ask Congress for authority to buy private debt if it wanted to pursue that option.
9. James Clouse, Dale Henderson, Athanasios Orphanides, David Small, and Peter Tinsley, "Monetary Policy When the Nominal Short-Term Interest Rate Is Zero," Finance and Economics Discussion Series, Federal Reserve Board, November 2000.
10. The paper presented by Woodford was coauthored with Gauti Eggertsson, and ultimately published as Gauti Eggertsson and Michael Woodford, "The Zero Bound on Interest Rates and Optimal Monetary Policy," *Brookings Papers on Economic Activity* 1 (2003): 139–233.
11. Woodford and Eggertsson recommended a specific form of a policy rule that they believed would allow monetary policymakers to avoid deflation or escape from deflation if necessary: a "history dependent" policy rule. An example of such a rule is a "price level" rule. Assume the FOMC sets a target for a constant price level. If the price level falls, the FOMC will have to implement a policy that would return the price level to its original position—that is, produce inflation for a period to offset the effect of the deflation on the price level.

    The longer the deflation lasted, the sharper and longer the period of ease that would be necessary to raise the price level back to its target. Thus, policy in the future was dependent on the history of the price level. The markets could judge how stimulative policy would be and for how long policy would remain stimulative by how far the price level had declined. In this case, a period of deflation would encourage markets to lower long-term interest rates as they became convinced that the funds rate would remain low longer than previously expected.

But the Fed didn't even have an inflation target and was clearly not ready to implement such a rigid and bold policy as Woodford had urged. Nevertheless, the market response to the May 6 statement suggested that a vaguer form of precommitment could still have a significant effect in lowering long-term rates.

12. Laurence H. Meyer, "After an Attack on Iraq: The Economic Consequences," Center for Strategic and International Studies, November 21, 2002.
13. The economy was absorbing the effect of the decline in household wealth, retrenchment in investment had unwound the capital overhang, and firms had made considerable progress improving their balance sheets. On the other hand, the savings rate remained very low, the household debt burden was relatively high, and the current account balance still seemed unsustainable. But the latter imbalances, while posing some risks for future prospects, did not appear to stand in the way of a self-sustaining recovery.
14. The Chairman's participation was by videoconference. In addition, this was not an official "speech"—only informal remarks made during a panel discussion—and, therefore, the text of the Chairman's remarks were not posted on the Board Web site. That was unfortunate, given the substance and perceived importance of the remarks.
15. An important question that affected the timing of any nonconventional policy was whether or not it would be prudent to set a floor to the funds rate and, therefore, stop short of driving the rate all the way to zero. The worry was that driving the funds rate to zero would seriously damage, if not destroy, the money market mutual fund industry, by driving the rate on money market mutual funds so close to zero that investors shifted their funds to banks. So the view, leading up to the June meeting, was that one more move of 50 basis points and the Fed might be ready to implement nonconventional policies.
16. John M. Berry, "Rate Cut Looking Like a Sure Thing: Economy's Continued Weakness, Possibility of Deflation Worry Fed Officials," *The Washington Post*, June 19, 2003, p. E1.
17. Greg Ip, "Next Fed Rate Cut May Be Smaller Than Expected—With Rates Nearing Zero, Fed Faces a Quandary: How Low Can They Go?," *The Wall Street Journal*, June 20, 2003, p. A1.
18. Ben S. Bernanke, "Some Thoughts on Monetary Policy in Japan," Federal Reserve Board, May 31, 2003.
19. In his July 15 semiannual monetary policy testimony, Greenspan clarified

the thinking about nonconventional policies. First, such policies were not likely to be implemented, given the Committee's expectations that the expansion was now strengthening. Second, if the economy did weaken further and additional stimulus was called for, the first line of action would be conventional monetary policy. The Chairman emphasized that the FOMC still had a considerable amount of room for further nonconventional policy, another 100 basis points of potential cuts in the funds rate. It was clear the Committee would first exhaust its conventional tool before even thinking about nonconventional policy.

20. The concern here was in part the effect of further declines in the federal funds rate on money market mutual funds and on the commercial paper market.
21. At the June meeting, the Committee reinforced the message about its concern with further disinflation, indicating that it expected that this concern would predominate for the "foreseeable future." Still, the new language was pretty well ignored as the markets responded to the disappointment of only a 25-basis-point cut in the funds rate.
22. See, for example, Ben S. Bernanke, "An Unwelcome Fall in Inflation," Federal Reserve Board, July 23, 2003.
23. Greg Ip, "Fed Parleyed on Its Communications—At Special Monday Session, FOMC Reviewed Its Policy of Relaying Assessments," *The Wall Street Journal*, September 19, 2003, p. A2.
24. We learned later that the Chairman had pressed the Committee to include this sentence in the statement and that although the Committee obliged, there was a lot of resistance. Seven of the Reserve Bank presidents allegedly opposed the move. By their September meeting, the Committee was already thinking about removing the controversial sentence. They worried that it gave the impression of a time-based commitment and that such a commitment was imprudent for a central bank, given uncertainties about how the economy will evolve in the future. In addition, they reminded themselves that they preferred never to talk about future policy prospects in their statements. However, they worried that dropping the sentence would give the impression that they had changed their views about the outlook and monetary policy prospects by more than had, in fact, been the case. So, they retained the language.

11: LOOKING FORWARD

1. Productivity is highly "cyclical." Specifically, it grows faster than its underlying trend when real GDP growth is rising and more slowly than its trend when GDP growth is slowing. It also trends to decline outright during recessions, when output is falling.
2. Don Kohn develops the interplay among productivity, aggregate demand,

and employment and the implications for monetary policy in Donald L. Kohn, "Productivity and Monetary Policy," Federal Reserve Board, September 24, 2003.

3. Roger W. Ferguson, Jr., "Lessons from Past Productivity Booms," Federal Reserve Board, January 4, 2004.
4. The Committee may also make some changes in the language it uses in its statement at the close of meetings. A subcommittee chaired by Roger Ferguson, Vice Chairman of the Board, is studying possible refinements. I expect the Committee may opt to simplify its current risk assessment language, returning to the single risk assessment it abandoned in 2003 (unbalanced either toward economic weakness or toward heightened inflation pressures). And I expect the Committee may reaffirm the decision it made in January 2000 to speak only about risks to the outlook, rather than commenting further on possible policy in the future (as it has returned to doing, beginning with the statement at the May 2003 meeting).

   Another direction for improved transparency would be for the FOMC to provide additional information about its forecast. FOMC members currently submit their forecasts twice a year, before the two-day meetings. The forecasts reveal a great deal about how the Committee views the outlook and also helps the markets better gauge the prospects for monetary policy. But the forecast detail could be improved to make them still more useful. For example, the forecast released in February covers only the remainder of the year, while the forecast released in July extends through the following year. Given the lags in the response to monetary policy, it would be more useful if the forecasts extended at least two years and preferably three. That would also help provide a clearer understanding of how the Committee interprets its objectives, in terms of price stability and full employment. In addition, it would be helpful if the Committee forecast core inflation, as this appears to be the measure that policymakers respond to most directly.
5. One concern is that Congress would insist on an explicit numerical target for full employment if the FOMC wanted to adopt an explicit numerical inflation target. That is certainly a possibility, but the Fed would surely reject such a package deal. It is possible for monetary policymakers to set and achieve an inflation target. They cannot, however, impose a definition of full employment. The NAIRU ultimately determines where full employment is, and the NAIRU cannot be set by policymakers. It must be estimated and ultimately respected.
6. I worked with most of the current members of the FOMC and have faith that they would carry on well after Greenspan retires. However, I don't have an equal amount of faith in the decisions of future presidents about their appointments to the Federal Reserve Board. For that reason, I can see some real value in institutionalizing at least this part of the disciplined policy of Greenspan.
7. In the United Kingdom, for example, the target is 2% for a measure of con-

sumer price inflation (changed from 2½% in December 2003, when they altered the price index on which the target is based). In New Zealand, it is 1%–3% for a measure of consumer price inflation.

8. There is also a question of whether the Fed can or should take the initiative in moving in this direction. Congress, after all, sets the objectives for monetary policy. In my view, Congress had already set price stability as an explicit objective of the Fed. The Fed could therefore operate within the statute by defining more precisely what it means by price stability. In practice, however, given the oversight role of Congress with respect to monetary policy, there should be consultations between the Fed and Congress if the Fed decides it wants to consider moving in the direction of an explicit numerical inflation target.
9. For example, the Bank of England Act of 1998, which provides the mandate for the Monetary Policy Committee of the Bank of England, reads, "In relation to monetary policy, the objectives of the Bank of England shall be (a) to maintain price stability, and (b) subject to that, to support the economic policy of Her Majesty's Government, including its objectives for growth and employment."
10. Lars Svensson argues that the earlier austere regimes have given way in practice to "flexible" inflation targeting, under which monetary policy is directed both at stabilizing output relative to potential and at achieving the explicit inflation target. See Lars Svensson, "Inflation Targeting as a Monetary Policy Rule," *Journal of Monetary Economics* 43 (June 1999): 607–54. Still, their mandates and rhetoric have not changed, and there is no reason for the United States to abandon the dual mandate that these countries seem to be converging toward.
11. The proposal I am offering here was first made in a speech while I was on the Board. See Laurence H. Meyer, "Perspectives on Inflation Targets and Inflation Targeting," Federal Reserve Board of Governors, July 17, 2001. This, by the way, is the regime under which the Reserve Bank of Australia operates. So I have suggested that the FOMC be more like the Reserve Bank of Australia. Not surprisingly, I have quite a few friends at the Reserve Bank of Australia!
12. There is some recent evidence, developed by Federal Reserve economists, that central banks with explicit inflation targets are more effective in anchoring inflation expectations than central banks without such an explicit inflation target. Andrew Levin, Fabio M. Natalucci, and Jeremy N. Piger, "The Macroeconomic Effects of Inflation Targeting," Annual Economic Policy Conference, Federal Reserve Bank of St. Louis, October 2003.
13. There have been conferences devoted to the subject, and a session of the American Economic Association featured a debate on this subject in January 2004.
14. Ben S. Bernanke, "Perspectives on Inflation Targeting," Federal Reserve Board, March 25, 2003.

15. Donald L. Kohn, "Panel Discussion," Inflation Targeting: Prospects and Problems, 28th Annual Policy Conference, Federal Reserve Bank of St. Louis, October 17, 2003.
16. The signals from the labor market, however, have been especially confusing in the last few months. The two different surveys of employment are flashing very different signals. The payroll survey, the one generally viewed as the most reliable indicator, suggests that employment growth remains very weak. The household report indicates stronger growth in employment and a continuing decline in the unemployment rate.

12: ALAN, I HARDLY KNEW YOU

1. He first introduced the risk management approach in his opening remarks to the Jackson Hole conference in August 2003, and further developed this theme in a presentation at the annual meetings of the American Economic Association in January 2004.
2. Stanley Fischer provides an excellent summary of the evidence on the relationship between inflation and economic growth in "Why Are Central Banks Pursuing Long-Run Price Stability?," in *Achieving Price Stability*, a symposium sponsored by the Federal Reserve Bank of Kansas City, Jackson Hole, Wyoming, August 29–31, 1996. He concludes, "It is not possible at this stage to draw any firm conclusion on the relationship between inflation and growth at the very low inflation rates" for the G-7 countries. Nevertheless, "These results leave little doubt that double-digit inflation is bad for growth."
3. Well, it is actually a chair that at one time was around the FOMC table. Departing governors get the older chairs that have since been replaced around the table.
4. Shortly before the party, the staff on the governors' floor put on a little skit for the governors at a holiday gathering. They sang their version of "The Twelve Days of Christmas." "On the first day of Christmas," it began, "my true love gave to me a Chairman in a bathtub." We all laughed, not quite prepared for the fact that there would be some barb for each of us along the way. For me it was the fifth day: "On the fifth day of Christmas, my true love gave to me a set of LONG Meyer papers." And every time this sentence was repeated, the LONG got longer and longer—and we all laughed louder and louder, especially me.

APPENDIX

1. Kendrick, John W. *Productivity Trends in the United States* (Princeton, N.J.: Princeton University Press for the National Bureau of Economic Research, 1961).

REFERENCES

THE FEDERAL RESERVE BOARD

Main page, http://www.federalreserve.gov

FOMC statements and minutes, http://www.federalreserve.gov/fomc/#calendars

FOMC meeting transcripts, http://www.federalreserve.gov/fomc/transcripts

Research and data, http://www.federalreserve.gov/rnd.htm

Speeches, http://www.federalreserve.gov/boarddocs/speeches/2004

Monetary policy report to Congress, http://www.federalreserve.gov/boarddocs/hh

Federal Reserve Districts and Banks, http://www.federalreserve.gov/otherfrb.htm

ECONOMIC DATA

Bureau of Economic Analysis, http://www.bea.gov

Bureau of Labor Statistics, http://www.bls.gov

St. Louis Fed economic data—Fred II, http://www.research.stlouisfed.org/fred2

NBER business cycles, http://www.nber.org/cycles.html

ECONOMIC NEWS

The Wall Street Journal, http://www.wsj.com

Financial Times, http://www.ft.com

Bloomberg, http://www.bloomberg.com

INDEX